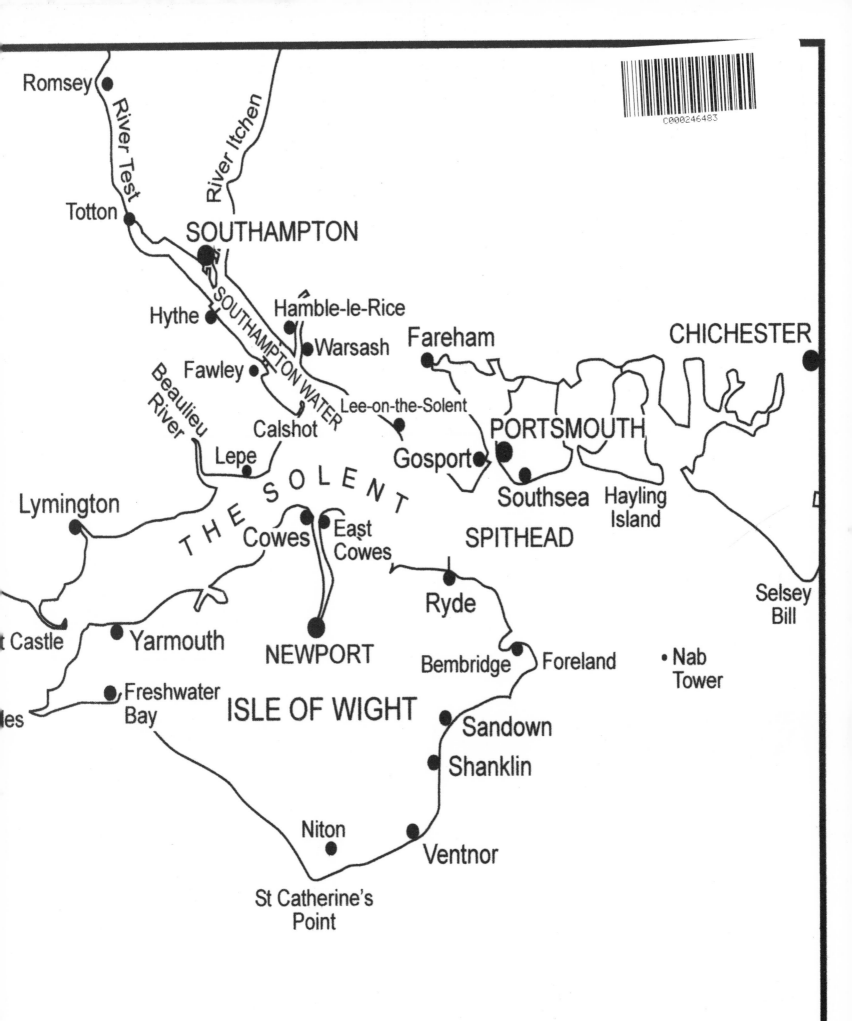

Romsey

River Test

River Itchen

Totton

SOUTHAMPTON

Hythe

SOUTHAMPTON WATER

Hamble-le-Rice

Warsash

Fareham

CHICHESTER

Fawley

Beaulieu River

Calshot

Lee-on-the-Solent

PORTSMOUTH

Lepe

Gosport

THE SOLENT

Lymington

Cowes

East Cowes

Southsea

Hayling Island

SPITHEAD

t Castle

Yarmouth

Ryde

Selsey Bill

NEWPORT

Bembridge

Foreland

Nab Tower

Freshwater Bay

ISLE OF WIGHT

les

Sandown

Shanklin

Niton

Ventnor

St Catherine's Point

CHANNEL

Map by Nigel V. Robinson, 2006

The fully-rigged Ukrainian-flag
*Khersones* awaits the start of the
Cutty Sark Tall Ships' Race at
Weymouth on the 20th July, 1994.

# SOUTHAMPTON SHIPPING

### (with Portsmouth, Poole and Weymouth)

CARMANIA PRESS

A Catalogue Record for this book is available from The British Library.

Art Director: Maurizio Eliseo
Printed by: Tisak Zambelli, Rijeka
First published: October 2006

**Carmania Press**
Unit 212, Station House,
49, Greenwich High Road,
London, SE10 8JL,
Great Britain

email: CarmaniaPress@transatlantici.com
web: www.carmaniapress.com

**ISBN**: 0-9543666-6-2 978-0-9543666-6-7

# SOUTHAMPTON SHIPPING

## (with Portsmouth, Poole and Weymouth)

The Maritime Photographs
of
**R. Bruce Grice**

With Text
by
**David F. Hutchings**

**CARMANIA PRESS, LONDON**

A spectacular but sad sight: (from left to right) *Windsor Castle*, *Queen Elizabeth*, *S.A. Vaal*, *Arcadia*, *Canberra*, *Good Hope Castle*, *Reina del Mar* and *Edinburgh Castle* laid up in the Western Docks, Southampton during the 45-day Seamen's Strike of 1966, which speeded the decline of the British liner industry.

# Contents

The Blue Star cargo liner
*Buenos Aires Star* in the
Western Docks, Southampton
in October 1976.

# Foreword

The name of R. (Bob) Bruce Grice has been well-known to readers of the popular shipping magazines for many years, especially the long-established *Sea Breezes* and its younger competitor *Ships Monthly*. He has been both a contributor of informed articles and, primarily, a frequent provider of photographs of the various shipping activities along the central southern coast of Britain – and sometimes further afield. He has recorded the great liners in Southampton, warships in Portsmouth, ferries in Poole and Weymouth – all are grist to the camera of Grice. Recording the southern shipping scene over the past twelve decades or more has been the self-appointed task of many photographers, both amateur and professional, but in the latter half of the twentieth century Bob Bruce Grice has ranked amongst the foremost of them.

He was born far from the sea, in Birmingham, on the 21st March, 1914. He recalls one of his earliest childhood memories, seeing one of the Kaiser's Zeppelin airship bombers caught in the crossbeams of searchlights over the city of his birth during the First World War. Prior to making a career in photography, Bob sailed as a crew-member aboard the coal-fired *Saxon* on her last round voyage on the Union-Castle Line's famous Cape Mail service.

He started his professional life in press and commercial photography before the Second World War and later served in the Royal Air Force Volunteer Reserve, passing through a wartime course at the R.A.F. School of Photography at Farnborough. After the War, he set up the photographic section for the Architects and Design Group for the famous 1951 Festival of Britain Exhibition, running the section from the Exhibition's office in Lennox Gardens, SW1. He had gained his Associateship in Illustrative Photography with the Institute of British Photographers and, in 1952, achieved Associateship of the Royal Photographic Society. In recognition of his work at the Aeroplane and Armament Experimental Establishment at Boscombe Down in Wiltshire, he was awarded the British Empire Medal in 1976, an accolade that he characteristically 'plays down'. Bob retired in 1979 whilst working in Public Relations at the United Kingdom Land Forces Headquarters at Wilton, Wiltshire but he has continued his passion for photography until the present day.

It was with great pleasure that I agreed to his request that I should caption this book of a selection of his shipping pictures, many taken from aboard working tugs. My pleasure was enhanced by the opportunity to re-discover vessels other than the ocean liners which had been my 'mainstay' since my childhood on the Isle of Wight. Working through this selection of images has been like becoming reacquainted with some old friends.

Faced with such an evocative collection of images, we had the onerous problem of selecting a minority and omitting a majority and of how to present the final choice. An arrangement of ships port by port would perhaps have been too topographical, so we chose to present the various ship types which have been seen around the South Coast, with an expected focus on the major ports of Southampton and Portsmouth. This volume does not purport to be an historical overview of the local shipping scene; nor is it a comprehensive study of all the ship types that could, or still can, be seen in the area. It does, though, give one man's idiosyncratic view, a particular view that has brought pleasure – and a taste of the sea – to many, over the years.

My sincerest gratitude and thanks go to Anthony Cooke of Carmania Press for his agreement to publish this book, his assistance in selecting the images we have used, his encouragement and his judicious and careful editing, thus adjoining this volume to his excellent series of already similarly themed works.

*David F. Hutchings,*
*Lee-on-The Solent,*
*Hampshire.*

# Preface & Acknowledgements

I am most grateful to David Hutchings for agreeing to co-author this volume showing a small selection of the many photographs that I have taken over the years. I must particularly thank him for the meticulous research included in his narrative and for obtaining authoritatively informed details for the various ships contained in this volume.

I first met David Hutchings one cold, damp day in September, 1967 on the occasion of the berthing of the magnificent *Queen Mary* – the most famous ship in the World – at the completion of her final eastbound transatlantic crossing. Since that sad but memorable event, David has, in his own words, tried in some small way to put back into his abiding interest some of the pleasure that he has derived from it since he used to watch from his birthplace on the Isle of Wight the comings and goings of the great liners. He has written several well-received books (sold at pocket-money prices), hoping to interest the young enthusiasts of tomorrow. Indeed, his books documenting the three *Caronia*s and the first three *Queens* achieved the accolade of being chosen as 'Book of the Month' in a popular shipping magazine.

Of course, I also particularly wish to acknowledge the great encouragement of my late wife Martha (whom I first met in a photographic environment) to make a collection of pictures for this book. Without that enthusiasm this volume would not have materialised. Martha would often accompany me on various shipping assignments, whatever the weather, sometimes just to stand waiting on a draughty pier or dock. I also greatly appreciate the help of my daughter Susan and her husband John Goldfinch, particularly for their keen observations and suggestions regarding my original submissions for this work.

I must thank, especially, the dockers of Southampton for their good humour and help when required. The tugmasters and crews should also receive a special mention, as it was through the good offices of Red Funnel's Tug Superintendent, Mr. A. Coslett-Derby, that I was often able to take photographs that would otherwise have been impossible. The deck boy during the delivery voyage of one ex-Red Funnel tug to Bermuda, the *Gatcombe*, went on to gain his Master's Certificate and to become Queen's Harbour Master in Bermuda whilst gaining experience in a different field. He is now a world-renowned marine artist – Stephen Card's paintings grace many a ship, including *Queen Mary 2*. Mr. D. A. Archdeacon, Secretary of The Southampton, Isle of Wight and South of England Royal Mail Steam Packet Company, Ltd. ('Red Funnel') should also receive a mention.

The Alexandra Towing Company was equally helpful and my appreciation goes to their Southampton Manager, Mr. C. J. Smith, for allowing me aboard their tugs. The steaming mugs of tea supplied to this photographer whilst standing on the bridge of many a tug forging through The Solent to meet an incoming ship are a particularly pleasurable memory – as are my recollections of deer crossing my 'bow' in the early morning light of a misty, verdant New Forest as I drove to be, often, the first on board a waiting tug!

The British Transport Docks Board and, later, Associated British Ports were also most accommodating to my requests for port access. Major G. J. F. Williamson of the Royal Corps of Transport allowed me on board the *Yarmouth Navigator* on her 'post boat' runs around the assembled ships at the Silver Jubilee Fleet Review, thus enabling me to obtain coverage of that important event.

R. Bruce Grice.

Other invaluable links include Major Peter Thompson, R.M., the First Director General of the Jubilee Sailing Trust and Kate Harris, his P.A.; John Waghorn, Ship Manager of the Jubilee Sailing Trust; the members of the Royal National Lifeboat Institution, Weymouth; Portland Borough Council; the Ministry of Defence; Southampton City Museums (Woolhouse Maritime Museum); the Fleet Air Arm Museum; and Maureen Attwooll of Weymouth Library. I especially wish also to thank Nigel Overton of Southampton Maritime Museum for his encouragement and help with regard to my coverage of *Shieldhall* and the tug *Galway Bay*, ex-Red Funnel *Calshot.*.

Both David and I would like to thank the following people for their expert help and generous encouragement: Nigel Allan of Oceancraft.co.uk (detailed card models); Rodney Baker, the Secretary of the Southampton branch of World Ship Society; Colin M. Baxter, marine watercolour artist of Lee-on-The Solent for his expertise on sailing vessels; Richard Clammer; Des Cox of Snowbow Productions' *Great Liners* video series; Philip J. Fricker; Norman Grice; Clive Harvey of the Ocean Liner Society; Roger Hardingham; David Hornsby; Ian Hutchings, crewmember of the Yarmouth lifeboat; Captain Peter Jackson; Richard de Kerbrech; Willem H. van der Leek; Robert Lloyd; Ron Mapplebeck; William H. Miller; Bert Moody, local historian *par excellence*; Robert John Ofield; George Robinson; Nigel V. Robinson, who produced the detailed maps which add to the clarity of this book; Robert Shopland; Solent Maritime Society; Southampton Reference Library; Margaret and Len Thompson; Robert L. Trillo; Kenneth Vard; Tony Westmore; David L. Williams; John F. Willows; Captain Robin Woodall; and Ron Young.

Finally, to Anthony Cooke, founder of Carmania Press and himself well-known as an author and lecturer, go my thanks for his patience and guidance.

David and I jointly hope that the following pages will evoke many memories of the southern shipping scene that, for many reasons, has sadly declined in some areas over the years but is thriving elsewhere in the region. We would be pleased to receive any updates, additions or corrections to the text through the Publisher.

*Bob Bruce Grice,*
*Morgans Vale,*
*Nr. Salisbury,*
*Wiltshire.*

The mighty *Queen Elizabeth* refuelling at night for the last time in the Atlantic Dock at Southampton on 7 November 1968.

# Introduction

The central southern coast of mainland Britain is washed by the English Channel and, in its midst, by the beautiful, sheltered waters of The Solent. The latter is confined between, to the north, the low-lying Hampshire coast, framed by the gently rolling hills of the South Downs, and, to the south, the verdant shores of the Isle of Wight. That beautiful little island is sometimes known as 'God's Garden Isle'.

Over numerous centuries, these waters have seen the arrivals and departures of thousands of vessels built for a myriad of voyages. There were the many-tiered galleys both of the Phœnicians and of Imperial Rome; the speedy high-prow'd ships of invading Danes and Normans; and the fleet of Henry V sailing from Southampton to victory at Agincourt. The ill-fated *Mary Rose* sank within King Henry VIII's sight off Southsea Castle and the same king's favourite, *Henri Grace à Dieu*, burned to the waterline a few miles away on the River Hamble. With his fleet, Nelson sailed on the *Victory* to gain honour and a hero's death at Trafalgar. Later, with the coming of steam, 'dirty British coasters with salt-caked smokestacks', as John Masefield so eloquently put it, traded through these waters by the score. Battlefleets sailed forth from Portsmouth en route to prestigious naval reviews at Spithead or, in deadly earnest, to fight Napoleon, the Kaiser or Hitler. Even more recently, ships have sailed with mindful intent to the Falklands and Iraq.

In The Solent nestled the mighty fleet that gathered prior to the D-Day invasion of 1944 and, in more peaceful times, gorgeous liners belonging to famous companies have brought the rich and famous to these shores, as well as taking thousands away in search of those new tomorrows that, in the 1950s, started with the 'Ten Pounds Assisted Passage'. In recent decades, huge container vessels – the 'box boats' – have efficiently and successfully – too successfully for some! – taken the sea-borne freight of the World away from the innumerable colourful and characterful cargo liners and tramps that for a century and a half had scoured the World's oceans for trade. Those earlier, smaller ships were swept away in the name of maritime progress by the latter-day leviathans.

Within the chosen geographic area of this book lie several ports of varying size and importance. To the west reside the ports of Weymouth and Poole and the pleasure piers and beaches of Bournemouth and Swanage. Centrally, Southampton, once famed as 'The Gateway to the World', still reigns supreme. (Southampton Water, with its double high tides giving it the advantage of prolonged deep water, is formed by the confluence of the rivers Itchen and Test.) Portsmouth, too, is a major, active port. The southern boundary of our area is formed by the northern shores of the Isle of Wight, with the ports and piers of Ryde, Fishbourne, Yarmouth and Cowes – the home of yachting and of the world-famous Cowes Week.

Thousands of ships over the centuries have served these ports, and have been served by them in return. Some of them found undying fame through notoriety or impressive achievement: *Mary Rose*, *Victory*, *Great Eastern*, *Mauretania*, *Titanic*, *Empress of Britain*, *Queen Mary*, *Hood*, *Queen Elizabeth*, *Oriana*, *Canberra*, *QE2* – and now *QM2*. All have graced these local waters and left their lasting impressions in the collective memory of a once-great maritime nation. Ships of other countries have also impressed: *Normandie*, *Nieuw Amsterdam*, *United States*, *Rotterdam*, *France* all created a stir in the local populace when they appeared. Beside the famous ships that have been household names, innumerable lesser-known, even obscure, vessels have played their part in the commerce of a great nation and its Empire-Commonwealth. Whether freighters arriving or sailing with myriad cargoes; or humble colliers and tankers bringing coal and oil fuel for their larger sisters; or 'just' tugs assisting in dozens of ship movements each day; or even specialised vessels taking out refuse of various sorts..... all have played important rôles both in the welfare of the local area and, ultimately, in that of the Nation in general.

# THE LINERS AND CRUISE SHIPS

## NEVASA

Completed 1956 by Barclay, Curle & Co., Ltd., Whiteinch, Glasgow. 20,160 gross tons. Length overall: 609 ft. 3$^{ins}$ / 185.7m (580 ft. 7$^{ins}$ / 177.0m between perpendiculars). Beam: 78 ft. 3$^{ins}$ / 23.85m. Draught: 26 ft. 3$^{ins}$ / 8.0m. Six Parsons-Pametrada turbines. 18,400 shp. Twin screw. Service speed: 17 knots. Call sign: GPQV.

Built as a troopship for the British India Steam Navigation Co., Ltd., London and delivered during their centenary year, *Nevasa* was their largest vessel. She was the first new British trooper to be built since the War and, as it turned out, the penultimate such vessel. *Nevasa* was an improvement on previous troopships, being fitted, for instance, with stabilisers. Nevertheless, by 1962, she found herself redundant due to the Government's decision to transport servicemen and their families by air. In consequence, she was withdrawn from service and laid up in Cornwall's River Fal.

However, two years later, British India – often known as BI – decided to reactivate her as a full-time educational cruise ship with room for 1,100 students and their teachers. There was also much more luxurious accommodation for 230 adult cruise passengers. BI was a subsidiary of P&O and in 1970 the operation of the revived *Nevasa* was taken over by the parent company's Passenger Division. As from the following year, she was fully owned by P&O.

Due to escalating fuel costs, an almost ten-fold increase, *Nevasa* again found herself redundant in 1974. This time it was final. When she arrived in Malta, she was sold. This fine-looking ship was sent to Nan Feng Steel Enterprises in Taiwan for breaking in 1975.

## UGANDA

Completed 1952 by Barclay, Curle & Co., Ltd., Whiteinch, Glasgow. 14,430 gross tons as built, later 16,907 gross tons. Length overall: 539 ft. 10$^{ins}$ / 164.5m (505 ft. 6$^{ins}$ / 154.1m between perpendiculars). Beam: 71 ft. 5$^{ins}$ / 21.8m. Draught: 27 ft. 6$^{ins}$ / 8.4m, later 25 ft. 3½$^{ins}$ / 7.7m. Six steam turbines by Wallsend Slipway Co., Ltd. 12,300 shp. Twin screw. Service speed: 17 knots. Call sign: GFRQ.

One of a pair built for British India (her sister being *Kenya*), *Uganda* was originally to have been called *Karatina*. She was launched as *Uganda* by Lady Hall, wife of the then Governor of Uganda, on the 15$^{th}$ January, 1952. On her trials, the ship substantially exceeded her design speed, achieving 19½ knots.

*Uganda* served on British India's London – East Africa route via the Suez Canal (except during 1956-7, when she was diverted by way of Cape Town because of the Suez Crisis). However, due to rising fuel costs and the incursion of jet travel on her route, she was sent to Hamburg in 1967 for conversion into an educational cruise ship. Cargo holds were rebuilt as additional passenger space; her original balanced and elegant profile took on a heavier aspect; her tonnage increased but, because she no longer carried cargo, her draught was reduced.

BI had first run educational cruises before the War and, over the years since then, had taken thousands of schoolchildren and their teachers to the Mediterranean and other places they might never otherwise have seen. Independent adult travellers also took advantage of these cruises and partook of the onboard lectures and the shore excursions, whilst retreating to quieter, panelled, more elegant quarters at other times. In 1971,

(Facing page.) The *Nevasa* photographed in Ocean Dock, Southampton in 1974.

management of *Uganda* was taken over by P&O, who became her registered owners in the following year. Whilst the ship was on a cruise to Egypt in April, 1982, her contingent of eager students was involuntarily disembarked at Naples because of the worsening crisis in the Falkland Islands. *Uganda* had been requisitioned for military service. Now a STUFT – Ship Taken Up From Trade – she sailed to Gibraltar where she was hastily converted into a NOSH – Naval Oceangoing Surgical Hospital. Called 'Mother Hen' by the British troops who had occasion to use her medical facilities, HMHS *Uganda* treated British and Argentinean wounded alike. She also took onboard survivors from the sunken HMS *Sheffield* for their repatriation to the U.K. After her triumphant return to Southampton on the 9th September, *Uganda* went back briefly to her educational cruising programme but within a few months she was chartered to the military to transport men and stores between the Ascension Islands and the Falklands for the next two years. On the conclusion of the charter, she did not return to her peacetime rôle but was sent to the River Fal for lay-up, remaining there for 13 months until June, 1986 pending her sale for further use or for breaking. Eventually, she was bought by the Triton Shipping Co. of Taiwan. Now called *Triton*, she finally sailed, rust-streaked but dressed overall, flying the flag of St. Vincent but with a British crew. Sadly, as she passed through the Carrick Roads that led to the English Channel, she was unable to return the salutes of honour from those who bade farewell to this very popular ship. A military helicopter made a very light and brief touchdown on her Falklands-installed heli-deck (in what Captain J. D. Coxe described as a kiss landing) in token memory of her sterling service in the South Atlantic.

She was not only virtually pirated as she passed through the Suez Canal but she was also denied bunkers at Jeddah because she had once sailed on educational cruises to Israel. Aden and its heat (so well-known to liners calling en route to posts of the old Empire) was hurriedly chosen as an alternative.

On arrival in the Far East, *Triton* anchored one mile off Kaohsiung on the 16th July, where, now poignantly flying a brand-new Red Ensign, she awaited yet another buyer. The scrapyard won her. However, a month later and before she could be beached, Typhoon Wayne claimed her as its own. She was blown towards the shallows where she capsized onto her starboard side, parallel to the shore, at an angle of 70°. Eventually breaking in two, the tragic wreckage of this well-loved ship was not scrapped until 1992.

# The Cunard Queens

## QUEEN MARY

Completed 1936 by John Brown & Co., Ltd., Clydebank. 81,237 gross tons. Overall length: 1,019 ft. 6$^{ins}$ / 310.8m (975 ft. 2$^{ins}$ / 297.2m between perpendiculars). Beam: 118 ft. 6$^{ins}$ / 36.1m. Draught: 41 ft. 4½$^{ins}$ / 12.6m. 16 Parsons steam turbines by John Brown. 200,000 shp. 24 Yarrow watertube boilers. Quadruple screws. Service speed: 31 knots. Call sign: GBTT.

A weekly service across the North Atlantic maintained by just two fast ships had been the long-desired goal of various shipping lines and it finally fell to the Cunard Steam Ship Co. to achieve this cherished ambition. Calculations had shown that the smallest vessels which could operate such a service would have to be at least 1,000 feet on the waterline. Accordingly, Cunard-White Star, as they had now become, introduced their new *Queen Mary* in 1936 and planned to follow her with the *Queen Elizabeth*.

Up to the launching of Yard No. 534, the first of the pair, her name had been kept a secret and when Her Majesty Queen Mary named the great liner after herself, a roar of approval went up from the throng witnessing the launch on a wet 26th September, 1934. Construction had been suspended for a time because of the Great Depression, a delay which gave the French a subsidised edge with which to complete their fabulous *Normandie* well ahead of her British counterpart. However, once in service, the less innovative *Queen Mary* proved to be more than a match for her French rival for the honours of the Blue Riband. The two ships would not actually race against each other as their sailings were timed to complement each other rather than compete.

The *Queen Mary* finally clinched the rivalry for the Blue Riband in August, 1938 but a year later the World was at war. *Normandie* never sailed again, being burnt at her pier in Manhattan while the U.S. Navy were converting her into a troopship. They had seized her in December, 1941 following America's entry into the War after the Japanese attack on Pearl Harbor. *Queen Mary* had arrived in New York on the 4th September, 1939, the day after war was declared between Great Britain and Germany, and there she remained, tied up at her berth and painted in wartime battleship grey.

Flying her 310-foot pay-ing-off pennant (10 feet for each year of service), the *Queen Mary* returned to Southampton on the 27th September, 1967 at the end of her 1,001st and final North Atlantic crossing.

Crowds watched in sombre silence but the reception at the Ocean Terminal was one of noisy celebration of a noble career. The *Oriana* (ibid) flew the signal 'Adieu, great Queen'.

Then, on the 21st March, 1940, she sailed, leaving behind her younger sister *Queen Elizabeth* (ibid), which had arrived in New York two weeks previously. The *'Mary'* headed towards Australia where, in Sydney, she was partially converted into a troopship. She then took ANZAC troops to Gourock and eventually went out to Singapore, where she entered the large drydock for maintenance and further conversion. Thereafter, she shuttled between Australia, India and Egypt, transporting Empire troops to various theatres of war.

Early in 1942, the *Queen Mary* was in New York for further conversion work. She returned to Sydney with thousands of GIs, who were needed to defend Australia from possible Japanese attack. Eventually ending up in New York again, she embarked on the 'GI Shuttle', ferrying huge numbers of American troops to Britain in the build-up to the invasion of Europe that began on the 6th June, 1944 – D-Day.

To the *Queen Mary* fell the unbeaten record of carrying the most people in a single ship – 15,125 troops and 863 crew on one eastbound voyage in August, 1942. But it was on one of these transatlantic dashes, on which she was met by escorting cruisers as she neared the end of her voyage, that disaster occurred when she rammed – and cut in half – HMS *Curacoa*. The huge troopship could not stop in those dangerous waters for fear of becoming a target for U-Boats or Nazi aircraft and, with a buckled bow and at reduced speed, she had to leave it to other escorts to pick up the survivors from the sunken warship.

After war's end, the *Queen Mary* not only assisted in repatriating U.S. troops but also made several trips taking war brides and their children to their new American homeland. It is sad to relate that during these trips several children died from gastric ailments as they were unused to such rich food after years of deprivation and rationing in war-torn Britain.

Whereas *Queen Elizabeth* was renovated for peacetime use at Tail o'the Bank on the Clyde, the *Queen Mary* was refitted for Cunard-White Star service at Southampton. On the 1st August, 1946, she left on her first post-War departure in the regular service to New York. The *'Mary'* instantly regained her old popularity and Cunard's coffers began to swell as her partnership with the *Queen Elizabeth* thrived.

The *Queen Mary* was fitted with stabilisers during the winter of 1957-58, to smooth your way across the Atlantic, as a leaflet proclaimed.

However, by 1958 as many people were travelling across the Atlantic by air as were crossing by sea. Thereafter, the new jet aircraft took more and more of the traffic and the number of passengers on the liners dropped precipitously. After losing a great deal of money in her final years, in spite of being sent on low budget cruising jaunts, the *Queen Mary* was put up for sale and, on the 27th September, 1967, she completed her last crossing from New York. Ten thousand people watched her arrival in Southampton. The 31st October saw thousands more lining the shores of Southampton Water and The Solent as the old 'Queen' bade the city a final sad farewell and headed off towards her new home in Long Beach, California. There, much of her machinery was stripped out and she was converted to become a hotel and convention centre, relying on land-based services for her power and water supplies while floating in her own rock-bound lagoon.

She is still there. During the long period of her retirement, she has seen much political infighting over her presence and even her very existence has sometimes been placed in jeopardy. One proposal was to take her out to sea and sink her, selling the film rights to Hollywood, and then using the wreck as an attraction for tourist submarines! At one time, it was decided to put her up for sale and she attracted bids from all over the World, including a viable one from Southampton put forward by a group that included the present author. However, she was later withdrawn from the market as she held too high an international profile for Long Beach to lose her. On another occasion, the famous ocean explorer Jacques Cousteau proposed to

The *Queen Mary* makes a night departure from Ocean Dock, Southampton on the 29th September, 1967 at the beginning of her final cruise. To most of us, it seemed that the age of the big ocean liners was almost over.

build a museum in the vast caverns of her by now emptied boiler rooms but the idea was dropped after a lot of initial work had been undertaken.

It is now hoped that the veteran liner may find a new lease of life as she is moored alongside a quay adjacent to a new terminal, a berthing place for visiting Carnival Group ships. In March, 2006 the new *Queen Mary 2* visited Long Beach for the first time (the old *Queen Mary* could fit inside the new one – including funnels!) and, amid joyful celebrations, the two great ships exchanged siren greetings. May the venerable *Queen Mary* find new strength as she is, assuredly, still the most famous ocean liner in the World.

# QUEEN ELIZABETH

Completed 1940 by John Brown & Co., Ltd., Clydebank. 83,673 gross tons. Overall length: 1,031 ft. / 314.2m. (1,004 ft. / 306.0m. at the waterline). Beam: 118 ft. 6$^{ins}$ / 36.1m. Draught: 39 ft. ½$^{ins}$ / 11.9m. 16 Parsons steam turbines by John Brown. 12 Yarrow-type boilers. 200,000 shp. Quadruple screws. Service speed: 29½ knots. Call sign: GBSS.

Launched on the 27th September, 1938 by Her Majesty Queen Elizabeth into a world beset by growing uncertainties, the *Queen Elizabeth* was the biggest and the longest liner yet built. Even after the launch of the slightly longer *France* in 1960, she could still claim to be the largest in terms of tonnage. Her size was not exceeded until the advent of the unthought-of new generation of super-sized cruise ships in the late 1980s. Such has been the phenomenal rate of growth since then that a vessel is now planned of 210,000 gross tons.

War was declared before the 'Elizabeth' was completed and to protect her from damage by Nazi aircraft, she sailed secretly to New York where, grey-painted in wartime drab, she arrived on the 7th March, 1940 after a dash across the North Atlantic for which most of those on board, including some shipyard workers, had been quite unprepared. The great liner languished in New York in company with the *Queen Mary* (for a short time), *Normandie* and *Mauretania*. At first, it was not known what to do with these leviathans. Indeed, a short-sighted suggestion was made that they should be scrapped for their steel and plans were even drawn up to convert the 'Elizabeth' into an aircraft carrier. It was realised, however, that they could be more gainfully used to transport vast numbers of troops to wherever in the World they were needed.

The *Queen Mary* went first but the *Queen Elizabeth* followed on the 13th November, 1940. She was taken to Singapore for initial conversion and then sailed from Sydney to Bombay and Egypt. However, the bulk of the service of these two huge troopships was on the North Atlantic after America's entry into the War. On each eastbound crossing, they transported thousands of GIs in a build-up to the invasion of Hitler's 'Fortress Europe'.

After Victory in 1945, the *Queen Elizabeth* and the *Queen Mary* were used to carry the surviving American forces back to the U.S.A. By the 15th October, 1946, the 'Elizabeth' had been restored after the rigours of her wartime

On the 31st October, 1967, the *Queen Mary* left Southampton for the very last time, while fourteen Westland helicopters from three Naval Squadrons flew over her in formation and the band of the Royal Marines played *Auld Lang Syne*. The retirement of the *Queen Mary* aroused a similar outpouring of sentiment to that which accompanied the withdrawal of another great icon, *Concorde*, thirty-six years later.

service and at last began her long-delayed maiden commercial voyage from Southampton to New York. Over the next two decades, she would ply this route together with the 'Mary', carrying the rich and famous who sought to cross 'The Pond' in style. One of the sisters was the World's biggest liner and, until the advent of the S.S. *United States* in 1952, the other was the fastest.

In the mid-1950s, the 'Elizabeth' was fitted with stabiliser fins but soon the jet airliners started to make incursions into all sea-borne passenger traffic. Finally, in a cost-cutting exercise, Cunard decided to sell the two 'Queens'. Again the 'Mary' was the first to go. It was intended that the *Queen Elizabeth* would be kept a while longer to run with the 'New Cunarder' (launched as the *Queen Elizabeth 2*) but this was not to be.

On the 7th May, 1968, a few months before her final voyage, Bob Bruce Grice was supplied with a pass to visit the great ship in order to take photographs when she docked at Southampton at 5.00pm. The liner's turn-round was only 24 hours (large vessels are these days in port for 10 hours or less!) and it was pointed out that Commodore Marr, whom Bob was to meet, would be anxious to leave as soon as possible, probably to catch a few hours' rest at his thatched cottage in Woodfalls, near the New Forest.

A classic view of the *Queen Elizabeth*, photographed on the 8th October, 1968 bound for New York on one of her last departures from Southampton. These were gloomy times for the port as, one by one, the familiar liners slipped away into oblivion.

**Commodore Geoffrey Thrippleton Marr**

Geoffrey Marr started his training on HMS *Conway* in 1922 at the age of 14. He began his sea-going career with Elders & Fyffes but obtained his master's certificate and joined the newly amalgamated

Commodore Geoffrey Thrippleton Marr, photographed on the bridge of the *Queen Elizabeth*.

(Top, right.) Quartermaster L. A. Perkins at the wheel of the *Queen Elizabeth*. He lived locally at Hythe on the western shore of Southampton Water. He had served for many years in various Cunard ships, including the *Mauretania*, and was with the *Queen Mary* during the War years 1941-1943.

Cunard-White Star Line in 1936. He became Junior Third Officer on the *Queen Mary* two years later and was still with her when she was temporarily laid-up in New York at the outbreak of the Second World War. Through the Royal Naval Reserve, he served on various small craft during the early years of the War before being appointed to the mighty battleship *King George V*. He was on her when she went in pursuit of the *Bismarck* in 1941. Stationed in the emergency conning position during the ensuing action, he broadcast a running commentary on the progress of the battle to the crew stationed below decks. Later, Marr served with other units of the Royal Navy, both as a Navigator and Staff Officer, and saw duty on the dreaded Russian convoys and on escort duty in the Atlantic, Pacific and Indian Oceans. He was awarded the D.S.C. for 'gallantry in the face of the enemy and for setting an example of whole-hearted devotion to duty'.

After the War, he joined the *Mauretania*, then moved to the *Queen Elizabeth* and (after acting as Staff Captain on various Cunarders), was given command of the 7,300-ton cargo vessel *Andria* in 1957. The *Scythia* was his first passenger liner command, followed by the *Ivernia*, *Carinthia* and *Caronia*. Then, after serving as Acting Captain on the two 'Queens', he was given the *Queen Mary* at the end of 1965. He was known variously – and affectionately – by his crew as either 'Danny Marr' or 'Tatty Marr', the latter, perhaps, an ironic comment on his always immaculate appearance.

On the 1st January, 1966, he was appointed Commodore-Captain of the Cunard Line and, as such, took over the company's flagship, *Queen Elizabeth*. In 1968, he had the sad task of taking her out of Southampton for the last time, to a supposedly peaceful retirement in Fort Lauderdale.

Commodore Marr retired at the end of 1969 after a lifetime of adventure and rubbing shoulders with royalty, politicians and film stars. But the sea still beckoned and he was recalled to take the *Queen Elizabeth*, now sold to C. Y. Tung and renamed *Seawise University*, to Hong Kong. Commodore Geoffrey Marr, DSC, RNR, RD* died in 1997 at the age of 88.

## Quartermaster L. A. Perkins

Typically, an Ordinary Seaman could rise to become Quartermaster by first achieving the rank of Able Seaman. To do this, he had to attain various certificates, including that for lifeboat proficiency.

One requirement of a Quartermaster's qualification was to be able to 'box the compass' in front of 'The Old Man' – the Captain. A pedantic skipper might also ask the applicant to box the compass in reverse! On the 2nd October, 1942, L. A. Perkins was off-watch when the *Queen Mary*, having picked up her naval escort off the northern coast of Ireland en route to the Clyde, collided with and cut in half one of the escorting cruisers, H.M.S. *Curacoa*. Of the 432 men on board the warship, 331 lost their lives. Quartermaster Perkins said that below decks on the *Queen Mary* not even a shudder was felt.

On the 4th November, 1968, the '*Elizabeth*' docked at Southampton at the end of Voyage 495, her final crossing from New York. A few days later, she was visited by Her Majesty, The Queen Mother, who had launched her over thirty years earlier. What Her Majesty did not see was that only one side of the ship, that which was visible from the quayside, had been repainted. Times were so bad for Cunard that this had become company policy for all their ships. After one brief

Butcher Trevor Jones at work in the Meat Room of the *Queen Elizabeth*. It was Bob Bruce Grice's foresight in recording scenes such as this, previously ignored by photographers, that brought to notice the below-decks workings of a large liner.

The starboard aft Engine Room platform (looking forward), showing ahead and astern manoeuvring valve controls and the bridge telegraph. The revolution indicator and counter are to the left of the engineering officer at the controls.

Night refuelling: a fine nocturnal study of the *Queen Elizabeth* at her berth, bejewelled in a myriad of shimmering lights. Alongside is the *Esso Brixham*, replenishing the liner's voracious fuel tanks.

cruise to the Canaries, the flagship of the British Merchant Navy was taken out of service.

On her disposal, the *Queen Elizabeth* was to have gone to a new rôle, moored in the Delaware River at Philadelphia, but, because her tall masts might have proved a danger to aircraft using the nearby airport, she was taken instead to Fort Lauderdale in Florida. She was to be a floating hotel. After an initial success, she soon fell on hard times and was sold to Hong Kong shipowner C. Y. Tung. She sailed, unlamented, from Fort Lauderdale on the 10th February, 1971 but broke down in the Caribbean a few days later. She anchored off the island of Aruba for three months while boiler repairs were carried out.

Seaworthy again, she sailed at last and arrived at Hong Kong on the 15th July. Major conversion work now commenced and by the 9th January, 1972 she was a mere week away from being transferred to a drydock in Japan for final preparation for her new career steaming the Pacific as a floating university and cruise ship, *Seawise University*. It was also planned that she would at some time visit her old home of Southampton. But fate – or maybe fate prompted by sabotage – dealt the old '*Elizabeth*' a deadly blow when she caught fire, with blazes starting in several places at once. With her upper decks flooded with water from firefighting tugs, the mortally wounded liner finally capsized, a wreckage of heat-twisted steel. Those who had loved this most gracious of ships felt her loss grievously.

(Previous page.) 'Topping Up' one of the plummer blocks, the castings that supported the propeller shafts. The inspection cover is raised as the engineering officer tops up the lubricating oil. The shaft had eight sections, each 33 feet long and with an outside diameter of more than 27 ins.

The *Queen Elizabeth*, flying her 280-feet long paying-off pennant, approaches the docks for the last time. Two navigational aids, a lozenge atop a pylon on the old Royal Pier and a triangle at the end of the Town Quay, provided the 'Queens' with a clear sight as they approached the Swinging Ground outside the entrance to the Ocean Dock. Illuminated at night, they are still used.

# QUEEN ELIZABETH 2

Completed 1969 by John Brown (Clydebank) Co., Ltd. / Upper Clyde Shipbuilders, Ltd., Clydebank. 65,863 gross tons. Length overall: 963 ft. 0$^{ins}$ / 293.5m. including bulbous bow (887 ft. 1in. / 270.4m. between perpendiculars). Beam: 105 ft. 3$^{ins}$ / 32.1m. Draught: 32 ft. 7½$^{ins}$ / 9.8m. Two sets of steam turbines. 110,000 shp (82,060 kW). Twin screw. Service speed: 28½ knots. Call sign: GBTT (inherited from the *Queen Mary*). 1986: re-engined with nine 9-cylinder MAN-B&W diesel engines, each coupled to a General Electric generator which, in turn, powers an electric propulsion motor. 118,000 bhp.

Photographed arriving alongside Southampton's famous Ocean Terminal for the first time, on 2 January 1969, the *Queen Elizabeth 2* was suffering from turbine problems which caused her delivery to her owners to be delayed until the following April.

The *Queen Elizabeth 2*'s entry into service occurred during very difficult times. Shipping lines and services were being cut back to extinction in many areas and the ship herself was almost a 'second best'. (The originally planned successor to the *Queen Mary* and *Queen Elizabeth* was to have been bigger in concept, as befitted the two mighty Cunarders she was designed to replace. She would, though, already have been obsolete by the time of her introduction.) The *Queen Elizabeth 2*'s first few months were troubled and almost proved her detractors to be right but her subsequent history has shown that she has been the equal of anything that has gone before.

Laid down and built with a shipyard appellation of a Queen-in-Waiting, the Q4 as she was then known (Q3 having been the abandoned design) was launched on 20th September, 1967 by Her Majesty Queen Elizabeth II. She named the ship after her beloved mother – and thus the new liner was the second vessel to bear the name Queen Elizabeth – hence *Queen Elizabeth 2*. The QE2, as she was called from the moment she entered service, had been designed for cruising as well as for Cunard's traditional transatlantic liner route. She has proved herself to be both a popular ship and a 'good sea boat', able to cope with whatever the North Atlantic has thrown at her.

Her career has not been without incident. She has been involved in some minor collisions with piers and uncharted reefs but the most serious occurred on 7th August, 1999, when she hit a group of shallow boulders after exiting the channel between Martha's Vineyard and Cuttyhunk Island on the northeast coast of the U.S.A. The damage was considerable and might have caused the demise of a lesser ship.

*QE2* has also brushed with human-inspired danger in her nearly forty years at sea. She was, for instance, the victim of a bomb scare in May, 1972. Despite the rough conditions, an R.A.F. Hercules parachuted four bomb disposal experts into the sea close to the liner, which had slowed to 2 knots and was able to pick them up. (This event later inspired a British film, *Juggernaut*, in which the Soviet liner *Maksim Gorkiy* (ibid) played the *QE2* rôle.) Eleven months after that, while the *QE2* was making a cruise to Israel, a threatened torpedoing by a Libyan submarine in the Mediterranean was only narrowly averted, thanks to the intervention of President Saddat of Egypt.

The *QE2*'s original engines were sometimes problematic. On her initial trials, for instance, she had to limp back to Southampton with turbine troubles. (Cunard at first refused to accept her.) In 1976, she had a serious boiler-room fire. Then, because of possible problems that could have occurred with her engines, her involvement in the Falklands campaign of 1982 was relatively limited. She transported personnel and supplies to the South Atlantic, but 'only' as far as South Georgia, where they were transferred to P&O's *Canberra* (ibid). Eventually, a decision was made to convert her into a diesel-electric ship and this huge task was undertaken at the Lloyd Werft in Bremerhaven over the winter of 1986-87.

Since then, Round-the-World trips and more 'local' cruises, transatlantic liner voyaging and special events have all kept the *QE2* a highly popular and highly visible ship. In spite of being eclipsed in many ways by larger, more modern and 'glitzy' purpose-built cruise ships, the Cunarder still retains the epithet of 'The most famous liner in the world to-day'. Of the many major events in which she has been involved, two took place locally in The Solent. The first was a celebration of the 150th Anniversary of the Cunard Line in 1990; and the second was the spectacular Review held in 1994 to commemorate the 50th Anniversary of D-Day. On that occasion, the waters of The Solent were churned white by hundreds of sightseeing craft. Both events were attended by Her Majesty the Queen in the Royal Yacht *Britannia* (ibid).

The *QE2* has now handed over her rôles as Cunard's flagship and the sole remaining regular transatlantic liner to her new fleetmate, *Queen Mary 2*. In April, 2004, the two ships sailed together from New York to Southampton, leaving the American port amid huge excitement and beneath a spectacular firework display and arriving in Southampton to equal acclaim. Although she is now inevitably overshadowed by the huge new liner, the *QE2* is still able to attract excited attention wherever she enters port. She now concentrates mainly on cruises for the British market but every year she still makes her customary World Cruise.

September, 2005 was significant for the *QE2*. In that month she broke the record of the *Scythia* (1921-57) as the longest serving Cunarder. Since 1969 the *QE2* had sailed 5.3 million nautical miles, which Cunard claimed was more than any ship in history and equivalent to travelling twelve times to the moon and back. She had carried nearly three million passengers on 1,383 voyages and had called at Southampton 651 times. Over her 36 years, she had sailed at an average speed of 24.75 knots and, it was said, can still sail backwards faster than most cruise ships can sail forwards!

Two shots from an escorting tug of the *Queen Elizabeth 2* proceeding up-river on arrival from New York.

Facing page. A rare 'real' shot of two masterpieces of British engineering seen together. On 29th April, 1987, *Concorde* over-flew the *QE2* as the liner sailed from Southampton. Following the replacement of her steam turbines by diesel engines, her original narrow, streamlined funnel has given way to a much more imposing one.

## QUEEN MARY 2

The last ocean liner? The mighty *QM2* photographed leaving Berth 106, Southampton, on 22 July 2004.

Completed 2003 by Chantiers de l'Atlantique, St. Nazaire, France. 148,528 gross tons. Length overall: 1,132 ft. / 345m. (988 ft. / 301m. between perpendiculars). Beam: 135 ft. / 40m. Draught: 32 ft. 10ins. / 9.9m. Four Wärtsilä 16-cylinder diesel engines and two General Electric gas turbines driving Brush generators which power four Alsthom-Rolls Royce propulsion pods (two fixed and two steering). Service speed: 28 knots (achieved 30.25 knots on trials). Call sign: GBQM.

"The biggest, the largest, the widest, the most expensive ocean liner in the World" were some of the hyperbolic claims surrounding the $800 million *QM2* when the intention to build her – and possibly a companion – was declared on board the *QE2* during celebrations to mark that latter ship's thirtieth birthday. Those claims are still true and will probably remain so for many years to come. Bigger, larger, more expensive *cruise ships* are currently being planned and built but it seems that, as an *ocean liner*, the *QM2* is unlikely to be surpassed. Designed by the British naval architect Stephen Payne, she is indeed an ocean liner, specially built to withstand the rigours of North Atlantic crossings.

*QE2's* popular captain, Ron Warwick, was chosen to stand by the gargantuan new vessel during her building in a massive dry dock at the Chantiers de l'Atlantique yard at St. Nazaire, the birthplace of such famous liners as the *Ile de France*, *Normandie* and *France*. Tragically, the construction of the *QM2* was marred by the deaths of several members of shipyard employees' families when a gangway collapsed during an open day. Otherwise, the project was a triumph.

Captain Warwick was created Commodore of the Cunard Line when – after successful sea trials during which the liner achieved a creditable 30 knots – the *QM2* arrived in Southampton on a misty, wet and windy Boxing Day (26th December), 2003. The port again thrilled to the mighty, nostalgic boom of the siren of a former Cunard 'Queen' as, amongst her array, the new ship sported a refurbished whistle from the legendary *Queen Mary*, now in retirement at Long Beach, California. This had been brought to the UK aboard the *QE2*. It is now powered by compressed air, but with a token wisp of steam to give it added authenticity.

The new ship was named by Her Majesty the Queen at Southampton on 8th January, 2004 during a spectacular ceremony. (Her Majesty apparently did not like the name *Queen Mary 2*. It had been her idea to call the previous liner *Queen Elizabeth 2* – with an Arabic 2 – after her mother – this being the second ship to be named after her beloved parent.) Four days later, the *QM2* left on her maiden voyage to Fort Lauderdale, Florida amid a non-stop display of fireworks that exploded in the Cunard colours of red and gold, the detonations of the rockets echoing from the ship's massive hull as if from a tall, solid cliff.

Her first traditional transatlantic crossing from Southampton to New York started on 16th April. On her arrival in the 'Big Apple' after a rough crossing, she was said to have attracted more attention from the media in that normally blasé city than any other ship in at least thirty years. The publisher of this book was on that crossing and remembers that even more exciting was the view of the ship departing for the return crossing four days later in company with her elder fleet-mate *QE2* against a spectacular evening background of the Manhattan skyline and yet another magnificent fireworks display.

Since her introduction, the new 'Queen' has experienced many gala arrivals and departures. Half a million people turned out to greet her maiden arrival in Hamburg, her disembarking passengers being treated like film stars. More surprisingly, the following year, her second arrival in the port attracted a similar welcome. Taking the hint, Cunard planned several future transatlantic crossings from Hamburg to New York. The *QM2* was even used as a static, grand luxury hotel during the August 2004 Olympic Games held in Athens. The British Prime Minister, Tony Blair, was one of her many guests.

On the 17th January, 2006, the *QM2* scraped one of her four propulsion pods against the bottom of the navigation channel outside Port Everglades, Florida. After a two-day delay for inspection, she was able to continue her round-South America cruise on three pods but had to miss three of her planned calls. Some passengers were discontented with the compensation they were being offered and, after much over-sensationalised coverage in the media, they eventually received 100% refunds – such is the present-day compensation culture.

Nevertheless, the World's love affair with the *QM2* – very similar to the response to the old *Queen Mary* nearly seventy years earlier – shows no sign of abating. Bob Bruce Grice (incorrigible even in his nineties) was determined to have photographs of this great liner included in this volume.

# OTHER CUNARDERS

## CARMANIA

Completed as *Saxonia*, 1954, by John Brown & Co., Ltd., Clydebank. 21,370 gross tons. Length overall: 608 ft. 4ins / 185.4m. (570 ft. / 173.7m. between perpendiculars). Beam: 80 ft. 4ins / 24.5m. Draught: 28 ft. 6¾ins / 8.7m. Two sets of geared steam turbines. 24,500 shp. Twin screw. Service speed: 20 knots. Call sign: GSJS. 1963: refitted, mainly for cruising service; re-named *Carmania*. 1974: became *Leonid Sobinov*.

Launched as the *Saxonia* in 1954, this handsome liner was one of a series of four intended for Cunard's Canadian service from Liverpool. In 1957, she was transferred to Southampton but returned to Liverpool in 1961. In the winter months, when the St. Lawrence was frozen, she mainly sailed on the New York route. Between 1962 and 1963, she was extensively refitted at her builders' yard at Clydebank and re-named *Carmania*, painted in the shades of green made famous by the *Caronia* of 1949. This was done to send her cruising. Her sister *Ivernia*, now called *Franconia*, was also converted and both proved to be very popular with their crews as well as with passengers. In 1967, the two ships were painted white.

The *Carmania* at Southampton in 1971 during her final season for Cunard.

Four years later, they were placed on the disposal list. Laid-up in the River Fal in Cornwall, they were finally sold in 1973. The buyers were Nikreis Maritime Corporation of Panama who, it emerged, were acting on behalf of the Soviet Union. The *Carmania* was re-named *Leonid Sobinov* and *Franconia* became the *Fedor Shalyapin*. As such, they were used on the Southampton to Australia route, earning valuable foreign currency for the Soviets. Later, these popular ships were sent cruising.

Both were laid-up at Ilichevsk in 1995, by now elderly and worn, but on 27th January, 1999, the *Leonid Sobinov* left her sister still at her berth and sailed for Odessa. She left there at the end of January, heading for the beaches of Alang and the burners' torches. But adventure awaited her as, after passing through the Suez Canal, she ran out of fuel in the Indian Ocean. Eventually, she was towed to an anchorage off the scrapping beaches, where dismantling commenced on 1st October but was interrupted by a strike in May, 2000. Subsequent events have exposed the appalling and dangerous conditions under which the scrapyard workers are employed and even Greenpeace has been involved in lobbying for safer working conditions for the labourers.

# CUNARD ADVENTURER

Completed 1971 by Rotterdamsche Droogdok Mij., (Rotterdam Drydock Co.) Rotterdam. 14,151 gross tons. Length overall, including bulbous bow: 485 ft. 11$^{ins}$ / 148.1m. (413 ft. / 125.9m. between perpendiculars). Beam: 71 ft. 11$^{ins}$ / 21.9m. Draught: 19 ft. 3½ $^{ins}$ / 6.6m. Four 12-cylinder Stork-Werkspoor diesel engines. 28,000 bhp. Twin screw. Service speed: 21½ knots. Call sign: GOZC.

This cruise ship was slightly unusual as she was one of two laid down to the order of an airline, Overseas National Airways. However, shortly into their construction, Cunard took a half-share in the contract. Eventually, Cunard took them over completely and placed them in Caribbean cruise service.

In June, 1973, *Cunard Adventurer* hosted a cruise entitled 'Voyage to Darkness', when 800 passengers witnessed a total eclipse of the sun which lasted just over four minutes, during which time 'Bailey's Beads', 'Diamond Rings' and several stars could be seen. One bizarre episode in her career involved her sistership, *Cunard Ambassador*, which caught fire during a Caribbean cruise. Half of her passengers transferred to the *Adventurer* and the *Ambassador* went off for repairs. Three days later, the repaired *Ambassador* sailed, only to receive a distress call from the *Adventurer*. The displaced passengers then had to be transferred back to their original ship. (In 1974, another fire caused the *Cunard Ambassador* to be declared a total

*Leonid Sobinov (ex-Carmania) departing Southampton for a North Cape cruise on the 7th June, 1975. With their low operating costs, Soviet liners were able to offer cheap cruises and became very popular in the Western market for a time.*

loss. In fact, she was sold and rebuilt as a livestock carrier, quite a come-down after her early career as a cruise ship.)

In 1977, *Cunard Adventurer* was involved in a collision off San Juan with the Costa Line's *Carla C.*, the former *Flandre* of the French Line. The *Adventurer* was repaired but later that year she was sold, having been replaced by the larger and rather better furnished *Cunard Countess*. The buyers were Klosters Rederi of Oslo (Norwegian Caribbean Line), one of the pioneering lines of the modern Miami-based cruise industry, who required her for their 'Bahamarama' jaunts. During an extensive rebuild by Lloyd Werft of Bremerhaven, her often-criticised tall funnel was replaced by a smaller, more shapely pair, side-by-side, and her interiors were lightened in style. She was now called *Sunward II*.

Fifteen years later, in 1992, and yet again replaced by larger tonnage, she was sold to Epirotiki Lines of Piraeus. Looking very smart in Epirotiki livery, she was renamed *Triton*. Although engaged in 'economy cruising', she built up an excellent reputation for her cuisine. In 1995, Epirotiki merged most of their operations with the Sun Line to form Royal Olympic Cruises, in which the Cypriot company Louis Cruises later held a stake for a short time. On the 22nd December, 2003, *Triton* hit the

The *Cunard Adventurer* photographed against the sun at Southampton on the 19th November 1971.

headlines. On a Mediterranean Christmas cruise, she missed two ports of call following the announcement of the detention of two other R.O.C. ships as a result of group companies defaulting on the payment of loan interest. *Triton* was the impounded at Patras in Greece. Eventually, R.O.C. was able to resume operations on a limited scale but in early 2005 it was declared bankrupt. In April, Louis Cruises bought the *Triton* for $9½ million and renamed her *Coral*.

# VISTAFJORD

Completed 1973 by Swan Hunter Shipbuilders Ltd., Neptune Yard, Newcastle-upon-Tyne. 24,292 gross tons. Length overall: 626 ft. 11ins / 191.1m. (550 ft 1in / 167.7m. between perpendiculars). Beam: 82 ft. 2ins / 25.0m. Draught: 27 ft. / 8.2m. Two 9-cylinder Sulzer-type diesel engines. 24,000 bhp. Twin screw. Service speed: 20 knots. Call sign: LFVI.

Built for Den Norske Amerikalinje, the Norwegian America Line, this well-proportioned ship – perhaps one of the most beautiful ever built – has been used mainly for cruising. Together with her equally lovely near-sister *Sagafjord*, she was sold to Cunard in 1983. Without undergoing changes of name, both ships were

later given Cunard colours on their funnels, while retaining the original dove-grey hulls from their Norwegian days. Some structural changes were made to the *Vistafjord*, especially at the aft end of her superstructure where two terraced decks were converted into a glazed-in nightclub. Fears were expressed that the takeover by Cunard would result in a lowering of the ships' famously high standards, but in fact it was generally agreed that, if anything, they were raised. *Sagafjord* was later sold to the Saga group, which specialises in travel and insurance for the over-fifties, and became their very popular *Saga Rose*. Cunard would come to regret breaking up this successful duo.

In 1999, in an attempt to give the rather mismatched Cunard fleet a corporate identity, the *Vistafjord* was repainted in the company's conventional livery and was renamed *Caronia* (after the fabled cruise ship of 1949) in a spectacular celebration-studded ceremony in Liverpool. She then sailed through a Force 10 in the Irish Sea to Southampton. This trip and her subsequent introductory excursion to France, also undertaken in rough conditions, caused Cunard, now a member of the Carnival group, to send her to the Lloyd Werft yard in Germany for the addition of a skeg extension to her stern at the waterline. Whilst probably improving her seaworthiness, this did nothing for her lines in that area.

Following the introduction of the gigantic *Queen Mary 2* in 2004, Cunard sold *Caronia* to Saga Cruises, where she joined her old fleet-mate and assumed the name *Saga Ruby*. It is to be hoped that these two delightful and comfortable ships will sail on in mutually elegant company for many years to come.

One of the most shapely passenger ships ever built, the *Vistafjord* is seen at Southampton on the 5th June 1987.

Seen here at Berth 38/39 on the 18th January 1974 in the last year of the Elder Dempster passenger service to West Africa, the *Aureol* was a much-loved ship.

## AUREOL

Completed 1951 by Alexander Stephen & Sons, Ltd., Linthouse, Glasgow. 14,083 gross tons. Length overall: 537 ft. 1ins / 163.7m. (480 ft./ 146.3m. between perpendiculars). Beam: 70 ft. 2ins / 21.4m. Draught: 25 ft. 1ins / 7.6m. Two 4-cylinder Doxford-type diesel engines. 9,400 bhp. Twin screw. Service speed: 16 knots. Call sign: GMGJ.

Built for Elder Dempster Lines of Liverpool, the elegant *Aureol* was launched on 28th March, 1951 and was the company's largest ship. As the flagship of the line, she remained in the mail, cargo and passenger service from Liverpool to Lagos in Nigeria until April, 1972, when Southampton became her British terminus. She had been the last liner in a regular service from Liverpool.

Her association with Southampton was short-lived, however. Arriving there for the last time on 14th October, 1974, she was sold to a company belonging to John S. Latsis, the Greek oil and shipping magnate, and was refitted in Piraeus and renamed *Marianna VI*. She was sent to Jeddah to be used as an office and leisure centre for workers on a construction project, returning to Piraeus early in 1979, her place being taken by the *Margarita L.*, the former *Windsor Castle*. The old *Aureol* remained in lay-up until sold for breaking in 2001, ending her days on the beach at Alang in India, where she arrived in June of that year.

She had been one of those rare, graceful, yacht-like ships, enjoying admiration both from those who sailed in her and those who saw her from afar. She even inspired parents to name their children after her and a railway to name a locomotive *Aureol* in her honour. Even now, she is not entirely forgotten: a collector in California has furnished much of his house with items from this beautiful ship.

# ORCADES

Completed 1948 by Vickers-Armstrongs, Ltd., Barrow-in-Furness. 28,164 gross tons. Overall length: 708 ft. 8ins / 216.0m. (666 ft. 9ins / 203.2m. between perpendiculars). Beam: 93 ft. 6ins / 28.5m. Draught: 31 ft. 0¼ins / 9.5m. Six Parsons steam turbines. 42,500 shp. Twin screw. Service speed: 22 knots. Call sign: MABA.

Launched on the 14th October, 1947, the *Orcades* was named after a previous Orient Steam Navigation Co. liner which had been torpedoed almost exactly five years previously. The first liner built after the War for the company's Tilbury-Australia service, the new *Orcades* commenced off-peak cruising in 1952. Because

Post-war Orient Line
ships had a very
distinctive appearance.
The *Orsova* was an early
example of a
mast-less ship.

soot tended to blow onto her after decks, a pipe extension was added to the top of her funnel, thus giving it a famously distinctive 'Welsh hat' appearance.

June, 1953 saw her not only represent her company at the huge Coronation Fleet Review at Spithead but lead a flotilla of two other liners full of distinguished guests to an anchorage at the head of the Merchant Navy contingent. She began round-the-World voyaging in 1955. In 1959, Harland & Wolff's Belfast yard were commissioned to fit her with the badly needed air-conditioning which would keep her viable in a competitive market. She was the first Orient Line vessel to be so equipped. In 1960, she was transferred to the newly combined P&O-Orient Lines. (Orient Line and P&O had been closely linked for many years.) Four years later, the lovely corn-coloured hull, a distinctive livery devised by the renowned Laurence Dunn, was painted over in P&O white. In 1966, the famous Orient Line name disappeared completely.

In 1964, with passenger numbers dwindling, the *Orcades* was designated a one-class ship catering for the tourist and migrant trades and she managed to sail on for another eight years. 1970 saw her increasingly rely on cruising, either from Sydney or from Southampton, from where in December, 1972 she sailed on her voyage of no return. She had been sold to Nang Feng Steel Enterprises Co., Ltd. of Kaohsiung in Taiwan for demolition, which started, appropriately, on the Ides of March.

# ORSOVA

Completed 1954 by Vickers-Armstrongs, Ltd., Barrow-in-Furness. 28,790 gross tons. Length overall: 722 ft. 10$^{ins}$ / 220.3m. (668 ft. 0$^{ins}$ / 203.6m. between perpendiculars). Beam: 90 ft. 7$^{ins}$ / 27.6m. Draught: 30 ft. 11½$^{ins}$ / 9.4m. Six Parsons steam turbines. 42,500 shp. Twin screw. Service speed: 22 knots. Call sign: GNDL.

Here seen leaving the King George V dry dock on the 7th August 1978, the *Oriana* was the last of the many ships built for the Orient Line by Vickers-Armstrongs at Barrow.

The third of a series of similar Orient liners, the *Orsova* differed from her peers, *Orcades* (ibid) and *Oronsay*, in not being fitted with a mast. Otherwise, she shared the same distinctive profile, with the bridge placed well aft, in front of the single almost upright funnel.

Like the *Orcades*, the *Orsova* was transferred to P&O-Orient Lines in 1960 but she was not fully registered under P&O ownership until 1965. She too had been fitted with air-conditioning shortly before the amalgamation. In the 1960s, the Orient Line vessels transferred their home port from Tilbury to Southampton and it was from here that the *Orsova* ended her days cruising. She followed the *Orcades* to the same breakers, arriving in Kaohsiung on St. Valentine's Day, 1974.

# ORIANA

Completed 1960 by Vickers-Armstrongs, Ltd., Barrow-in-Furness. 41,915 gross tons. Length overall (including bulbous bow): 804 ft. 0ins / 245.1m. (740 ft.0ins / 225.6m. between perpendiculars). Beam: 97 ft. 2ins / 29.6m. Draught: 30 ft. 11½ins / 9.4m. Six Pametrada-Vickers steam turbines. 80,000 bhp. 2 thrusters forward and 2 aft. Twin screw. Service speed: 27½ knots. Call sign: GVSN.

While still on the drawing board, this ship had to be given a name – beginning, of course, with the traditional Orient Line *Or......*. Because of her intended route, someone in the design office suggested, with a slight Australian twang and a great deal of humour, *Orstralia*! However, *Oriana* was the official choice (an epithet for Queen Elizabeth I, 'Good Queen Bess').

This radical new ship was launched on the 3rd November, 1959 by Princess Alexandra in a blaze of publicity and to the accompaniment of 'Fanfare for *Oriana*', specially composed by Benjamin Britten. She was a departure from the previous post-War designs of the Orient Line. Tiers of superstructure built onto an excellent hull were surmounted by two funnels of differing size on different levels. In actual fact, the after 'funnel', looking rather like an upturned flower pot, was a dummy. After decades of courtship, Orient Line and P&O finally 'tied the knot' on the 2nd May, 1960, when the two companies cemented their long-term relationship by becoming P&O-Orient Lines, each partner keeping its own ships and its own identity. Orient Line ships would continue with their lovely corn-coloured hulls for a few more happy years until 1963-4, when P&O took over the entire operation, discarding both the Orient name and the Orient hull livery, preferring their own white-painted uniform.

Oriana's maiden voyage from Southampton to Australia started on a cold, wet 3rd December, 1960. The ship was partly lit against the prevailing murk but the sounds of her band were carried by the cold wind to the few hardy watchers on the Royal Pier. It would, at least, be summer when she made her maiden arrival in Australia. She was not only the biggest ship Orient had ever owned but she was also the largest in the Pacific and the fastest in the U.K. to Australia and U.S. West Coast service. Her patrons gradually lost their initial surprise at her almost eccentric appearance and took her to their hearts. She became very popular. Although the austerity of the post-War years had eased, many Britons were still seeking new lives in Australia and New Zealand, which needed to increase their populations. By the early 'sixties, although the jet airliner was taking its toll of the passenger lists of the Atlantic ships, long-haul flights had not yet impacted on the shipping services to the other side of the World and the Oriana thrived. Later, by 1973, as the aircraft finally took hold on the antipodean routes, she became a full-time cruise ship, operating out of both Southampton and Sydney during their respective summers. In 1981, she was permanently transferred to Sydney. She undertook her final cruise from that port in 1986.

Saved from the scrapyard, she began a series of placements which kept her afloat for many years, albeit in a static rôle. Firstly, she went to Japan and, after having her rudder and propellers removed at the Hitachi Zosen shipyard, she became a hotel, leisure centre and museum moored (welded to the adjacent pontoon) at Oita on the island of Kyushu. Now with a pink funnel, she remained there until 1996 when her owners, Daiwa House Group, collapsed. She was then towed to China where new owners, Hangzhou Jiebai Group, used her as a hotel at Qinhuangdao, 180 miles east of Beijing. November, 1998 saw her in a deteriorated condition and being moved to Shanghai, where she was given an extensive renovation. Opened again in 1999 by Oriana Entertainment Corporation, her fortunes took a further downturn after the Millennium celebrations were over and Song Dynasty Town Groups bought her in September, 2000. Oriana was once again in poor condition, awaiting either an injection of capital or a journey to the breaker's yard. In fact, now at Dalian, she capsized during a storm on the 18th June, 2004. She was later salvaged but was finally scrapped at Zhanjiagang.

# HIMALAYA

Completed 1949 by Vickers-Armstrongs, Ltd., Barrow-in-Furness. 27,989 gross tons. Length overall: 708 ft. 8ins / 216.0m. (666 ft. 9ins / 203.2m. between perpendiculars). Beam: 90 ft. 10ins / 27.7m. Draught: 31 ft. 0¼ins / 9.4m. forward and 40 ft. / 12.2m. aft. Six geared steam turbines. 42,500 shp. Twin screw. Service speed: 22 knots. Call sign: GBDK.

Part of the P&O Line's post-War rebuilding programme, the handsome Himalaya was the company's third ship to bear that name. She was the first sign that luxury and a sense of normality had returned to P&O after the bleak austerity of wartime. She spent the first nine years of her career on the Tilbury to Sydney route, making the occasional break to go cruising – the first ship to do so for P&O since before the War.

In 1958, her itinerary was extended across the Pacific to Vancouver and San Francisco. The *Himalaya* achieved a form of lasting fame when, following a shore excursion at Trieste in July, 1952, a passenger, Mrs. Rose Adler, fell sixteen feet after the gangway to the liner slipped. It was alleged that the gangway was faulty – and therefore improperly maintained. Because Mrs. Adler's ticket contained a non-responsibility clause exempting the company, the ship's bosun and her master, Captain Bob Dickson, were sued. Judgement in the case of Adler versus Dickson resulted in legislation introduced in 1954. From then on, international sea carriers have used a clause, which has become known as the *Himalaya* clause, as an exemption in their bills of lading.

A Thornycroft funnel cap with internal but visible fins within its parameters was fitted in 1953 to help obviate the sooty smuts which were falling onto the *Himalaya*'s after passenger decks. This 12-foot extension slightly improved her good looks by giving additional height. Some other liners, notably the *America* and *United States*, had an external fin. Following the example of the Cunard 'Queens', the *Himalaya* was given stabilisers during a dry-docking at Tilbury in 1959, thus improving her passengers' comfort.

Misfortune had visited the liner in 1956, when five crewmembers were killed and another twelve injured by an explosion in a refrigeration chamber. During a call into a Ceylonese port on the 10th October, 1960, local police visited the ship and arrested a passenger, Stephen Bradley, who was travelling with his wife and family. Bradley was flown back to Sydney, where he was tried and found guilty of the kidnap and murder of 8-year old Graeme Thorne, whose father had won £100,000 on the very first Opera House Lottery.

In 1963, following the retirement of the *Orion*, the *Himalaya* was converted from a two- to a one-class ship at Tilbury. She now carried 1416 passengers as against her previous 758 1st class and 401 Tourist. Her tonnage was now measured at 27,989, a figure which was revised to 28,047 in 1969. A year later P&O moved its passenger operation from Tilbury to Southampton and it fell to the *Himalaya* to make the service's last departure from the River Thames.

In November, 1974, the ship arrived at Kaohsiung, Taiwan for breaking and this unhappy work started two months later. However, her name lives on: in the current cruise ship *Aurora* there are two small rooms that can be used for private functions. They are sited either side of the now traditionally named Crow's Nest Bar and one is called after the *Uganda* and the other after the *Himalaya*.

The ultra-modern *Canberra*, with her engines positioned aft, her twin side-by-side funnels and her low-slung lifeboats, was not at first successful. Later, she achieved great popularity as a cruise ship. Here she is leaving for Sydney via Panama on the 10<sup>th</sup> November 1984.

# CANBERRA

Completed 1961 by Harland & Wolff, Ltd., Belfast. 45,270 gross tons. Length overall: 818 ft. 6<sup>ins</sup> / 249.5m. (740 ft. 0<sup>ins</sup> / 225.6m. between perpendiculars). Beam: 102 ft. 6<sup>ins</sup> / 31.2m. Draught: 41 ft. 6<sup>ins</sup> / 12.6m. Turbo-electric (2 steam turbines driving alternators). 88,000 shp and 32,200 kW. 2 electric motors.) Twin screw. Service speed: 27½ knots. Call sign: GBVC.

The *Canberra* was built for the Peninsular & Oriental Steam Navigation Co., Ltd. (P&O Passenger Division). She aroused a lot of excitement in the U.K. and a children's television programme, 'Crow's Nest', was hosted by her young designer, John West, and demonstrated how to build a quite passable model of her over a six-week period. (The present author was amongst the many prize winners in a weekly identify-and-sketch competition.) The *Canberra* was then known as 'The Ship That Shaped the Future'.

Her maiden voyage left Southampton on a very hot 2<sup>nd</sup> June, 1961 and was a gala occasion (in spite of an unsightly slick along her starboard waterline!) that assured her place in the affections of the city. By 1973, with sea travel to Australia in decline, P&O tried cruising her out of New York but this proved to be a failure. After only two cruises, she was laid up at the mouth of Cape Fear River in North Carolina. She actually returned to New York for nine more cruises but P&O announced that, after only 12 years service, she would be sent to the breakers. The reason given was that her deep draught made it impossible for her to berth at many cruise destinations. Fortunately, she was reprieved but on the date that the good news was received she celebrated by running aground.

An eventful career included a serious switchboard fire whilst in the Mediterranean in January, 1963, causing her to be returned to Belfast for repairs; another visit to New York on the 4<sup>th</sup> July, 1979, dressed overall in a parade to celebrate 'Operation Sail'; and a change from liner voyaging to profitable and highly popular full-time cruising. She achieved lasting fame with an heroic tour of duty in the 1982 Falklands Campaign when she acted as both troopship and hospital ship, under which guise she repatriated Argentinean prisoners of war to the country whose newspapers had previously described her destruction in flames. A banner slung over her side proclaimed 'Canberra cruises where QE2 refuses' when, on the late morning of the 11th July, 1982, she finally returned to Southampton in high-profile triumph carrying the men of 40 Commando, Royal Marines.

Later major events in her career included a noble rôle during the D-Day Anniversary commemorations in 1994 when she took veterans on a return to the seas off the Normandy beaches where so many of their comrades had sacrificed their lives; and, following an ignominious loss of power off the Isle of Wight in a storm-force gale also in 1994, she drifted to within four miles of the island's southern shore. All ended with her equally memorable last return to Southampton, emerging from a foggy Solent on the 30th September, 1997. She was then laid up to de-store, unusually at the Queen Elizabeth II Terminal at Berth 38/39, with preservation as a hoped-for but ultimately unfulfilled possibility.

After much conjecture as to her future, the well-loved old ship, popular with both passengers and crew, was made to steal away at 9 o'clock at night with only her navigation lights burning, to meet her appointment with Indian shipbreakers. Dappled clouds and her own shadowy, ghost-like bulk reflected the partial moonlight of the 10th October but other ships – and not a few motor cars lining the shores of Southampton Water – decided that her final departure should not go un-noticed and lamented her passing with their sirens.

# SEA PRINCESS

Completed 1966 by John Brown & Co. (Clydebank) Ltd., Clydebank, Scotland. 27,670 gross tons. Length: 660 ft. 2[ins] / 201.2m. including bulbous bow (569 ft. 10[ins] / 173.7m. between perpendiculars). Beam: 87 ft. 0[ins] / 26.5m. Draught: 28 ft. 1[ins] / 8.6m. Two Götaverken 9-cylinder oil engines. 25,200 bhp. Twin screw. Service speed: 21 knots. Call sign: GBBA.

This fine ship was originally built as the beautiful *Kungsholm* of the Swedish American Line, for whom she was the fourth vessel to bear that name. Later, after a brief spell with Flagship Cruises, she was bought by P&O in 1978. The following year, with her well-balanced profile now rather spoiled by the unfortunate removal of her forward funnel and the somewhat unsympathetic rebuilding of the after one, she was given the name *Sea Princess*.

She then cruised in British and Australian waters but later joined Princess Cruises' American-based fleet. For this P&O subsidiary she wore their funnel emblem of a girl's stylised profile with flowing, wavy hair ('The Sea Witch'). This at least broke up the uninspired, almost vertical symmetry of her new funnel for a short while. Later, on returning to Britain, she reverted to P&O colours. In February, 1992, she rescued over 370 passengers from the cruise ship *Ocean Pearl* which had caught fire off Sumatra.

*Sea Princess* was renamed *Victoria* in April, 1995, thus avoiding confusion with the vessels of the Princess Cruises division and also releasing her name for a Princess newbuilding. It was perhaps fortunate that, unlike *Oriana*, the vessel she replaced, she had been given a royal name rather than a royal pseudonym. (*Oriana* was a term of affection for Queen Elizabeth I; *Victoria* might have been called 'The Widow of Windsor'.)

In the winter of 1999-2000, *Victoria* was given a red funnel with a black top prior to sailing on a chartered voyage to South Africa commemorating the centenary of the old Union-Castle service. In 2001, she was sold out of the fleet to become the *Mona Lisa* under Greek ownership, appearing with yet another female face on her funnel – a huge facsimile of the portrait of La Gioconda (the Mona Lisa), faithfully reproduced.

The picture overleaf shows the still-elegant *Sea Princess* being passed by the inbound Red Funnel hydrofoil *Shearwater 2* in August 1985.

During a cruise in late July, 2003, the *Mona Lisa* was returning to Bremerhaven from Spitsbergen when she went aground whilst leaving the Magdalena Fjord. Her propellers and parts of her hull were damaged, her passengers were flown home and she sailed under her own power for Hamburg, where she was repaired. She hit the headlines again in early May, 2004, this time grounding in thick fog in the narrow channel waters of the canal basin near St. Mark's Square in Venice. Although she was refloated an hour later, the mishap prompted the city's mayor to complain that cruise ships were coming in too close to the historic square.

Two generations of P&O group cruise ships: the *Canberra* of 1961 and the *Royal Princess* of 1984 make an interesting comparison on the 10th November 1984.

# ROYAL PRINCESS

Completed 1984 by O/Y Wärtsilä, Helsinki. 44,348 gross tons. Length overall: 756 ft. 7$^{ins}$ / 230.6m. including bulbous bow (633 ft. 10$^{ins}$ / 193.2m. between perpendiculars). Beam: 95 ft. 9$^{ins}$ / 29.2m. Draught: 25 ft. 7$^{ins}$ / 7.8m. Four 6-cylinder Pielstick oil engines. 31,543 bhp. Two controllable-pitch propellers. Service speed: 20 knots. Call sign: GBRP.

The *Royal Princess* was the first cruise ship to feature all-outside staterooms and created quite a stir when she was named in Southampton by HRH the Princess of Wales on a sunny 19<sup>th</sup> November, 1984. A member of the Princess Cruises fleet, the new ship then set off on a positioning voyage to Miami, from where she made her maiden cruise.

In 2000, the UK government introduced tax incentives to encourage British shipping companies to re-register their ships under the Red Ensign. The P&O group, of which Princess was a member, led the way by re-flagging their *Royal Princess* and *Pacific Princess* and the rest of their fleet soon followed. Until then, the numbers of the British-flagged fleet had been gradually dwindling, with the *QE2* accounting for quite a high proportion of the total tonnage. Many old merchant mariners were horrified when, in 2004, there was a proposal that the stars of the European Commission should deface the Red Ensign, but this idea was soon dropped.

In 2003, Princess Cruises, which – in a rôle reversal – had become the parent company of all the P&O group's cruising subsidiaries, was taken over by the giant Carnival Corporation. Princess's Southampton headquarters now manage all the enlarged Carnival group's British subsidiaries, including P&O and its old rival Cunard. In 2005, *Royal Princess* was renamed *Artemis*, now flying the P&O flag. Although not considered to be as 'glitzy' as some of her more modern counterparts, she is still regarded as a very comfortable ship.

The Italian-designed and -built *Crown Princess* is seen in mid-stream after leaving the Queen Elizabeth II Terminal at Southampton on the 13<sup>th</sup> September 1990.

# CROWN PRINCESS

Completed 1990 by Fincantieri Cantieri Navali SpA, Monfalcone. 69,845 gross tons. Length overall: 805 ft. 0<sup>ins</sup> / 245.4m. including bulbous bow (670 ft. 7<sup>ins</sup> / 204.4m. between perpendiculars). Beam: 105 ft. 9<sup>ins</sup> / 32.2m. Draught: 25 ft. 9<sup>ins</sup> / 7.9m. Four 8-cylinder MAN-type oil engines coupled to electric generators and motors. 52,860 bhp. Two controllable-pitch propellers. Service speed: 19½ knots. Call sign: ICBB.

Sadly, there are no longer
any British yards building
large passenger ships.
The very popular second
*Oriana* is dressed overall
as she arrives from her
German builders on the
3rd April 1995.

*Crown Princess* was the first of the P&O group's 70,000-tonners but she and her sister, *Regal Princess*, had actually been ordered by Sitmar Cruises, which P&O took over in 1988. These ships signalled their Italian builders' return to the market for deep-sea passenger ships after an absence of many years. Under a deal with the government in Rome, they flew the Italian flag and had Italian officers. The unusual profile of these vessels had been devised by the famous Genoese architect Renzo Piano.

Until 2002, the *Crown Princess* was operated within the P&O group by Princess Cruises, but she was then transferred to a German subsidiary, becoming their *A'Rosa Blu*. Distinctive additions were made on either side of her small, cylindrical funnel and gaudy artworks were painted onto her hull. In a group re-organisation she was later renamed *AidaBlu*. Meanwhile, the name *Crown Princess* has been revived for a huge new cruise ship of the *Grand Princess* class.

# ORIANA (II)

Completed 1995 by Meyer Werft, Papenburg, Germany. 69,153 gross tons. Length overall 853 ft. 0$^{ins}$ / 260.0m. including bulbous bow (735 ft. 2$^{ins}$ / 224.1m. between perpendiculars). Beam: 105 ft. 7$^{ins}$ / 32.2m. Draught: 26 ft. 10$^{ins}$ / 8.2m. Four MAN-B&W oil engines (two 9-cylinder and two 6-cylinder). 78,100 bhp. Two controllable-pitch propellers. Service speed: 24 knots. Call sign: GVSN.

Built as a replacement for the beloved *Canberra* (ibid), the new *Oriana* was even given a recessed funnel that represented the twin uptakes of her predecessor. A considerable amount of thought was given to this new P&O flagship. She was intended to cater for British tastes and instead of the enclosed structures of the American-orientated cruise ships, with their chrome and glass décor and vast, open-spaced interiors, she was given terraced open decks, wood and brass interiors and smaller, more intimate public rooms.

The *Oriana* received a spectacular welcome when she arrived at Southampton from the builders. She was named by Her Majesty Queen Elizabeth on the 6th April, 1995 during a lavish ceremony (unusually, alongside the site of the by-then demolished Ocean Terminal, with *Canberra* moored nearby). Benjamin Britten's *Fanfare for Oriana*, composed for the earlier ship of that famous name (ibid), was included among the other musical offerings of the day.

Deservedly, *Oriana* has proved to be a most popular cruise ship. It has to be said, though, that when she is in a rough sea her bluff underwater form forward does tend to be a noise-maker for those berthed in the crew's quarters. It is said that a crack 'like cannon fire' arises when a sea hits the knuckle at the turn of the bow. Hence, like many cruise ships, she is not totally suited for sailing on a turbulent North Atlantic. This was proven during a crossing from New York in September, 2000 when a 40-foot wave hit her during a Force 10 gale. Three windows on deck five and three on deck six were broken and three passengers were treated for cuts from glass flying into their flooded cabins. The *QE2*, specially designed for such seas, had met the same storm but rode it beautifully.

# SOUTHERN CROSS

Completed 1955 by Harland & Wolff, Ltd., Belfast. 20,204 gross tons. Length overall: 603 ft. 10ins / 184.0m. (560 ft. 0ins / 170.7m. between perpendiculars). Beam: 78 ft. 5ins / 23.9m. Draught: 25 ft. 10ins / 7.9m. Four Pametrada geared steam turbines. 20,000 shp. Twin screw. Service speed: 20 knots. Call sign: GSWW.

At the time of her appearance, the Shaw, Savill & Albion Line's *Southern Cross* was hailed as a revolutionary ship, with her engines sited aft. In fact, this feature was not new to passenger liners. As early as 1908, the Matson Line had taken delivery of the first of a series of engines-aft ships for their service between San Francisco and Hawaii and, in the Second World War, the United States Army commissioned no less than thirty 13,000-ton troop transports (Class C4-S-A1) with this profile. Subsequently, smaller engines-aft ships appeared in the Far East, on the French cross-Mediterranean routes and in the famous Norwegian Coastal Express service.

However, the *Southern Cross* was still a landmark liner. (She was identified by some as a tanker when she first appeared in The Solent but also received the accolade of being reproduced as an early Airfix plastic model construction kit.) Since then, innumerable modern liners and cruise ships have followed her example in having their engines, and therefore funnels, located aft. The Shaw, Savill company's forward-thinking chairman, Basil Sanderson, had realised the value of strategic engine placement and the elimination of cargo space to produce a liner which could carry larger numbers of passengers and would have vast, uninterrupted expanses of deck space.

Launched on the 17th August, 1954 by Her Majesty, The Queen (who had chosen the ship's name from a short-list), the £3,546,000 *Southern Cross* commenced her maiden voyage from Southampton on the 29th March, 1955. This took her on an east-about circumnavigation of the World via Australia and New Zealand. She remained on this route until the introduction of her near-sister *Northern Star* in 1962, when her itinerary was reversed.

In 1971, feeling the effects of the incursions of the airlines into the seaborne passenger trade, the *Southern Cross* was used for cruising voyages from Liverpool but these were not very successful and at the end of the year she was laid up in Southampton. The following year, she was moved to a berth between the wooded

A stern view of Shaw, Savill's round-the-World passenger liner *Southern Cross*, now laid up at berth 46 in the old Ocean Terminal in 1971. With her is the cable-layer *Stanley Angwin*.

banks of the River Fal in Cornwall. Spending over a year there, she made a splendid sight to those commuting across the river on the nearby King Hal Ferry. Her companions astern at the buoys were for some time the Cunarders *Franconia* (ex-*Ivernia*) and *Carmania* (ex-*Saxonia*).

But Fate would stay its hand and, as her old fleetmates disappeared to the breakers, the *Southern Cross* found a new lease of life. Bought and massively up-dated internally by the Greek-owned Ulysses Line, she was renamed *Calypso* and sailed as a cruise ship between 1975 and 1980, when, at the stroke of a brush, she became *Calypso I*. Because of her popularity she was considered by some to be a 'Butlin's afloat'. In 1980, she was sold again, this time to Eastern Steamship Lines of Panama, and later transferred to the associated Western Steamship Lines. She was now called *Azure Seas* and operated in the American cruise market. Later, amalgamation brought her into the fleet of the new Admiral Cruises.

By 1992, she was sailing as the *OceanBreeze* of Dolphin Cruise Lines until another amalgamation saw her in the handsome new livery of Premier Cruise Lines – a dark blue funnel (with logo) and a similarly coloured hull with a fetching gold band along her sheer line. Still later, she was chartered to Imperial Majesty Cruises with the logo on her funnel being changed to a white crown. In 1999, Imperial Majesty bought her outright and spent $3½ million on a refit, which left her with the company name written in stylish graphics along her aft quarters. She was steadily employed in two- and three-day cruises between Miami and Nassau.

The old *Southern Cross* was very popular in all her incarnations and, in spite of her 1950s 'radical' appearance, she came to be regarded as a classic ship, an impression enhanced by her graceful sheer. But in 2003, she was superseded by another classic, the 1953-built *Regal Empress* (ex-*Olympia*). She was sold for breaking, originally it was thought on the steel-hungry beaches of Alang in India, but eventually she went to Chittagong in Bangladesh.

But before she arrived at her final destination, a leak occurred. She shipped a lot of water and developed a 20° list. Fortunately, the floodwater was pumped out and she was soon sitting upright once more. The 26th November, 2003 was to have seen the commencement of her demolition but, that same day, a possible buyer boarded her to start a week's survey and evaluation. Finally, however, the old ship was grounded in December and breaking began.

# NORTHERN STAR

Completed 1962 by Vickers-Armstrongs (Shipbuiulders) Ltd., Walker-on-Tyne. 24,733 gross tons. Length overall: 650 ft. 0$^{ins}$ / 198.1m. (595 ft. 0$^{ins}$ / 181.4m. between perpendiculars). Beam: 83 ft. 8$^{ins}$ /25.5m. Draught: 26 ft. 1¼$^{ins}$ / 8.0m. Four geared steam turbines. 22,000 shp. Twin screw. Service speed: 19½ knots. Call sign: GHZB.

The *Northern Star*, launched by Her Majesty, the Queen Mother in 1961, was introduced into the Shaw, Savill & Albion round-the-World service seven years after her smaller sister, the *Southern Cross*. She incorporated many design changes resulting from experience with the older ship. On her entry into service, the *Northern Star* took over the east-about sailings, while the *Southern Cross* adopted a west-about route.

In 1966, the *Star*'s funnel colour was changed from buff to a light green and incorporated a raised, elongated four-pointed star on each side. This easily distinguished her from her sister and did not go un-noticed by some of the engineers from the *Cross* who, on one occasion, sneaked onto the *Star* and fixed a pair of engineer's white overalls to the emblem with arms outstretched, thereby upsetting those of a more religious persuasion.

In 1969, *Northern Star* began a series of cruises from Southampton but was increasingly dogged by mechanical troubles. One cruise had to be terminated at Tunis after a severe machinery breakdown. The ship carried on for a few more years but by 1975 her owners had had enough and decided to give up the carriage of passengers. At a very early age, the *Northern Star* was sent to Kaohsiung to be scrapped.

The *Northern Star* was a development, but not an improvement, of the *Southern Cross*. Here she is seen at Southampton on the 25$^{th}$ May, 1974.

# OCEAN MONARCH

Completed 1957 by Vickers-Armstrongs (Shipbuilders) Ltd., Walker-on-Tyne. 25,585 gross tons. Length overall: 640 ft. 0[ins] / 195.0m. Beam: 85 ft. 4[ins] / 26.0m. Draught: 29 ft. 0[ins] / 8.8m. Six geared steam turbines. 30,000 shp. Twin screw. Service speed: 20 knots. Call sign: GVSV.

Built as the *Empress of England* for Canadian Pacific's service from Liverpool to the St. Lawrence, she was launched on the 9th May, 1956 by Lady Eden, the wife of the then Prime Minister. One of a trio of liners that have since became known as the 'Last White Empresses', the *Empress of England* was the first ship to carry this name in the Canadian Pacific fleet. (Her sister, the *Empress of Britain* which came out a year earlier, had been the first British-built liner to be fully air-conditioned and the *Empress of England* was also notable in this respect.)

In April 1970, the *Empress of England* was sold to Shaw, Savill & Albion for £5 million. Renamed *Ocean Monarch*, she was intended for their service to Australia and New Zealand and for cruising. After one voyage from Liverpool to Australia and a cruise to Japan to coincide with Expo '70, she was sent to Cammell Laird's yard at Birkenhead for conversion for full-time, one-class cruising.

The ten-month conversion started in September, 1970 and was to have cost £1½ million but it escalated to thirteen months and £4 million. Of the many problems that arose, including labour disputes, some were of unforeseen structural origin, especially in the area of the forward cargo holds. These had not been anticipated by the expert engineers from Cammell Laird who had sailed with the vessel from Cape Town to assess the work required. As the costs rose, they found themselves out of a job.

The *Ocean Monarch*'s return to service was postponed from July to October, 1971, thus giving the *Southern Cross* a temporary reprieve from her imminent disposal. Once the *Ocean Monarch* settled into her cruise routine, she became popular at the family end of the cruise market but was constantly beset by unpleasant troubles among the crew. It was unfortunate, too, that both *Northern Star* and *Ocean Monarch* should suffer from recurring mechanical problems. Shaw, Savill quit the cruise market and the *Ocean Monarch* left Southampton on the 13th June, 1975 for shipbreakers in Taiwan.

# REINA DEL MAR

Completed 1956 by Harland & Wolff, Ltd., Belfast. 20,501 gross tons, after rebuilding. Length overall: 600 ft. 9ins / 183.1m. (560 ft. 0ins / 170.7m. between perpendiculars). Beam: 78 ft. 5ins / 23.9m. Draught: 27 ft. 11ins / 8.5m. Six Parsons geared steam turbines. 18,700 shp. Twin screw. Service speed: 18 knots. Call sign: GTYN.

Built for the Pacific Steam Navigation Co., Ltd. for their Liverpool – Valparaiso route, the *Reina del Mar* (i.e. *Queen of the Sea*) went on to have two more owners but, unusually, never suffered a change of name. With her South American service in decline, she was chartered to the Travel Savings Association. Owned jointly by its South African founder and the Canadian Pacific, Royal Mail and Union-Castle lines, this concern ran a scheme whereby people could make regular payments so as to accumulate a fund which could then be used to pay for cruises. In 1964, to fit her for her new service, the *Reina del Mar* was sent to Harland & Wolff and was extensively rebuilt. Her passenger accommodation was extended forward over her redundant cargo holds, thus unfortunately destroying her original well-balanced appearance.

The Travel Savings Association scheme collapsed and the charter of the *Reina del Mar*, by now owned by Royal Mail Lines, was taken over by Union-Castle. Painted in their lavender-hulled livery, she became their only full-time cruise ship, dividing her time between the British and South African markets. She was very popular and could often be seen well down on her marks as she sailed through The Solent, heavily laden with passengers and stores. In 1973, she at last came under Union-Castle's complete ownership but by 1975 the cost of fuel had risen so much that this much-liked vessel was sold to Japanese shipbreakers, who in turn passed her on to breakers in Taiwan.

*Reina del Mar* sails from Southampton on the 25th May 1975. A strong gust of wind not only makes her flags snap smartly to attention but causes some of the farewell streamers to break loose and blow along the ship's hull to her forefoot.

# WINDSOR CASTLE

Completed 1960 by Cammell Laird & Co., Ltd., Birkenhead. 37,640 gross tons. Length overall: 783 ft. 1in / 238.7m. (730 ft. 0$^{ins}$ / 222.5m. between perpendiculars). Beam: 92 ft. 6$^{ins}$ / 28.2m. Draught: 32 ft. 1½$^{ins}$ / 9.8m. Four Parsons-type geared steam turbines. 49,400 shp. Twin screw. Service speed: 22½ knots. Call sign: GVGT.

Built for the Union-Castle Mail Steamship Co., Ltd. to replace the venerable *Winchester Castle*, the *Windsor Castle* was not only the company's largest mail, passenger and cargo liner but assuredly continued their policy of ordering handsome ships, internally attractive as well as externally. Launched by Her Majesty, the Queen Mother on the 23$^{rd}$ June, 1959, in a ceremony which was broadcast live on television, the new ship was the largest liner yet to be built in an English yard (a distinction to be usurped a few months later by *Oriana*) and the first to be built for the line by Cammell Laird.

As her maiden voyage started from Southampton at the then traditional Union-Castle time of 'Every Thursday at 4 o'clock' on the 18$^{th}$ August, 1960, all the port's cranes dipped their booms in salute as she passed. Her departure also broke the grip of an unofficial seamen's strike that had even the mighty *Queen Mary* tied up at her berth, her side doors acting as a platform for members of her crew as they fished in the pea-green waters. The *'Windsor'* sailed to Cape Town in a record 11½ days.

After a relatively brief career that spanned only seventeen years, this fine ship had the sad distinction of bringing to an end the long tradition of Union-Castle mail and passenger sailings between Southampton and Cape Town, her final sailing from the latter port on the 6$^{th}$ September, 1977 being a particularly poignant event. (The very last mail service voyage, by the cargo liner *Southampton Castle*, ended at Southampton on the 24$^{th}$ October.)

The *Windsor Castle* was quickly sold to the Greek oil and shipping magnate John S. Latsis and renamed *Margarita L.* after one of his daughters. When the liner sailed from Southampton on the 3$^{rd}$ October, the so-familiar red of her funnel had been painted yellow and the famed lavender colour of her hull had by now become almost a shade of grey.

After a slight conversion in Piraeus, *Margarita L.* was sent to Jeddah, there to become an accommodation ship and then, later, an office and leisure facility for Latsis's employees. Eventually, she returned to Greece and was laid up at Eleusis, near Piraeus. Mr. Latsis died in 2003 and shortly afterwards the ship was offered for sale. Plans for preservation were received from both the United Kingdom and South Africa but in December, 2004 she sailed for Alang in India, where she was scrapped.

# S.A. ORANJE

Completed 1948 by Harland & Wolff, Ltd., Belfast. 28,705 gross tons. Overall length: 747 ft. 5$^{ins}$ / 227.8m. Beam: 84 ft. 0$^{ins}$ / 25.6m. Draught: 32 ft. 0$^{ins}$ / 9.7m. Six geared steam turbines. 35,000 shp. Twin screw. Service speed: 22 knots. Call sign: GOAE.

This handsome, sturdy-looking ship, then the Union-Castle Line's *Pretoria Castle*, was launched over a radiotelephone connection by Mrs. Jan Smuts, the wife of the South African premier. *Pretoria Castle* was the first liner to be built for the Southampton – South Africa mail service after the War. The company's sailing time of 'Every Thursday at 4 o'clock' became a byword for regularity in Southampton – that is, until Friday at 12 was substituted in later years.

(facing page.)
The magnificent *Windsor Castle*, photographed on the 4$^{th}$ of August, 1977, as she prepares for her final voyage from Southampton to South Africa.

Another famous liner prepares for her last sailing to South Africa: the *S.A. Oranje* at Southampton on the 19th September, 1975.

The liner's big red and black funnel, together with those of the other Union-Castle ships, became part of the Southampton skyline as it loomed over the sheds that lined the Western Docks. But, in January, 1966, the *Pretoria Castle* was sold to the South African Marine Corporation (Safmarine), who now became partners in the mail service. She was renamed *S.A. Oranje* and repainted in Safmarine's white livery. She still looked very smart but their grey-based funnel livery never had the same impact as the Union-Castle colours. In a refit, she lost her mainmast but was given a signal mast just aft of the bridge, rather spoiling her balanced profile. In November, 1975, the *S.A. Oranje* arrived at Kaohsiung to be broken up by Chin Tai Steel Enterprises. Demolition started two months later.

# S.A. VAAL

Completed 1961 by John Brown & Co., Ltd., Clydebank. 32,697 gross tons. Length overall: 760 ft. 2$^{ins}$ / 231.7m. Beam: 90 ft. 2$^{ins}$ / 27.5m. Draught: 32 ft. 0$^{ins}$ / 9.7m. Four Parsons-type geared steam turbines. 44,000 shp. Twin screw. Service speed: 22½ knots. Call sign: GBQE.

Launched as *Transvaal Castle*, this liner was a near-sister to the *Windsor Castle* (ibid). They were the largest and fastest ships to be built for the Union-Castle mail service. Unfortunately, they were also the last.

The *Transvaal Castle* started her maiden voyage from Southampton in the English winter, on the 18$^{th}$ January, 1962, arriving at Durban in the South African summer on the 1$^{st}$ February. Unlike the 'Windsor', she was a one-class 'hotel ship' and carried stewardesses, the first to be employed by Union-Castle. She did not last for long in the company's service as in 1966 she was sold to Safmarine. She was now renamed *S.A. Vaal* but, like *S.A. Oranje*, she continued to be British-flagged and British-crewed until 1969, when she was registered at Cape Town.

Withdrawn from service in 1977 when competition from aircraft and container ships finally prevailed, she was sold to Festivale Maritime, Inc. of Panama for operation by the fledgling Carnival Cruise Lines as the third ship of what would eventually become the biggest cruise corporation in the World. Now called *Festivale*, she was sent to Japan for conversion, her redundant cargo holds being transformed into passenger accommodation and her superstructure being extended, so that her passenger-carrying capacity was increased from 728 to 1,300. A further rebuild in 1987 saw it grow yet again, to 1,750.

For eighteen years, the *Festivale* was very successful but in 1996, with Carnival now introducing ever bigger and more modern vessels, she was chartered to Dolphin Cruise Lines, who began operating her as their *IslandBreeze* from New York. (A flash of *déja vu*, as she, or the *Windsor Castle*, had been shown on a beer mat in the early'70s, improbably sailing from that port in Union-Castle colours.) In 1996, she carried fare-paying passengers in an expedition to observe the eventually unsuccessful attempt to raise a large piece of hull-plating from the debris field surrounding the wreck of the *Titanic*.

As *IslandBreeze*, she later came under the ownership of Premier Cruise Lines, a company that specialised in

On the 19$^{th}$ October 1977 the magnificent *S.A. Vaal*, ex-*Transvaal Castle*, is still wearing Safmarine colours but has already been sold.

running older, 'classic' ships such as the *Rembrandt* (ex-*Rotterdam*). Things seemed to be going well until they painted the hulls of most of their once-dignified ships in a dreadful red livery and disastrously renamed them with a prefix *Big Red Boat*. The *IslandBreeze* was scourged with the name *Big Red Boat III*. Following the collapse of Premier Cruise Lines, *Big Red Boat III* was laid up at Freeport in the Bahamas next to the *Rembrandt* (ex-*Rotterdam*). In November, 2002, there was a suggestion that she be used as a floating shelter for many of New York's homeless; then, an Australian consortium was said to be interested in her. But February, 2003 brought the news that she had been sold for breaking. On the 4th June, she departed Freeport, her name truncated to an even more deplorable *Big Red* but at least under her own steam. She arrived at Alang on the 9th July after a call into Gibraltar for fuel. In spite of being in reportedly good condition, she was beached and breaking began by early August. By the end of January, 2004, the nefarious work was almost complete.

## ST. HELENA

Completed 1963 by the Burrard Drydock Co., Ltd., North Vancouver. 3,150 gross tons. Length overall: 329 ft. 0ins / 100.3m. Beam: 48 ft. 0ins / 14.6m. Draught: 18ft. 0¾ ins / 5.5m. One 6-cylinder Stork oil engine. 4,200 bhp. Single screw. Service speed: 14 knots. Call sign: CYJX.

The *St.Helena* lies at Southampton in 1978 prior to her refit for service to St. Helena and Ascension. Her new name has been painted over the welded letters of her previous one.

This small, engines-aft passenger-cargo vessel was built as the *Northland Prince* to serve the isolated communities along the coast of British Columbia. In 1976, she was laid up when the government subsidy which had kept her going was withdrawn. However, the following year she was bought by a private bank on behalf of a little-known Cornish company, Curnow Shipping, Ltd., for another government-subsidised service – between Avonmouth and the British-owned islands of St. Helena and Ascension, way out in the South Atlantic. After calling there, she would then continue to Cape Town. This new service had become necessary because the withdrawal of the Union-Castle Line from the Cape run, with occasional calls at St. Helena, had left that tiny British outpost almost completely isolated. In comparison with the imposing Union-Castle liners, the St. Helena seemed minuscule but she soon established herself as a valued link for the islanders with the outside world. She was commonly known as 'The RMS' – Royal Mail Ship.

After an initial proving voyage, she was brought to Southampton for a thorough conversion by Vosper Shiprepairers and it was not until September, 1978 that she started her regular service after being renamed by Princess Margaret. Once a year, this tiny vessel would take supplies to the even more distant and remote island of Tristan da Cunha. In view of her experience in the South Atlantic, she was an obvious choice to act as mother ship to a number of minesweepers during the Falklands War of 1982 and she performed admirably during and after that conflict.

She was eventually replaced on the St. Helena run by a new ship of the same name and, in anticipation of the arrival of that much over-budget vessel, she was renamed St. Helena Island in 1989. The following year, she was sold to a firm called Sea Safaris (Malta) Ltd. and used, as the Avalon, for a service from Durban to Mombasa via Mauritius and the Comores Islands. Unfortunately, this was not a success and she then became the Indocéanique for Mauritian owners. She was scrapped at Alang in 1996.

# UNITED STATES

Completed 1952 by the Newport News Shipbuilding & Dry Dock Co., Inc., Newport News, Virginia. 53,329 gross tons. Length overall: 990 ft. 0$^{ins}$ / 301.7m. (905 ft. 4$^{ins}$ / 276.0m. between perpendiculars). Beam: 101 ft. 7$^{ins}$ / 31.0m. Draught: 32 ft. 4$^{ins}$ / 9.9m. Four sets of Westinghouse geared steam turbines. 240,000 shp. Quadruple screw. Service speed: 30 knots. Call sign: KJEH.

Designed by the renowned American naval architect William Francis Gibbs, the United States was to be the largest liner built in the U.S.A. Because both her designer and the U.S. Navy had a penchant for secrecy, her underwater form was not revealed for many years.

Built during the Cold and Korean Wars, this true superliner was constructed to naval standards, with two engine rooms and, in order to reduce flammability, very little woodwork (except, as was famously advertised, in her butcher's chopping board and her piano – although it was later revealed that her bilge keels were filled with balsa wood!) These precautions were undertaken in case the military should ever require her to be converted into a high-speed troopship. Uniquely at the time in such a large vessel, aluminium was used extensively in her superstructure in order to reduce top weight.

She was built in a dry dock that was then flooded so that the lower part of her hull should be concealed during her naming ceremony. Her trials took place in choppy seas that added to the impression of absolute power which she created. Her maximum speed remained a secret for years until in the April, 1978 edition of Marine Technology, the journal of The Society of Naval Architects and Marine Engineers, the retired vice-president of her builders, John R. Kane, revealed that the United States had achieved 38.32 knots during her trials – a staggering 44 miles per hour. (Later claims have been made, perhaps mistakenly, that a speed of 44 knots was achieved.)

The great ship left New York at the start of her maiden voyage on the 3$^{rd}$ July, 1952. She crossed the North Atlantic in 3 days, 10 hours and 40 minutes, an average speed of 35.59 knots, easily beating the Queen Mary's fourteen-year old record. Arriving in The Solent en route for Southampton, having already called at Le Havre, the new holder of the prestigious Blue Riband passed the outward bound Queen

(Following pages.) The imposing United States arrives at Southampton early in her career. For the first time in a century an American-built ship could outpace the great European speed champions on the North Atlantic run.

*Elizabeth* whilst off the Prince's Green at Cowes. That event, on a warm summer's evening, has remained in the author's cache of fond childhood memories ever since.

Trying to put a brave nationalistic face on the loss of the Blue Riband, the satirical magazine *Punch* commented, 'After the loud and fantastic claims made in advance for the liner *United States*, it comes as something of a disappointment to find them all true.' On a later occasion, when overtaking the *Queen Mary* in mid-Atlantic, the *United States* sent a signal apologising for overtaking such a stately lady. Brushing aside the ignominy of the moment, the Cunarder made reply that 'a lady does not like to be seen in fast company'.

In spite of the comparatively austere decoration of her fireproofed interiors, the American liner enticed quite a few regulars, including the Duke and Duchess of Windsor, away from the Cunard 'Queens' and the French Line ships. Her almost antiseptic atmosphere did not appeal to those who preferred to be cosseted in more obvious luxury but she had speed and she had glamour, especially when seen abeam from her aft quarters.

Her designer had calculated a swift conversion into a troopship should the necessity arise and she was put on stand-by during the Cuban missile crisis of 1962, when the World held its breath. Her use as a military transport was also considered during the ghastly Vietnam War.

This mechanically reliable liner kept her speed record throughout her sadly short seventeen year career. But falling passenger numbers, the need for rising subsidies and increasing crew troubles, that caused several voyages and a cruise to be cancelled, sounded her death knell. Under the pretence of taking an early winter overhaul, she was docked at Newport News in November, 1969. Her boilers were never to be fired again.

In 1973, she was placed under the U.S. Federal Maritime Administration who, five years later, sold her to a company called United States Cruises, Inc. for $5 million. (She had cost $79 million to build.) A proposed conversion into a floating cruising condominium fell through, as did plans to convert her boilers to burn pulverised coal. The great ship lay idle, steadily deteriorating and eventually being stripped of her interior fittings, which were auctioned off. With her owners now bankrupt, she was sold to Marmara Marine, Inc. for $2.6 million – basically her scrap value. There were plans to operate her in partnership with Cunard's *QE2* (ibid) and she was towed to Turkey for conversion and to have vast amounts of asbestos removed. The Turkish government refused to allow this deadly insulation to be stripped by its people and so the *United States* was towed across the Black Sea to Sebastapol for the work to be done. But the *QE2* plan fell through and, four years later, 'The Big U' was towed back across the Atlantic in July, 1996, to languish in lay up at Philadelphia.

Pitted with rust and with her paint peeling, the almost empty husk of the once-great liner presented a pathetic sight as she lay alongside her fenced-off pier with no apparent hope of a future, even with the goodwill of preservationists behind her. The few visitors who managed to get aboard left her with sorrow at the neglected state of this American icon.

However, on the 14th April, 2003, a press release proclaimed that 'Norwegian Cruise Line announced today it has purchased the *United States*, one of the country's most venerable ships' and..... 'intends to convert the vessel to a state-of-the-art, modern cruise ship and to add her to NCL's planned US-flagged Homeland fleet.' There was an irony here: years earlier, NCL, then trading as Norwegian Caribbean Lines, had failed to buy the *United States* at auction and had purchased the former *France* instead, converting her into their giant cruise ship *Norway* (ibid). Now, NCL, which had passed into Malaysian ownership, also acquired the old *Independence*, hoping that the two famous ships would give them a patriotic American image, perhaps at the expense of the damaged and laid-up *Norway*. Time, of course, will tell but so far there have been few signs that America's greatest liner, one of the loveliest to ply the Atlantic, will ever sail again.

# AMERICA

Completed 1940 by Newport News Shipbuilding & Dry Dock Co., Inc., Newport News, Virginia. 26,414 gross tons. Length overall: 723 ft. 0$^{ins}$ / 220.4m. (663 ft.7$^{ins}$ / 202.3m. between perpendiculars). Beam: 93 ft. 6$^{ins}$ / 28.5m. Draught: 30 ft. 5$^{ins}$ / 9.3m. Six Parsons-type geared steam turbines. 37,400 shp. Twin screw. Service speed: 22 knots. Call sign: WEDI.

This sturdy liner was hailed at the time of her introduction as the 'largest and fastest merchantman ever built in the United States'. Initially, her funnels were low and streamlined, giving her a very racy appearance, but almost immediately they had to be heightened by 15 ft. to obviate the nuisance of smuts falling on the after decks. She made her début as the War in Europe approached its first anniversary and, consequently, United States Lines used her only for cruising in American waters. With the darkness of Nazism spreading across Europe, the new *America* sailed on in an aura of glamour and glitz and light. Whilst cruising along the western seaboard, she hosted the first film première afloat. Unfortunately, many of the stars of *The Sea Wolf* were laid low by seasickness!

Later, when the Japanese attack on Pearl Harbor embroiled the United States in the conflict, the *America* was enlisted by the U.S. Navy, converted into a troopship and renamed *West Point*. She served her country well and then, some time after the War's conclusion, she was returned to United States Lines and again assumed her original name. She now ran on the line's express service from New York to Southampton and Le Havre, which was later extended to Bremerhaven. After 1952, she

The greatly-liked *America*, forerunner of the *United States*, leaves the Western Docks on the 23$^{rd}$ April 1951, passing the British India troopship *Dilwara*.

ran in tandem with the bigger, faster *United States* but many less hurried passengers preferred her warm, comfortable atmosphere to her running mate's somewhat clinical ambience.

In 1960, demonstrating that ship measurement is not an exact science, she was re-assessed and her gross tonnage was now said to be 33,961 – quite a change from the original 26,414. Four years later, with Atlantic liner services in precipitous decline, she was offered for sale and was bought by Okeania SA, a Greek registered company belonging to London-based Anthony Chandris who, under the name Chandris Lines, was running an emigrant service between Europe and Australia. She was refitted to carry up to 2,300 passengers – double her previous capacity – and renamed *Australis* (Greek for 'Australian Lady').

She made her first dazzling appearance in The Solent as the *Australis* on a fine summer's afternoon in 1965, looking splendid in her all-white livery with black-capped funnels painted dark blue and bearing the Greek letter X (pronounced *Ch*, for Chandris). Later, her hull below the sheer line was painted dove grey. She was said to be immensely profitable, often sailing full to capacity. In 1970, she suffered a serious fire whilst in the Pacific but was quickly repaired. However, by 1977 the Australian emigrant trade was being poached by the jet airliners (some years later than the jet-inspired decline of the Atlantic services). In 1978, the *Australis* was sold – into imminent humiliation.

Her new owners were a company called Venture Cruise Lines, who returned her to the States and revived her old name of *America*. She was in an extremely poor condition and, amid a public outcry, she was withdrawn after two disastrous cruises. Chandris bought her back at a bargain price, restored her, removed her forward (dummy) funnel and named her *Italis*. After one season of cruising, she was laid up and from then on she was a fated ship, passing under various names through the hands of several different owners but never seeing further service. At one time, she almost sank at her moorings in Eleusis Bay and would have been broken up had not the scrap merchant defaulted on half the $2 million price tag.

Sold to Thai buyers (Chapeya Transport Company) for $1 million in 1994, she was intended to become a floating hotel in Phuket and seemed destined for a new life. Refurbished in a dry dock, the ex-*America* was renamed *American Star*. But, whilst under tow on the 15th January, 1994, she broke loose during a storm and grounded off Fuerteventura in the Canary Islands. Plundered of her fittings, art, non-ferrous metals and transportable wood, she remained stranded until her well-picked carcass split apart just aft of the remaining funnel. Although the stern section eventually broke away and sank, her battered forward section remained in defiant isolation until finally disappearing in 2005.

Two successful emigrant ships, the *Australis*, ex-*America*, and the *Fairsky*. In the picture with the *Fairsky* on the 25th April, 1972 is the Blue Star cargo liner *Gladstone Star*.

# FAIRSKY

Completed 1942 by Western Steel & Pipe Co., Inc., San Francisco. After conversion to *Fairsky*, 1958: 12,464 gross tons. Overall length: 502 ft. 0ins / 153.0m. (465 ft. 3ins / 141,8m. between perpendiculars). Beam: 69 ft. 8ins / 21.2m. Draught: 25 ft. 6ins / 7.8m. Two sets of General Electric geared steam turbines. 8,500 shp. Single screw. Service speed: 17½ knots. Call sign: HPIB.

*Fairsky* was a ship which had an interesting and varied career. Starting life on the slipway as a C3-S-A2 standard American freighter, she was launched – sideways – as the *Steel Artisan* for Isthmian Lines but was subsequently taken over by the U.S. Navy and completed as an auxiliary aircraft carrier, a 'baby flat-top', the U.S.S. *Barnes* (CVE7).

In 1942, she was transferred to the Royal Navy, becoming HMS *Attacker* (DO2). As the War progressed, she was often in action. In the Mediterranean, her fighter planes provided cover for the Salerno landings and later, by now converted into an assault carrier, she took part in the landings near Toulon. She was then involved in the attacks on the enemy entrenched in Crete, Rhodes and mainland Greece. Earlier, she had narrowly escaped an aerial torpedo attack whilst at Gibraltar. HMS *Attacker* later sailed for the Pacific, where she arrived in time to help cover the final assaults on the Japanese and had the honour to be the first British warship to enter Singapore after the surrender. The crew gallantly gave up their quarters so that recently released prisoners of war might be comfortably berthed for their return to England after their harrowing experiences.

On the 14th December, 1945, HMS *Attacker* left Southampton carrying GIs returning to the U.S.A. Three weeks later, she was handed back to the American government. For a while, she was laid up. In 1947, there were plans by National Bulk Carriers, Inc. to convert her into a tanker but they did not reach fruition. Three years later, she was sold to a subsidiary of the expanding, cosmopolitan Vlasov group (hence the letter V on her bow in the photographs). They at first intended to convert her into a 'reefer' (refrigerated cargo vessel), the *Castelforte* (later *Castel Forte*), but although some work was done at the Newport News shipyard it was soon abandoned and the vessel lay idle for several years. However, a Vlasov subsidiary, the Italian-based Sitmar Line, was active in the booming migrant trades and in 1957 they took her over and had her converted into a passenger ship, the final stages of the work being completed at Genoa. She emerged as the *Fairsky* and sailed from Southampton on the 26th June, 1958, bound for Australia. She quickly acquired the reputation of being one of the most comfortable ships in the trade. In 1970, Sitmar lost the lucrative Australian emigrant contract to Chandris and for eighteen months in 1972-73 the *Fairsky* was laid up at Southampton but, with Sitmar turning its attention increasingly to the cruise market, she was transferred to Australia for full-time cruising. A previous plan to convert her into a passenger-car ferry to operate between Singapore and Fremantle had been abandoned.

Her Australian cruising career came to an abrupt end in 1977 when she struck the submerged wreck of the *Klingi* off Djakarta. Holed and suffering considerable flooding, she was beached at Tanjung Priok. Sold to Fuji Marden, she was reprieved whilst lying in Junk Bay, Hong Kong, being bought for service as a hotel and casino ship in the Philippines. Her new owners, Peninsula Tourist & Shipping Co., had her repaired and refitted at Manila and called her *Philippine Tourist*. Unfortunately, she lasted for only six months before being gutted by fire. She was sold back to Fuji Marden for demolition, which began in June, 1980.

# ANGELINA LAURO

Completed 1939 as the *Oranje* by Nederlandsche Scheepsbouw Mij., Amsterdam. After conversion to *Angelina Lauro*, 1966: 24,377 gross tons. Length overall: 674 ft. 0 ins / 205.4m. Beam: 83 ft. 9ins / 25.5m. Draught: 29 ft. 0ins / 8.8m. Three Sulzer oil engines. 37,500 bhp. Triple screw. Service speed: 21 knots. Call sign: IBHO.

Built to the order of Stoomvaart Mij.'Nederland' (the Nederland Line) for their service from Amsterdam to the Dutch East Indies, the *Oranje* was a handsomely solid-looking ship with an accentuated tumblehome (i.e.: an inward slope of the sides of the hull so that the ship was wider at the waterline than higher up, thus improving stability). At the time, she was said to be the fastest motorship in the World, having a maximum speed of 26½ knots. She started her maiden voyage on the 4th September, 1939, one day after the declaration of the Second World War and, on arrival, she was laid up at Sourabaya, although The Netherlands were still neutral. In 1941, she was sent to Sydney for conversion into a hospital ship for the Royal Australian Navy but continued to fly the Dutch flag.

After the War, she returned to her intended route but a rebellion was raging in the East Indies, which eventually resulted in independence for the new state of Indonesia, and trade declined. By 1950, the *Oranje*

The *Angelina Lauro* embarking passengers for Australia at Berth 43 at the old Ocean Terminal, Southampton on the 11th April, 1972. In this photograph she is in the background, framed by Sitmar Line's *Fairsky* and Union-Castle's *Reina del Mar*.

The *Achille Lauro*, running-mate to the *Angelina Lauro* and like her of Dutch origin, is here seen sailing from Southampton on the 29th November, 1979.

was employed in a new round-the-World service via Panama, New Zealand, Australia and Suez. In 1953, she lost much of her prow when she was involved in a collision in the Red Sea with the *Willem Ruys* of the rival Royal Rotterdam Lloyd.

Like many liners, the *Oranje* was affected by the inroads on the passenger trade being made by the jet aircraft and by the rising cost of oil fuel. By 1964, she was being offered for sale. She was bought by the Neapolitan shipowner Achille Lauro, who named her *Angelina Lauro* after his wife. A major rebuild was undertaken at a Genoese shipyard, increasing her length by the addition of a raked bow. A striking new funnel, tall, winged and tapered, now surmounted her superstructure and both hull and funnel were painted in her owner's blue livery. Despite delays caused by a serious fire, possibly the result of arson, the *Angelina Lauro* was placed on the emigrant route between Southampton, Australia and New Zealand. In 1972, she became a full-time cruise ship.

In 1978, she was chartered to the Costa Line and her funnel was accordingly painted in their yellow livery with a blue "C,, motif on either side. The following year, whilst still under charter and berthed alongside at St. Thomas in the U.S. Virgin Islands, she caught fire. Most of her crew were ashore at the time and, with many of her ports left open, the conflagration soon spread. The cruise ship *Cunard Princess* was moored ahead of the smoke-billowing and listing liner and members of the Cunarder's crew boarded the burning vessel in an attempt to fight the fire. Unfortunately, their efforts proved futile. Eventually, whilst being towed to the scrapyards of Taiwan, the charred hulk of the *Angelina Lauro* defeated the breakers and sank.

# ACHILLE LAURO

Completed 1947 as *Willem Ruys* by N.V. Koninklijke Mij. 'De Schelde', Vlissingen. After conversion to *Achille Lauro*, 1966: 23,629 gross tons. Length overall: 643 ft. 0ins / 196.0m. Beam: 82 ft. 0ins / 25.0m. Draught: 24 ft. 2ins / 7.4m. Eight Sulzer-type 8-cylinder oil engines. 38,000 shp. Twin screw. Service speed: 22 knots. Call sign: IBHE.

Laid down for Rotterdam Lloyd's service to the Dutch East Indies a few months before the outbreak of the Second World War, this fine vessel was still on the stocks when the Nazis invaded The Netherlands. Although they had tried to bomb her as she lay on the 'ways, the Germans now decided to complete her on their own account. The Dutch shipyard workers thought differently and caused delays by committing various acts of sabotage. They also built false bulkheads inside her to hide materials from the occupying forces. She was apparently used as a navigational aid by both Nazi aircraft and marauding Allied 'planes as they passed over and, perhaps for this reason, she escaped aerial bombardment. The people living around the yard reportedly sheltered under her during air raids as they deemed her to be safer than the official bomb shelters.

She was still uncompleted at the end of the War but was eventually launched as *Willem Ruys* in 1946. She had a distinctive appearance with two unusual but nicely shaped black funnels and a light grey hull. Like her great rival the *Oranje*, later *Angelina Lauro* (ibid), she had an accentuated tumblehome. The *Willem Ruys* was in service for Royal Rotterdam Lloyd for only seventeen years. (The prefix 'Royal' had been bestowed on the line in recognition of its wartime activities and the bravery of many of its employees.) With Indonesia becoming an independent nation, trade for Dutch ships on the route to the East Indies soon declined sharply. For a time the *Willem Ruys* was diverted to round-the-World voyaging and also saw brief service on the North Atlantic, sailing to New York and Canada. In 1953, she was in collision with the *Oranje*, fortunately without fatality.

Like many splendid liners, she began to suffer from a fall in passenger traffic and in December, 1964 Royal Rotterdam Lloyd sold her to the Flotta Lauro of Naples. Taking her new owner's name, *Achille Lauro*, she underwent a rebuild that resulted in a new, sleek bow and two remarkable tall funnels and she was painted in the line's distinctive blue livery. 1972 saw her employment change from liner voyaging between Europe and the Antipodes to full-time cruising.

As the *Achille Lauro*, she had an eventful career but what befell her over the years did not detract from her popularity. While being rebuilt in 1965, she suffered an explosion and fire, almost certainly caused by arson – work on her running mate *Angelina Lauro* had also been disrupted by a serious fire a few days earlier. Another fire in 1972 caused damage to the bridge and to some of her accommodation. In 1975, whilst on passage through the Dardanelles, she collided with and sank a Lebanese livestock carrier, the *Youssef*. There was one fatality. In 1981, a fire in a bar resulted in three fatalities during the evacuation. In 1982, following the Lauro Line's bankruptcy, the ship was arrested and laid up for a year in Teneriffe. She re-entered service after outstanding debts had been settled.

There followed two major incidents that ensured the *Achille Lauro* of world headlines and lasting fame, even notoriety. On the 7th October, 1985, whilst cruising in the Mediterranean under charter to the Chandris Line, she was hijacked by four heavily armed Palestinian terrorists who held the 400 passengers hostage. The hi-jackers demanded that 50 Palestinian prisoners in Israeli gaols be released. They shot and killed a wheelchair-confined American passenger, 69-year old Leon Klinghoffer and both he and his wheelchair were thrown overboard. It was a brutal act that outraged world opinion. After two days of negotiation, the ter-rorists surrendered on the promise of a safe passage but their aircraft was forced to land in Italy and they were arrested. The mastermind behind this murderous episode was not caught until eighteen years later.

The Russian *Alexandr Pushkin* sailing from the North Mole, Gibraltar, bound for Casablanca, 10th March, 1977.

The *Achille Lauro* incident spawned various works of differing merits, the best being a gripping opera by the talented American minimalist composer John Adams, entitled *The Death of Klinghoffer*. There was also a film, *Voyage of Terror*, starring Burt Lancaster. This low-rated TV movie was filmed on the ship itself and in the actual location where the incident occurred.

1987 saw Flotta Lauro becoming StarLauro Cruises, the predecessors of the present day MSC Cruises (a subsidiary of the big container line Mediterranean Shipping Co.). The *Achille Lauro* sailed on for the next seven years but on the 30th November, 1994, with over a thousand passengers on board, the old ship caught fire off the coast of Somalia. The passengers were evacuated (the rescue operation being co-ordinated in faraway Stavanger, Falmouth and Rome), leaving the vessel to burn for three agonising days. In full view of the World's media, she finally sank on the 2nd December.

A final bizarre note was added in 1995 when the *Daily Telegraph* reported that a man had been fined £16 by his local library for an overdue book that had been lost on the *Achille Lauro*. He later claimed a refund.

# ALEXANDR PUSHKIN

Completed 1965 by Mathias Thesen Werft, Wismar, East Germany. 19,861 gross tons. Length overall: 577 ft. 10ins / 176.1m. (508 ft. 6ins / 155.0m. between perpendiculars). Beam: 77 ft. 5ins / 23.6m. Draught: 27 ft. 3ins / 8.3m. Two 9-cylinder Sulzer-type oil engines. 21,000 shp. Twin screw. Service speed: 20 knots. Call sign: URRU.

Built with an ice-strengthened hull for the Baltic Shipping Company of Leningrad, the *Alexandr Pushkin* sailed regularly from that port and Copenhagen to London (or sometimes Southampton) and Montreal. She was the second of five sisters that, with their large storage capacity and long cruising range, were, one suspects, convenient hard currency-earning troopships-in-waiting. In addition to her liner voyages, she was also used for cruising. With their low labour and other costs and consequent low fares, she and her Soviet fleetmates were able to carve out a big share of the British cruise market.

In 1985, she was refurbished by Koyo Shipyards in Japan and transferred to another Soviet state-owned concern, the Far Eastern Shipping Co. of Vladivostock. Following the collapse of the Soviet Union, she was sold in 1991 to Shipping & General Services, Ltd. of London for their subsidiary Orient Lines (not to be confused with the previous famous line of that name). Now renamed *Marco Polo*, she was sent to one of the several small yards at Perama in Greece for a lengthy two-and-a-half year rebuild which saw her original engines being overhauled, her funnel heightened on a lengthened superstructure and stabilisers fitted.

Cruising from 1993, the *Marco Polo* has sailed to destinations that hold the appeal of being both interesting and unusual, such as Antarctica, the South Pacific, etc. She carries several 'Zodiacs', rigid inflatable boats ('ribs'), and a helicopter to take passengers to more difficult locations and to observe wildlife at sea and has proved to be a very popular ship. However, an attempt in 1996 to use her for cruises in the eastern Mediterranean met with problems when Greek cabotage laws created some prolonged and unpleasant incidents. The following season, the company chartered the Greek-flagged *Ocean Majesty* for these cruises.

Orient Lines were bought by Norwegian Cruise Lines which, in turn, has been taken over by Star Cruises of Malaysia. They briefly provided the *Marco Polo* with a running mate, *Crown Odyssey* (ibid), but she is now once again a single ship operation.

# MAXIM GORKIY

Completed 1969 by Howaldtswerke-Deutsche Werft AG, Hamburg. 25,022 gross tons. Length overall: 639 ft. 0$^{ins}$ / 194.8m. including bulbous bow (557 ft. 5$^{ins}$ / 170.0m. between perpendiculars). Beam: 87 ft. 4$^{ins}$ / 26.6m. Draught: 27 ft. 2$^{ins}$ / 8.3m. Two sets of AEG geared turbines. 22,660 shp. Twin screw. Service speed: 22 knots. Call sign: UYAD.

As the *Hamburg* of the German Atlantic Line (Deutsche Atlantik Linie), she was the first major passenger ship to be built for a German owner since the Second World War. Her unique funnel with three outward-branching exhausts radiating from the top and capped by a circular, flat plate makes this not-unattractive vessel easily identifiable. In 1973, she was renamed *Hanseatic* for a few months before being sold to the Soviet-owned Black Sea Shipping Company in 1974, for whom she became the *Maxim Gorkiy*, sometimes transliterated as *Maksim Gorkiy*. In 1974, she featured in the United Artists film *Juggernaut*, sailing out of Southampton with many Sotonians aboard, volunteers to act as extras. The film was based on a real event concerning a mid-Atlantic bomb threat to the *QE2* in 1972. A real life disaster was averted in June, 1989 when, whilst on a cruise to Spitsbergen with 950 people on board and steaming at 18 knots, the *Maxim Gorkiy* collided with an undetected ice floe and sustained serious damage. With two holes in her bow, she listed badly but she was later trimmed but was nevertheless in danger of foundering until additional pumps were brought in. Photographs showed passengers adrift in lifeboats with the ship in the distance, down at the head. The passengers were eventually picked up by the Norwegian Coast Guard. Happily, the *Maxim Gorkiy* was repaired and lived to sail another day.

She later had the honour of hosting Summit talks between U.S. President George Bush, Senior and the Soviets' Chairman Gorbachev that heralded the era of 'Perestroika' and the collapse of the Soviet Union. Now owned by Belata Shipping, the *Maxim Gorkiy* has been on charter to the German company Phoenix Reisen since 1993.

# FRANCE / NORWAY

Completed as *France* 1961 by Chantiers de l'Atlantique, St.Nazaire. 66,348 gross tons. Length overall: 1,035 ft. 6ins / 315.6m. Beam: 110 ft. 7ins / 33.7m. Draught: 34 ft. 4¾ins / 10.5m. Eight CEM-Parsons geared steam turbines. 160,000 shp. Quadruple screw. Service speed: 31 knots. Call sign: FNRR. Completion of her conversion to *Norway*, 1980. 70,702 gross tons. Four of her eight turbines disabled. Twin screw. Service speed: 25 knots. Call sign: LITA.

Launched by Mme. de Gaulle, the wife of the charismatic French president, this fine ship caused quite a stir when she appeared in Southampton. She was, for instance, the only contemporary liner to exceed Britain's *Queen Elizabeth* in length. The author had been eagerly anticipating her arrival ever since he had seen a special edition of *Paris Match* which featured her.

An early opportunity to see the new liner in the flesh occurred when she arrived at the port in January, 1962 during a pre-maiden voyage cruise to the Canaries during which she underwent berthing trials. After this first call, and after rounding Calshot Spit as she left Southampton Water, she was obscured by a blanket of fog which descended over The Solent to a distance of about two miles off the Isle of Wight. Suddenly, her bow thrust through the fog's edge into clear water. Her bridge followed and then her forward funnel, painted in that wonderful, black-topped, deep French Line red. As the rest of the ship emerged from the mist, the impact was utterly unforgettable.

Her maiden voyage arrival took place the following month on a cold, dark and windy evening that deterred many would-be spectators. She passed, outward bound, through the black, choppy waters of The Solent

The *Maxim Gorkiy* (page 71) passes the *Royal Viking Star* (page 81) at Southampton on the 9th September, 1978. They have both proved to be very successful survivors in the cruise market.

just before midnight, the light from her decks illuminating the blue-grey wisps of smoke emanating from the wings of her unique funnels. The wide spacing of those finely shaped funnels accentuated her graceful length. Her appearances in Hampshire waters were occasions that were always keenly anticipated.

The *France* was a successful ship but neither popularity nor state subsidies could shield her from the rising costs of oil fuel and it was announced that, after a career of not much more than twelve years, she would be withdrawn from service in October, 1974. However, a month before that could happen there was a veritable mutiny by her crew, whose jobs were due to disappear with the ship. The mutineers forced a thirteen day anchorage off Le Havre and even after docking they continued to occupy her until December, when she was at last taken to a backwater for lay-up.

After several further occupations by groups who used the high-profile liner to protest their various grievances (and after CGT – better known in Britain as the French Line – amalgamated with Messageries Maritimes to form the Compagnie Générale Transatlantique Maritime in 1977) it was decided to put this famous liner up for sale.

She was initially sold in October, 1977 to Saudi business interests but plans to convert her into a floating casino resort and to moor her either off Florida's Daytona Beach or at the Red Sea port of Jeddah never came to fruition. Finally, in June, 1979, the *France* was purchased by Klosters Rederi of Norway for $16 million and renamed *Norway* for their Norwegian Caribbean Line. Klosters had her towed from Le Havre to the Lloyd Werft shipyard in Bremerhaven, where she underwent an $80 million refit. She reappeared as a a full-time cruise ship.

A new livery dominated by shades of blue now graced this exceptionally beautiful ship. (Over the coming years, her funnels would sport no less than three changes of livery.) She now had just two screws instead of her original four, her crew was cut by a quarter and her passengers were able to enjoy the entire ship as she was now a single class vessel. The Norwegians took their new flagship to their hearts. She was not only the (by then) largest passenger ship in service but also the longest, a distinction she retained until the advent of Cunard's *Queen Mary 2* in 2004.

The former *France*, the now the much-converted *Norway* arrives in Southampton Water for the first time in her new guise on the 7th May, 1980. Note the extension to her after decks.

In 1990, the *Norway* received a further drastic rebuild that increased her gross tonnage to 76,049 but somewhat marred her graceful lines, with two new decks being added atop her superstructure. But her pedigree could not be hidden – her two distinctive, winged funnels were relocated above the new, high steelwork. (Later, although those funnels retained their trademark aerofoils, they actually exhausted through pipes which were added to their tops.)

For nearly two decades, *Norway* was one of the most notable ships in the cruise market but by 2001 she was becoming outclassed by the new generation of vessels. In September, 2001, she left Miami on what was going to be her last western cruise, a nostalgic transatlantic crossing. It was planned that she would then be sent to Asian waters, where she would become a vast floating casino. But this 'final' trip was such a sell-out that the now re-styled Norwegian Cruise Lines (actually Malaysian-owned, by Star Cruises) decided to keep her in the American market, at least for a while longer.

However, while moored at Miami on the 25th May, 2003, during Memorial Weekend, the *Norway* suffered a serious explosion. She had arrived in the port just over an hour earlier with a full complement of nearly 2,000 passengers. One of her boilers was destroyed and four crew members were killed (three others died later in hospital). Twenty two others were injured. Doors as much as three decks above the explosion were either blown off their hinges or were flung open.

In late June, following a considerable amount of technical debate, the ship left Miami, towed by a Smit Wijsmuller tug bound for the Lloyd Werft shipyard at Bremerhaven. It was hoped that she would be back in service by late September or early October but the damaged boiler proved problematic. It was estimated that it would take up to a year to build and deliver a replacement.

Other alternatives were considered: re-engining her with diesels; basing her at Rotterdam as a casino/hotel/nightclub; selling her to French interests who briefly toyed with the idea of preserving her at Honfleur. In the event, Norwegian Cruise Lines' Malaysian parents decided that they could find unspecified employment for her 'Out East' and on the 10th August, 2005 she arrived under tow at Port Klang. However, after a year, she was sold to the voracious Indian shipbreakers of Alang and beached there on the 15th August 2006 to be broken up.

# ARGONAUT

Completed 1929 by Friedrich Krupp Germania Werft AG, Kiel. 3,097 gross tons. Length overall: 333 ft. 3ins / 101.6m. Beam: 46 ft. 8ins / 14.2m. Draught: 16 ft. 0ins / 4.9m. Two 8-cylinder Krupp oil engines. 3,600 bhp. Twin screw. Service speed: 13 knots. Call sign: MHNT.

This long-lived vessel was launched as the *Orion*, a schooner-rigged private motor yacht. At the time, she was the second largest privately-owned pleasure craft in the World and boasted a salt-water swimming pool, an on-board physician and a crew of no less than fifty-six. She was built for Julius Forstmann, an American woollen textile magnate and philanthropist born in Germany but of Dutch descent. Like a number of the super-rich in the heady days of the late 1920s, Mr. Forstmann ordered his yacht from the Germania shipyard, an offshoot of the mighty Krupp combine. Yachting was, in fact, his hobby and he took his 'pride and joy' around the World during her first season.

In 1933, the *Orion* was slightly damaged when, during a hurricane, she was driven onto rocks at Hamilton, Bermuda. In 1942, after the United States' entry into the Second World War, she was requisitioned by the US Navy and renamed *Vixen*. As such, she was used as a flagship by the Commander-in-Chief of the US Atlantic Fleet. After the War, this attractive little vessel was transformed into a luxury cruise ship for a company called Pacific Cruise Lines, who registered her under the Panamanian flag.

Survivor from a previous age, the small cruise ship *Argonaut* is seen in Southampton on the 9th June, 1985.

She reverted to her original name in 1950. For nine years from 1954, *Orion* cruised for the McCormick Shipping Corporation but in 1964 she was sold to Epirotiki Lines, run by the Greek Potamianos family. They had her extensively rebuilt and in 1965 she emerged as the *Argonaut*, with accommodation for about 200 passengers. Epirotiki kept her for thirty years during which time she sailed under charter to various companies and academic institutions, including in later years Phoenix Reisen, the German tour company.

Sold in 1995 to Regina Maris Cruises, she was again refurbished and renamed, appropriately, *Regina Maris*. She was still powered by her original Krupp diesel engines, by now nearing 70 years old, but she could still achieve a speed of 15 knots. For a time, she was again chartered by Phoenix Reisen but this employment came to an abrupt end in 2002 and the ship was laid up in Alexandria. She was briefly used as an accommodation ship at Faliron, near Piraeus, during the 2004 Olympics but the following December the career of this notable veteran ended when she arrived at Aliaga in Turkey for scrapping.

# NAVARINO

Completed 1957 by Ansaldo SpA, Sestri-Ponente, Genoa. 23,191 gross tons. Length overall: 631 ft. 0ins / 192.3m. Beam: 81 ft. 8ins / 24.9m. Draught: 27 ft. 10ins / 8.5m. Two Götaverken 9-cylinder oil engines. 18,800 bhp. Twin screw. Service speed: 18 knots. Call sign under her original owners: SLQT.

This beautiful ship was launched in Genoa on the 8th April, 1956 as the *Gripsholm* for the Swedish American Line. Later that year, the line's *Stockholm* (ibid) was involved in a fatal collision with the Italian *Andrea Doria*. The loss of the *Andrea Doria* was deeply felt in Italy, where she was a symbol of the nation's revival after the War, and although the former captain of the *Stockholm* was appointed to the command of the new *Gripsholm*, it was felt advisable that he should not go to Genoa to take delivery of her.

The elegant Greek cruise ship *Navarino* departs Southampton on the 10th January, 1980 accompanied by the Red Funnel tug *Dunnose*.

*Gripsholm* became very popular not only as a transatlantic liner but also as a luxurious cruise ship. However, in 1975 Swedish American closed their passenger business and she was laid up in Vestlefjord in Norway. She was quickly purchased by Michael A. Karageorgis of Piraeus. Renamed *Navarino*, she cruised for him for six years. In 1981, she suffered considerable damage during a grounding off Patmos but was purchased by Sally Shipping of Finland, who intended to have her repaired and to sail her under the Commodore Cruise Line banner.

However, not only did she catch fire but, while she was in floating dock undergoing repairs in 1982, the dock collapsed. This caused the ship to partially capsize and she suffered even more damage. In spite of being declared a Constructive Total Loss, she was sold to a firm called Multiship Italia and was renamed *Samantha* but was then quickly re-sold to become the *Regent Sea* of Regency Cruises. Restored, she soon became recognised as the finest ship in their fleet of veteran ex-liners.

In 1995, Regency Cruises was declared bankrupt and *Regent Sea* was arrested at Nassau, Bahamas and was laid up at Freeport. She was eventually bought by a company called American Cruise Line, who intended to use her as a casino ship under the simply truncated name of *Sea*, but work on her conversion ceased and she remained idle at Tampa. It was hoped in Sweden that she could be returned to her home waters to be used as a hotel in Stockholm but this was not to be and she was sold to Indian breakers in May, 2001. She never reached that final destination. En route under tow, she encountered heavy seas off South Africa and, denied shelter, had to ride out the storm. She sprang a leak, developed a 30º list and foundered.

# MONTEREY

Completed 1952 as the cargo ship *Free State Mariner* by Bethlehem-Sparrows Point Shipyard, Inc., Sparrows Point, Maryland. Converted into a passenger ship, 1956. 14,799 gross tons. Length overall: 563 ft. 8ins / 171.8m. (529 ft. 7ins / 161.4m. between perpendiculars). Beam: 76 ft. 1in / 23.2m. Draught: 29 ft. 5ins / 9.0m. Two geared steam turbines. 19,250 shp. Single screw. Service speed: 20 knots. Call sign: KFCN.

Launched for the U.S. Maritime Commission as a C4 'Mariner'-class freighter, ostensibly built for use in the Korean War, she was bought by the Matson Line in 1956. They had her converted into a passenger and cargo liner by the Williamette Iron & Steel Corporation of Portland, Oregon and used her in their San Francisco – Hawaii – Australia service. She was renamed *Monterey* and a sister ship, formerly *Pine State Mariner*, became the *Mariposa*. (An earlier *Monterey* had been a four-masted iron ship built locally in Southampton in 1878 as the *Cypromene*.)

Sold in 1971 to the Pacific Far East Line, the sisters continued to trade on their old route until 1978, when they

A rare visitor to Southampton, the *Monterey*, then still American-owned, is seen on the 24th May, 1974.

were laid up. The *Monterey* was purchased the following year by President World Airways and, a few months later, sold to Royal Hawaiian Cruises. Before the ship had even sailed for them, the company went bankrupt and she passed into the hands of the Marine Engineers' Beneficial Association.

She remained idle until in 1987 she was taken over by Aloha Pacific Cruises, who sent her for a rebuild (begun in the United States but completed in Finland) which somewhat spoiled her very pretty lines. Not only did a forward-projecting lido deck now cover part of her foredeck but an ugly square open deck was built over her stern. Within a few months, her owners were also bankrupt and the ship began another period of idleness.

After nearly two years, she was purchased by StarLauro, the successors to Achille Lauro, and cruised mainly in the European market.

After five years, StarLauro was reorganised as Mediterranean Shipping Cruises, an offshoot of a big Italian-Swiss container shipping line. As this is written, she remains in service, although now a true veteran.

# EUROPA (III)

Completed 1953 by N.V. Koninklijke Mij. 'De Schelde', Vlissingen.  21,141 gross tons.  Length overall: 600 ft. 0$^{ins}$ /182.9m.  Beam: 77ft. 2$^{ins}$ / 23.5m.  Draught: 26 ft. 10$^{ins}$ / 8.2m.  Two Burmeister & Wain 8-cylinder oil engines.  18,600 bhp.  Twin screw.  Service speed: 19 knots.  Call sign under her original owners: SKUA.

Another very attractive liner built for the Swedish American Line, she made her maiden voyage from Gothenburg to New York as the *Kungsholm* in November, 1953.  In 1964, she was sold to the North German Lloyd and was delivered to them in the following year, becoming their *Europa*.  (She was the third ship of that name in their fleet and recalled their pre-War Blue Riband holder which, as a result of post-War reparations, became the French Line's *Liberté*).  This latest *Europa* was employed on liner voyages between Bremerhaven and New York.  North German Lloyd was amalgamated with the Hamburg-America Line in 1970, becoming Hapag-Lloyd, and from 1972 *Europa* was used solely for cruising.

Another former Swedish American liner, the German *Europa* is seen arriving at Southampton on the 18$^{th}$ August, 1980.

She completed her final cruise for Hapag-Lloyd in October, 1981, being sold to the Costa Line of Genoa, who named her *Columbus C.*  Unfortunately, this lovely ship collided with rocks near a breakwater in Cadiz in July, 1984, badly damaging her keel.  She managed to reach a quay, where her passengers were disembarked but, listing, she sank at her berth.  Although raised a year later, she was sold to Spanish breakers.

# EUROPA (IV)

Completed 1981 by Bremer Vulkan, Vegesack. 33,819 gross tons. Length overall: 655 ft. 11$^{ins}$ / 200.0m. including bulbous bow. Beam: 93 ft. 6$^{ins}$ / 28.5m. Draught: 27 ft. 7$^{ins}$ / 8.4m. Two MAN 7-cylinder oil engines. 28,920 bhp. Twin screw. Service speed: 21 knots. Call sign: DLAL.

Built for Hapag-Lloyd as a replacement for the third *Europa* (see opposite), this fourth vessel to bear the famous name achieved a very high reputation in the German-speaking cruise market. Her record was marred only by a collision with a containership in Hong Kong which resulted in her being sent to Kaohsiung in Taiwan for repairs. She continued to voyage worldwide until 1999, when she was replaced by yet another *Europa* and was sold to Star Cruises.

She was originally to have been renamed *Superstar Europe* but in fact became *Superstar Aries*. Briefly, she was transferred to Orient Lines, a member of the Star Cruises group, sailing to adventurous destinations like her fleetmate *Marco Polo* (ibid). However, in 2004 she was sold to the Spanish company Pullmantur, who have called her *Holiday Dream* and employ her mainly for Mediterranean cruising.

# ROYAL VIKING STAR

*The fourth Europa, photographed arriving at Berth 38/39, Queen Elizabeth II Cruise Terminal, Southampton, 1st July, 1985.*

Completed 1972 by O/Y Wärtsilä A/B, Helsinki. 21,847 gross tons. Length overall: 583 ft. 0$^{ins}$ / 177.7m. including bulbous bow. Beam: 82 ft. 8$^{ins}$ / 25.2m. Draught: 24 ft. 1in / 7.3m. Four Sulzer-type 9-cylinder geared oil engines by Wärtsilä. 18,000 bhp. Twin screw. Service speed: 21½ knots. Call sign: rather poetically, LILY.

*Royal Viking Star* departing Southampton Water in 1978. Many years later she is a familiar habitué of the port as Fred. Olsen's *Black Watch*.

This stylish ship was built for Det Bergenske Dampskibsselskab (better known as the Bergen Line), one of the three Norwegian shipping companies who jointly established the new Royal Viking Line in the early 1970s. Each of the partners contributed one ship. They all came from the same yard and operated at the de luxe end of the worldwide cruising market, catering particularly for wealthy American passengers. They were very attractive vessels, each with a *QE2*-influenced funnel and a pronounced clipper bow (see page 71). The author recalls seeing *Royal Viking Star* sailing down Southampton Water in the late '70s. She had recently encountered exceptionally heavy seas and her battered prow was turned up at quite an acute angle!

Between 1981 and 1983, each of the three ships was lengthened by 91 feet / 27.7m. (a cheaper, quicker option than building new vessels). The Royal Viking Line had built up a very loyal following but some of their regular passengers did not like having 'their' ships enlarged. They felt they had become less exclusive and so they transferred their custom to the new generation of smaller, yacht-like cruise ships.

As a result, the company suffered financially and in 1984 it was sold to Kloster Cruises, owners of the Norwegian Caribbean Line. Eventually, two of the sisters were transferred to other companies within the Kloster group. *Royal Viking Star* went to the Norwegian Cruise Line in 1991 and was renamed *Westward*. Then, in 1993, she became the *Star Odyssey* of the Royal Cruise Line and was given a lengthy refit which lasted into 1994.

Klosters encountered a financial crisis and sold the ex-*Royal Viking Star* in 1995. She was bought, through an intermediary, by Fred. Olsen Cruise Lines and called *Black Watch*. She was heavily refitted and some reworking of her after deck was undertaken locally by Vosper Thornycroft (UK), Ltd. and A&P in Southampton. She has proved extremely popular and is still sailing for Olsens, who in 2005 had her re-engined and upgraded. She now has a number of cabins with balconies – a facility demanded by many cruise passengers these days.

# VÖLKERFREUNDSCHAFT

Completed 1948 by Götaverken, Gothenberg. 12,165 gross tons. Length overall: 524 ft. 8ins / 160.0m. Beam: 69 ft. 1in / 21.0m. Draught: 24 ft. 9ins / 7.5m. Two Götaverken 8-cylinder oil engines. 12,000 bhp. Twin screw. Service speed: 19 knots. Call sign: SEJT.

When launched for the Swedish American Line (A/B Svenska Amerika Linien) as the *Stockholm*, this vessel was one of the first passenger liners to be built after the War. Although she was the largest ship yet constructed in Sweden (previous, bigger Swedish American vessels had been ordered abroad), she was one of the smallest liners on the North Atlantic. To cope with winter conditions in the Baltic, her hull had been strengthened, especially at the bow, for navigation through ice.

Even though her enclosed superstructure gave her an almost slab-sided appearance, she still presented a modern, yacht-like profile. Her maiden voyage in February, 1948 took place in stormy winter conditions and resulted in one fatality among her passengers.

Fame, or infamy, came to the *Stockholm* in 1956. She had sailed from New York on the 25th July and was approaching Nantucket Island and a distant bank of fog. Coming westward in the opposite direction was the beautiful Italian liner *Andrea Doria*. As they closed, the watchkeepers on both ships made a judgement that proved to be fatal. The *Stockholm* turned to starboard to pass the *Andrea Doria* whilst the latter turned to port. The ice-strengthened bow of the *Stockholm* easily sliced through the hull of the other vessel just aft of her bridge. A few hours later, the *Andrea Doria* sank whilst the *Stockholm* limped back into New York minus her bow. 52 people died as a result of the accident.

With luxurious new liners joining their fleet, Swedish American no longer had room for the rather austere *Stockholm*. So, in May 1959, she was sold to a trade union organisation in Communist East Germany, the Freier Deutsche Gewerkschaftsbund, and registered at Rostock, being handed over on the 3rd January,

One of the most photographed prows in shipping history: the rebuilt ice-strengthened bow of the former *Stockholm* which sank the *Andrea Doria*. Now *Völkerfreundschaft*, the ex-*Stockholm* is laid up at Berth 46 in the Ocean Dock, 24th January 1986.

The *Astor* leaving Berth 38/39 for Cape Town on the 2nd October, 1984. The attempt to re-start a regular UK-South Africa passenger service was unsuccesful.

1960. Having now become the *Völkerfreundschaft*, she was devoted to holidays for trade unionists, during which some of her passengers took the opportunity of 'jumping ship' and escaping from Communist rule. She was sometimes chartered to the Swedish Stena Line. Her career was not without incident - on the 13th August, 1960 she suffered serious bottom damage after a grounding near Sandhamn and on two occasions she collided with West German naval vessels.

*Völkerfreundschaft* sailed for the East Germans for 25 years until April, 1985 when she was sold to a firm called Neptunus Rex Enterprises. Officially, she was now called *Volker* but, as can be seen in the photograph on page 83, her former name remained welded on her bow. At first, she was laid up in the Oslofjord but later she was brought to Southampton to continue her hibernation. In 1986, she was taken to Oslo where, under the name *Fridtjof Nansen*, she acted as an accommodation vessel for asylum seekers.

In 1989, she was sold yet again, this time to StarLauro of Naples and towed to Genoa for a major rebuild. The Italian press gave the old liner a hard time as her rôle in the *Andrea Doria* tragedy was still vividly remembered. In 1993, she was renamed *Italia 1* (later spelled out in full – *Italia Prima*) in the ownership of Nina Compagnìa di Navigazione. After many delays, her reconstruction was completed. Now a sleek modern cruise ship, she was hardly recognisable as the old *Stockholm*. Over the following years, she was chartered to several travel firms, including the Valtur organisation of Italy for whom she was re-named *Valtur Prima*. She now ran regular Caribbean cruises based on Havana in Cuba.

Following the terrorist attack on the World Trade Centre in New York on the 11th September, 2001, which caused an abrupt fall in tourist travel, the ship's owners collapsed into bankruptcy and she was laid up in Havana. Later, she was chartered to Festival Cruises, although remaining in lay-up for many months. They renamed her *Caribe* but they too went bankrupt. In October, 2004, she passed into the hands of Arcalia Shipping of Lisbon who renamed her *Athena*. Like their *Arion* (ibid), she now runs for Classic International Cruises.

# ASTOR

Completed 1981 by Howaldtswerke-Deutsche Werft AG, Hamburg. 18,835 gross tons. Length overall: 539 ft. 3ins / 164.4m. including bulbous bow. Beam: 74 ft. 2ins / 22.6m. Draught: 20 ft. 2ins / 6.1m. Four MAN 6-cylinder oil engines. 13,200 bhp. Twin screw. Service speed: 20 knots. Call sign: C6SI2

Laid down as *Hammonia* for Hadag Seetouristik und Fahrdienst AG, a local Hamburg pleasure boat company who were moving into deep-sea cruising, she was renamed on the stocks and launched as the *Astor* in December, 1981. Her maiden voyage was delayed due to water damage after a fire.

The cruising venture was not a success and in 1984 the ship was sold to the South African Marine Corporation of Cape Town, retaining the name *Astor* and operating both cruises and Union-Castle-style liner voyages to South Africa. Within a year, though, she was back in German hands – this time, Communist East German – having been sold to a subsidiary of the government-owned VEB Deutfracht Seerederei of Rostock as a successor to the *Völkerfreundschaft* (ibid). She was renamed *Arkona*, and later *Astoria*, and has become a popular cruise ship in the German-speaking market.

# ISTRA

Completed 1965 by Brogladiliste Uljanik, Pula. 5,645 gross tons. Length overall: 383 ft. 3ins / 116.8m. (344 ft. 6ins / 102.0m. between perpendiculars). Beam: 54 ft. 2ins / 16.5m. Draught: 17 ft. 5ins / 5.3m. Two 10-cylinder Sulzer oil engines. 7,500 bhp. Twin screw. Service speed: 16 knots. Call sign: YTMI.

Ordered by the Yugoslav state-controlled Jadrolinija (Jadranska Linijska Plovidba, or Adriatic Line) this shapely little passenger ship was built at Pula on the northeast tip of the Istrian Peninsular and was thus aptly named. She and her sister *Dalmacija* were the largest ships to be built in Yugoslavia for the Adriatic and Mediterranean trade. The *Istra* was frequently chartered to German travel firms and, indeed, she was on charter to TUI Cruises when she made her first call at Southampton in June, 1979. She was en route from Venice to Bremerhaven.

The attractive Yugoslav *Istra* photographed at Berth 38/39 while on a German charter, 21st May, 1985.

In 1991, her name was slightly changed to *Astra* when she passed into Ukrainian ownership. She now cruised for Caravella Shipping Company, still often carrying German passengers. In 1997, she became *Astra 1* and later *Nautilus*. She passed into the hands of Portuguese-based owners and now operates as the *Arion* for Classic International Cruises, managed by Arcalia Shipping Company. In 1999-2000, she was refitted at Lisbon and was given stabilising sponsons at her stern. She has proved to be a popular ship and has cruised in many areas, ranging from Canadian waters to the Far East.

# HORIZON

Completed 1990 by Jos. L Meyer GmbH, Papenburg. 46,811 gross tons. Length overall: 681 ft. 2$^{ins}$ / 207.6m. including bulbous bow. Beam: 95 ft. 1in / 29.0m. Draught: 23 ft. 7$^{ins}$ / 7.2m. Four MAN oil engines (two 9-cylinder, two 6-cylinder) in a 'father and son' configuration. 27,200 bhp. Twin screw. Service speed: 19½ knots. Call sign: ELNG.

*Horizon* was one of three ships which established Celebrity Cruises, an offshoot of the more down-market Chandris Cruises. The other two were *Meridian*, a conversion of the beautiful former Lloyd Triestino *Galileo Galilei*; and *Zenith* of 1992, *Horizon*'s sister ship. (*Meridian* was later sold to Far Eastern owners and, by then called *Sun Vista*, burned in May, 1999.) The Celebrity ships, bearing the famous Chandris X on their funnels, quickly established a good reputation at the higher end of the American cruise market. The company has since become a subsidiary of the big Royal Caribbean International group.

The *Horizon* at Southampton on the 4$^{th}$ May, 1990 during an unscheduled call shortly after leaving her builders' yard.

In 1998, *Horizon* was given a refurbishment at the Newport News shipyard in Virginia to bring her more into line with Celebrity's newer ships and became well-known for her cruises to Bermuda from New York and from Philadelphia. In 2005, however, she was transferred to another Royal Caribbean associate, Island Cruises, and now often sails in the Mediterranean under the name *Island Star*, carrying mainly British passengers.

# FASCINATION

Completed 1994 by Kvaerner Masa-Yard, Helsinki. 70,367 gross tons. Length overall: 855 ft. 7$^{ins}$ / 260.8m. Beam: 103 ft. 4$^{ins}$ / 31.5m. Draught: 25 ft. 4$^{ins}$ / 7.7m. Diesel-electric (Two 8-cylinder and four 12-cylinder Sulzer-Wärtsilä oil engines driving generators and, in turn, electric motors). 57,425 bhp. Twin screw. Service speed: 18 knots. Call sign: C6FM9.

The *Fascination* is the fourth of the eight-ship *Fantasy* class of 'fun ships', built for Carnival Cruise Lines between 1991 and 1998. As on her sisters (*Fantasy*, *Ecstasy*, *Sensation*, *Imagination*, *Inspiration*, *Elation* and *Paradise*), her interiors are based on a 'theme' – in her case Hollywood. Mannequins depicting famous film stars adorn her lounges and it is said that they soon became quite well-handled as countless passengers posed alongside them for photographs. The ship's interior colour scheme is described as 'Sixties Retro' with green, mauve and purple paint schemes being highlighted by chrome and a myriad of small coloured lights.

It may all be too much for passengers of delicate sensibilities but there can be no denying that the Carnival ships have become hugely popular in the American market. The line's reputation of catering for the young and noisy seems to be something of the past as an increasing number of older 'guests' are now said to be booking on their ships.

The *Fascination* has mainly been used for short 3- and 4-day cruises, at first from San Juan in Puerto Rico and more recently out of Miami. So fast has been the pace at which the size of cruise ships has increased that the 70,000-ton *Fantasy* class ships are now being dwarfed by a later generation of 140,000-tonners and 180,000-tonners are under construction. A 220,000-ton ship is in an advanced planning stage.

The face of things to come: *Fascination*, here seen calling at Southampton on the 9th July, 1994 during her delivery voyage, was one of the early highly-succesful Carnival Cruise Lines mega-ships.

# CROWN ODYSSEY

Completed 1988 by Jos. L. Meyer GmbH, Papenburg. 32,242 gross tons. Length overall: 615 ft.10ins / 187.7m. including bulbous bow. Beam: 92 ft. 6ins / 28.2m. Draught: 22 ft. 8ins / 6.9m. Four MaK oil engines (two 4-cylinder and two 6-cylinder). 28,955 bhp. Twin screw. Service speed: 22 knots. Call sign: RCLB.

Another high-class product of the Meyer Werft at Papenburg in North Germany, this strikingly modern-looking cruise ship was built for the up-market, Greek-owned Royal Cruise Line. In 1992, the line was taken over by the Kloster group but the new owners' attempts to 'improve' the ships reportedly caused a drop in standards. In May, 1996 financial difficulties led to the Royal Cruise Line being closed down and the ship was transferred to the group's Norwegian Cruise Line under the name *Norwegian Crown*. In 2000, by which time NCL had become a subsidiary of the Malaysian-owned Star Cruises group, she was sent for a refit at the Sembawang Shipyard in Singapore and was transferred within the group to Orient Lines under her original name of *Crown Odyssey*.

Given Orient Lines' dark blue hull, she joined *Marco Polo* (ex-*Alexandr Pushkin* (ibid)) in providing cruises with a little more adventure in their itineraries, releasing *Marco Polo* to spend more time exploring the Polar reaches for which her ice-strengthened hull is well-suited.

In 2003, because of the Iraqi War, the *Crown Odyssey* returned west via Cape Town. It was now decided to switch her back to NCL. She thus did a 'second take', being again named *Norwegian Crown* and being given a major refurbishment. That September, she experienced some propeller damage whilst sailing from Quebec en route for Baltimore, where she was to be re-introduced to the press and the travel trade. Missing, her own party, she had to be drydocked at Boston for repairs. Back in service, she was marketed as a 'Freestyle Cruising' vessel, catering for passengers who prefer a more informal atmosphere. In another change of ownership, she is due to become Fred. Olsen's *Balmoral* in 2008.

The Greek-owned *Crown Odyssey* departing Southampton for Piraeus on the 3rd September, 1990.

# MONARCH OF THE SEAS

Completed 1990 by Chantiers de l'Atlantique, St. Nazaire. 73,937 gross tons. Overall length: 880 ft 4ins / 268.3m. including bulbous bow. Beam: 105 ft. 7ins / 32.2m. Draught: 24 ft. 10ins / 7.6m. Four 9-cylinder Pielstick-type oil engines. 29,365 bhp. Twin screw. Service speed: 20 knots. Call sign: LAMU4.

One of the increasingly massive cruise ships built for Royal Caribbean Cruises, *Monarch of the Seas* came from the great shipyard at St. Nazaire on the River Loire. That, of course, is the yard which, more recently, produced the new Cunard flagship *Queen Mary 2*. Delivery of *Monarch of the Seas* took place on the 17th November, 1990, having been delayed by a fire whilst she was fitting out. Her 'Godmother' was the actress Lauren Bacall, famous for *The Big Sleep* among other films.

The ship's career has not been without incident. At 00.30 hours on the morning of the 15th December, 1998 she made an unscheduled arrival outside Great Bay, St. Maarten (in the Leeward Islands in the Caribbean) as an ill passenger ('guest') required urgent 'shore-side' medical attention. At 01.30 hours, shortly after disembarking the patient, the ship was proceeding at 12 knots when she hit the Proselyte Reef with a glancing blow. Crew and passengers were assembled at their emergency stations whilst the captain turned the ship, which was making water, and headed towards a sandbar in Great Bay, where she grounded an hour later. By 05.15, all passengers had been safely landed. The ship's bottom plates had been severely cracked, buckled and dented and seventeen compartments were affected by flooding. The subsequent repairs cost a staggering $40 million. The Norwegian Maritime Investigator and the U.S. Coast Guard later jointly issued a 62-page report.

June, 2003 saw *Monarch of the Seas* emerge from a further $26 million refit that began at sea in April and was completed during a major rebuilding in Freeport in May. Amongst her new attractions is a rock-climbing wall added to her funnel, bringing her in line with some of the company's later ships.

The appearance in The Solent of giant, modern cruise vessels such as the *Monarch of the Seas* and, recently, even bigger ships, is a certain sign that Southampton still retains its old position as 'Gateway to the World'.

*Monarch of the Seas* departing Southampton after a promotional visit to the Queen Elizabeth II Terminal, 18th October, 1991. Although massive she has a more shapely stern than most modern cruise ships; it is not dis-similar from that of the famous *Normandie*.

# FERRIES

## From Poole

## FERRY No. 3

Completed 1959 by J. Bolson & Son, Ltd., Poole.  400 tons dwt.  Length overall: 157 ft.0$^{ins}$ / 47.9m.  Beam: 42 ft. 6$^{ins}$ / 13.0m.  Draught: 3 ft. 6$^{ins}$ / 1.1m., fully loaded.  Diesel-electric with three Ruston oil engines. 135 bhp.

The current Sandbanks Ferry service across the 350 yard-wide mouth of Poole Harbour, between Studlands and Shell Bay, began in 1923 when an Isle of Wight businessman, Frank Aman, and his two sons founded the Bournemouth-Swanage Motor Road & Ferry Company.  Their first vessel, coal-fired and driven by steam, also came from the Isle of Wight, being built by J. Samuel White at Cowes. Like her successors, she was a chain ferry.  The chains along which the ferries are pulled are 1,235 feet long and last from 15 to 18 months before requiring replacement due to wear (especially at the landward ends) and to 'stretch', for which two links are removed every two weeks.  Each passage takes approximately 4 minutes.

The 'floating bridge' *Ferry No. 3* ran on two of her three engines at a time, enabling any necessary maintenance work to be carried out on the third.  Her final sailing was the last crossing on the 17th January, 1994.  She was replaced by *Ferry No. 4*, the *Bramble Bush Bay*, the first of the company's ferries to have a name.

Locally built *Ferry No. 3* crossing the mouth of Poole Harbour with a full load in April, 1993.

# ROZEL

Completed 1974 by Cammell Laird Shipbuilders, Ltd., Birkenhead. 8,987 gross tons. Length overall: 427 ft. 10$^{ins}$ / 130.4m. including bulbous bow. Beam: 70 ft. 10$^{ins}$ / 21.6m. Draught: 17 ft. 1in / 5.2m. Four 8-cylinder Stork-Werkspoor oil engines. 20,400 bhp. Twin controllable-pitch propellers. Service speed: 21 knots. Call sign: GUKB.

This well-proportioned ferry was built as the *St. Edmund* for the British Rail (later Sealink) Harwich to Hook of Holland service. She was the flagship of the line and proved well able to cope with rough conditions on the North Sea. She was noted for her broad funnel capped with a narrow extension, typical of the British Rail ferries of that era, and for her ultra-modern interiors.

In 1982, the *St. Edmund* was requisitioned on charter (STUFT – Ship Taken Up From Trade) by the Ministry of Defence to carry troops and equipment to the battle zone during the Falklands crisis. For this task, she was given a rapid refit at Devonport Dockyard, which included the fitting of a helicopter pad. The following year, in the aftermath of the crisis, she was purchased outright by the Ministry and converted on the Tyne into a fully-fledged troopship to shuttle between Ascension and Port Stanley in the Falklands. For this

*Rozel* in the King George V Drydock, Southampton, undergoing conversion work by Thew Marine, 24$^{th}$ January, 1989.

Although German-built, the Beauport was of a very typical Scandinavian design. Here she is outward bound from Poole 9th March, 1993.

purpose, she was managed by the Blue Star Line and was renamed HMS *Keren*. Made redundant by the opening of Port Stanley Airport, she was sold to Cenargo Navigation, Ltd., then one of the younger and more enterprising British shipping companies. They operated her in the charter market as the *Scirocco* and over the next few years she saw Mediterranean service with Italian, Moroccan and Tunisian ferry companies. In 1989, she was renamed *Rozel* for a charter to British Channel Island Ferries, who used her on their service between Poole and the islands. The biggest ship yet seen on the Channel Islands routes, she became very well-liked. She may, in fact, have been too large for the amount of traffic on offer and, when her charter ended after three years, it was not renewed.

In 1992, once again called *Scirocco*, she found summer employment running between Melila and Malaga under charter to the Spanish company Trasmediterránea. The following year, Cenargo tried to enter the Morocco-Spain trade themselves, forming a new subsidiary, Ferrimaroc, to run between Nador and Almeria. The Spanish government blocked the service, delaying the disembarkation of the *Scirocco's* first passengers for 18 hours. An acrimonious battle through the courts followed and it was not until November, 1994 that the new service finally got underway. The *Scirocco* established it successfully, much of her trade consisting of carrying Moroccan workers seeking employment in Spain. In 2004, Ferrimaroc, now running a more modern ship, sold the *Scirocco* to Greek owners. She quickly passed to a company called United Pacific Navigation, who have named her *Santa Catherine I*. Ironically, Ferrimaroc has since been sold to Trasmediterránea.

# BEAUPORT

Completed 1970 by Schichau-Unterweser AG, Bremerhaven. 7,747 gross tons. Length overall: 388 ft. / 118.25 m. (338 ft. / 103m.between perpendiculars). Beam: 58 ft. 7$^{ins}$ / 17.85m. Draught: 16 ft. 9$^{ins}$ / 5.1 m. Two SEMT-Pielstick V12-cylinder oil engines. 12,000 bhp. Twin screw. Twin rudders. Service speed: 17 knots. Call sign as built: SHGA.

Launched as *Prince of Fundy* for Lion Ferry and used on the summer service across the Bay of Fundy on the East Coast of America and Canada, this handsome vessel was sold in 1978 to Brittany Ferries to become, first, their *Prince of Brittany* and then, in 1988, *Reine Mathilde*. Three years later, she was running as the *Beauport* for British Channel Island Ferries. Although a good ship in many ways, she attracted criticism in the islands, where she was compared unfavourably with the *Rozel* (ex-*Scirocco*) (ibid). Retaining the name *Beauport*, she later sailed under the banners of Stern Maritime Line (1994) and Hellenic Inter Ferries (1994-95). She also saw winter service with other companies. Between 1995 and 1999, she attracted summer charters ferrying Moroccan citizens crossing to work in Europe and returning for holidays. Managed by ISP (International Shipping Partners of Miami), she was operated by COMUNAV (Compagnie Marocaine de Navigation).

For a time, she was registered in the name of Beauport Shipping, Ltd., still managed by ISP, and ran for the Government Shipping Service of Trinidad and Tobago in an inter-island service, in which she proved to be a popular, if sometimes controversial, vessel. (There were episodes of non-payment of crew wages and on one occasion berths were cancelled which had been allotted to 200 'panners' – steeldrummers – from Trinidad and Tobago who were heading for the inaugural Caribbean Steelband Panorama Championships in Grenada.) In 2005, she was broken up at Alang in India.

# BARFLEUR

Completed 1992 by Kvaerner-Masa Yards, Helsinki. 20,133 gross tons. Length overall: 517 ft. 3$^{ins}$ / 157.65 m. over bulbous bow. Beam: 76 ft. 6$^{ins}$ / 23.3 m. Draught: 17 ft. 9$^{ins}$ / 5.4 m. Four Wärtsilä 8-cylinder oil engines. 16,303 bhp. Twin controllable-pitch propellers. Service speed: 19½ knots. Call sign: FNIE.

Lengthened by 7.2 metres before completion, *Barfleur* was launched for Truckline Ferries France S.A. of Cherbourg, an associate of Brittany Ferries, for their Poole – Cherbourg route. She was the largest vessel to have been placed in that service and made a defiant gesture towards the new Channel Tunnel.

For her first month of service she carried only truck-based traffic but, on receipt of her passenger certificate, she proceeded to carry 'non-truck' passengers. In 1999, the Truckline identity was dropped and she assumed the Brittany Ferries livery. She suffered damage to her stern ramp-operating machinery in June, 2001 whilst at Poole and was out of action for some weeks.

A much larger vessel than most which have sailed out of Poole, the French-owned *Barfleur* is here seen with Brownsea Island astern on the 21$^{st}$ May, 1993.

# ST. PATRICK

completed 1925 by Alexander Stephen & Sons, Ltd., Glasgow. 1,922 gross tons. Length overall: 281 ft. 4$^{ins}$ / 85.8m. Beam: 41 ft. 2 $^{ins}$ / 12.5m. Draught: 16 ft. 4$^{ins}$ / 5.0m. Four steam turbines. 887 nhp. Twin screw. Call sign: MUNY.

Although built for the Irish sea service of Fishguard & Rosslare Railway & Harbours, Ltd. (a joint venture between the Great Western Railway and the Great Southern Railway of Ireland), the *St. Patrick* actually made her maiden voyage from Weymouth to the Channel Islands for the Great Western. On arrival, she damaged her rudder, which took three weeks to repair at Southampton. It was not until the September that she joined the Fishguard – Rosslare service for which she was intended. Although she spent most of her time on that route, she did return to Weymouth each July and August. It was in the latter month of 1932 that she was damaged on rocks off Jersey during thick fog.

The *St. Patrick* was attacked twice by German bombers in August, 1940 and then met a dreadful end on Friday the 13th June, 1941. Having left Rosslare that morning, she was approaching Strumble Head when German aircraft discovered her at 04.20, in the early light twenty minutes before dawn. Passengers were still asleep below decks when the first machine gun attack came.

The ship's 12-pounder gun fired back, but to no avail. The 'plane turned and dropped four bombs which found their target forward of the hapless ship's funnel. Fuel tanks were broached and set on fire and the boat deck was in ruins, as was the First Class accommodation. All but one of the thirteen passengers in this area lost their lives during the onslaught, as did seventeen of the crew. Only one lifeboat could be launched. Meanwhile, the radio officer kept at his post but seven minutes after the attack the ship started to break in two before disappearing beneath the waves, still belching black smoke from the burning oil. Of the ninety people on board, one-third were lost. RAF aircraft arrived to drive off the attackers and, two hours later, rescue craft arrived on the scene. Because a suitable replacement ferry could not be found, the route was abandoned until 1946.

# MONARCH

completed 1888 by R. & H. Green, Blackwall, London. 315 gross tons. Length overall: 210 ft. 4$^{ins}$ / 64.1m. Beam: 32 ft. 3$^{ins}$ / 9.8m. Draught: 9 ft. 0$^{ins}$ / 2.7m. 2-cylinder simple, diagonal, direct-acting, condensing engines by John Penn & Son, Greenwich. 179 nhp. 850 ihp. Paddles. Call sign: KSMG.

This hardy veteran, an early steel-built ship, was ordered by Cosens & Co., Ltd., for their cross-Channel service from Bournemouth to Alderney and Cherbourg, a trip of some 5½ hours. Over the years, she made long-distance excursions from Weymouth or Bournemouth Pier to Cherbourg, Torquay or the Channel Islands as well as to the Isle of Wight. When she appeared, she was the largest excursion vessel on the South Coast. Her machinery had an unusual configuration, with two boiler rooms, one for'd and one aft of the engine room, hence the fact that her two slender funnels were so widely spaced. Her engines were of the non-compound diagonal type – the first and last time that Cosens used such machinery.

During the Great War, she was commissioned as a minesweeper, HMS *Monarch*, serving in the Bristol and St. George's Channels. After the War, she returned to civilian service but now venturing less abroad – she mainly plied her trade in local waters with Swanage, Bournemouth and sometimes the Isle of Wight being her prime destinations, although on occasion she also went a little further afield to Seaton and Torquay.

Earlier, on the 1st April, 1902, *Monarch* had the distinction of being the first steamer to use the new 170 ft.-long Victoria Pier at Cowes. Ten years later, in 1912, she visited Southampton to see *Titanic* depart on her maiden voyage – at her next refit she was given additional lifeboats. Over the years, damage occurred through colliding with a pier in stormy weather and through hitting some wreckage with one of her paddles. More happily, she was chartered by the Supermarine aviation company to watch the Schneider Trophy races in The Solent.

A reboilering and some restyling by John I. Thornycroft's yard in 1929, including the fitting of larger diameter funnels, saw her through to the Second World War, in which she again served her country. This time she became HMS *Exway*, an Admiralty examination and contraband control vessel, reputedly the oldest ship to fly the White Ensign during the War. Afterwards, she returned to civilian service but only for another five years before being sold for breaking up. Both the rôle and the name of this beloved old ship passed to the ex-*Shanklin*.

An early Bob Bruce Grice photograph taken at Weymouth in the late 1930s. The *St. Patrick* turns off the harbour entrance while the paddle steamer *Monarch* splashes by with a shipload of excursionists.

# CONSUL

Completed 1896 by R. & H. Green, Ltd., London. 257 gross tons. Length overall: 175 ft. 0ins / 53.3m.
Beam: 20 ft. 7ins / 6.3m. Draught: 8 ft. 3ins / 2.5m. 3-cylinder compound diagonal steam engine by J. Penn
& Son, Greenwich. Paddles. Call sign: GWMW.

The lovely paddle-driven excursion steamer *Consul* moored at Weymouth in August, 1964.

Built as the *Duke of Devonshire* for the Devon Dock, Pier & Steamship Co., Ltd., this small paddler ran excursions from Torquay, etc. in competition with the ships of Cosens & Co. of Weymouth. She had a strengthened forefoot so that she could put her bow ashore in Lulworth Cove. In 1902, she attended King Edward VII's Coronation Naval Review at Spithead. In the Great War, she was requisitioned as a minesweeper and managed to steam as far as Mesopotamia and back.

In 1933, she passed into the hands of P. & A. Campbell, Ltd., who laid her up until the following year when they sold her to a new owner, a Mr. Dwyer, for excursion work from Cork in the Irish Free State. However, she returned to home waters in 1936, now under the ownership of Alexander Taylor of Torquay who, in December, 1937, sold her to the competition, Cosens & Co. She arrived at her new homeport of Weymouth the following April and was renamed *Consul*.

On the 2nd September, 1939, a day before the outbreak of the Second World War, it fell to the *Consul* to make the company's last peacetime sailing. The Cosens fleet initially acted as examination and inspection vessels. In July, 1940, *Consul* had the unpleasant experience of passing near to the burning wreckage and carnage of the anti-aircraft vessel *Foylebank* which had been bombed at her moorings. *Consul* herself narrowly missed destruction during an air raid the following August: shortly after she left her coaling berth, a bomb fell in the position she had occupied just minutes previously. On another occasion, a mine was detected beneath her causing her to make a hurried but cautious departure from her anchorage.

De-activated from patrol duties in December, 1940, she was used as a training vessel but saw light duties during the D-Day period in 1944. The Cosens fleet survived the War unscathed but the now elderly *Consul*, very much in need of a virtual rebuild, did not resume her peacetime work until 1949. Her structure had been extensively modified (although her new deckhouse would be removed in 1957) and there had been much replating of her hull. She had also been converted to burn oil fuel. She emerged from it all, looking smarter than ever. In 1953, she made excursions from Southampton to Spithead for the Coronation Review and the following year she was there again to welcome Her Majesty home after her Commonwealth Tour.

By 1957, she could claim to be the oldest paddle steamer in the U.K. After 1960, when the *Glen Gower* was scrapped, she also had the oldest set of paddle engines. Her last call at Bournemouth Pier occurred during the 1962 season and, in 1963, it was decided to withdraw her from service as she had become unprofitable. She was first sold to W. Smyth, who then quickly sold her on to South Coast & Continental Steamers, Ltd. They painted her hull green and operated her out of Newhaven. Because of mechanical troubles, she made only a handful of excursions from the Sussex port along with a successful week's charter in the Thames before returning to a winter berth in Weymouth. She was still steaming in 1964 but this truly vintage ship was sent to the breakers early in 1965 after a short stint with her last owners, Sailing & Travel Club of Dartmouth, under her original name of *Duke of Devonshire*.

# MONARCH (II)

Completed 1924 by John I. Thornycroft & Co., Ltd., Woolston, Southampton. 412 gross tons. Length overall: 197 ft. 9$^{ins}$ / 60.3m. Beam: 26 ft. 1in / 7.9m. Draught: 8 ft. 8$^{ins}$ / 2.6m. Compound diagonal engine by her builders. 1116 hp. Paddles. Service speed: 13.3 knots. Call sign: MNBC

This paddle steamer started her life as the *Shanklin* on the Southern Railway's Portsmouth to Ryde route. She remained on station throughout the Second World War before being laid up in 1949, having reached her quarter century. It was some time before she was finally sold. However, in 1951, she was purchased by Cosens, inheriting the name *Monarch* from a much-loved ship which had been withdrawn during the previous year (ibid). Cosens sent their new purchase to be refitted by her original builders and then placed her on their Bournemouth to Swanage service. She was one of three paddlers from their fleet that were based in Southampton for five days to run excursions during the Coronation Review of the Fleet in June, 1953. She was seen to her best advantage during her visits to Cowes Week and, in what proved to be her final season, was one of the flotilla that greeted Princess Margaret and Anthony Armstrong-Jones as they returned from their honeymoon on board the Royal Yacht *Britannia* (ibid).

*Monarch* was the youngest of the Cosens fleet and it came as a surprise when she was withdrawn from service, laid up with her windows boarded over and finally, having been sold for £2,500, towed to Passage West in Cork at the beginning of March, 1961. There she was broken up by Haulbowline Industries.

This photograph of the second *Monarch* returning to Poole of the evening tide was taken in 1952 by Sue Goldfinch, Bob Bruce Grice's daughter.

# ST. HELIER

Completed 1925 by John Brown & Co., Ltd., Clydebank.  1,885 gross tons.  Length overall: 282 ft. 3$^{ins}$ / 86.0m.  Beam: 40 ft. 0$^{ins}$ / 12.2m.  Draught: 16 ft. 4$^{ins}$ / 5.0m.  Four steam turbines.  819 nhp.  Twin screw.  Service speed 18 knots.  Call sign: GBT.

Built for the famous Great Western Railway, the *St. Helier* and her sister *St. Julien* originally sported two funnels but the second was removed in 1927 – along with the docking bridge – in an effort to reduce both vessels' disconcerting propensity to hang on the roll in choppy seas.

In 1926, double trouble came to the Channel Islands port of St. Helier when, on the 10$^{th}$ March, *St. Helier* rammed the pierhead.  The very next day, in a sisterly fashion, *St. Julien* did exactly the same thing.  *St. Helier* was one of the heroic vessels involved in the evacuation from Dunkirk in 1940.  She made eight crossings, bringing back over 10,000 Allied troops and 1,500 civilian refugees.  During this hectic time, she was involved in two collisions, one being with the paddle steamer *Princess Helena* and the other with HMS *Sharpshooter*.  She also suffered damage from enemy gunfire whilst attempting an evacuation of personnel from La Pallice.

As HMS *St. Helier*, she saw service on the Clyde and at Dartmouth (as 'mother ship' to a group of motor torpedo boats).  In June, 1942 she was converted to an Assault Landing Ship (LSI(H)) in readiness for the D-Day invasion of Hitler's 'Fortress Europe'.  When the landings eventually occurred, she made several trips, on the first of which she carried Canadian troops.

In June 1946, it fell to *St. Helier* to make the first post-War crossing, re-establishing the mail link to the Channel Islands from Weymouth.  In 1948, she was transferred to the Southern Region of the by-then nationalised rail network.  This plucky little steamer left Weymouth for the last time on the  12$^{th}$ September, 1960, and three months later sailed for shipbreakers in Belgium.

The *St. Helier* loading cargo and embarking passengers at Weymouth, circa 1954.

# SARNIA

Completed 1961 by J. Samuel White & Co., Ltd., East Cowes, Isle of Wight. 3,989 gross tons. Length overall: 322 ft. 0$^{ins}$ / 98.1m. (302 ft. 0$^{ins}$ / 92.0m. between perpendiculars). Beam: 52 ft. 7$^{ins}$ / 16.0m. Draught: 13 ft. 7½$^{ins}$ / 4.2m. Two geared steam turbines. 9,000 shp. Twin screw. Service speed: 19½knots. Call sign: GHNF.

The steamship *Sarnia* alongside at Weymouth with the boat train arriving, 4th September, 1977.

*Sarnia* (the Latin name for Guernsey) and her sister *Caesarea* (Jersey) were one-class vessels, the last passenger ferries and the last steamships to be built for the Channel Islands service of the British Railways Board, the government-owned successors to the former Great Western Railway. (Later, the service came under the auspices of British Ferries and, later still, Sealink.) With the introduction of these new sisters, the Channel Islands services were concentrated on Weymouth and the sailings from Southampton were abandoned.

*Caesarea* continued in the service until October, 1975 and the *Sarnia* sailed on until September, 1977. But the old *Falaise*, converted into a car ferry, tolled the death knell for conventional passenger ships on the route. After leaving Weymouth, both sisters saw some service on cross-Channel routes but eventually *Sarnia* was sold for rather undignified employment as a floating supermarket called *Aquamart*, based at Ostend. The venture failed and she was further sold to a company with the surprising name of Grecian Fertility, Inc., becoming their *Golden Star* in 1979. She later passed to Hitta Establishment, Jeddah who, calling her *Saudi Golden Star*, had her rebuilt to load vehicles through a stern door and placed her in Red Sea service. She was finally sent for breaking on Gadani Beach in Pakistan in 1987.

The author (then a schoolboy in West Cowes and whose uncle, Edgar Way, was J. Samuel White's Electrical Design Manager and was thus involved in the building of these vessels) well remembers the launching and shipyard departures of both ships, with Red Funnel tugs in attendance on each occasion.

## MAID OF KENT

Built 1959 by William Denny & Bros., Ltd., Dumbarton. 3,920 gross tons. Length overall: 373 ft. 0ins / 113.7m. (348 ft. / 106.1m. between perpendiculars). Beam: 60 ft. 3ins / 18.4m. Draught: 13 ft. 0ins / 4.0m. Two sets of geared steam turbines. 11,500 shp. Twin screw. Service speed: 20 knots. Call sign: GCHU.

This fine little turbine steamer was named after Elizabeth Barton, 'The Maid of Kent', who was publicly hanged at Tyburn by order of Henry VIII. Given to trances, she had predicted that he would abdicate should he divorce and re-marry.

Ordered by the British Railways Board as a car-carrier loading through a stern door, the *Maid of Kent* originally ran on the Dover to Boulogne route. In 1974, she was transferred to Weymouth for the cross-Channel service to Cherbourg, for which her stern door had to be modified to fit the shoreside ramps. After just three days on this route, she embarrassingly suffered a severe mechanical breakdown and spent eight hours at anchor in Weymouth Bay. With the arrival of the tug RMAS *Sheepdog*, she was towed back to Weymouth but, such was her popularity, many of her passengers did not seem to mind having spent so long in a sunny Dorset bay being well looked after. Those were the days when an official letter of apology for the inconvenience which had been caused actually appeared in the local paper.

A year later, she was moved again – this time to the Stranraer – Larne service. Then, in 1976, she

The car ferry *Maid of Kent* did not change her name when in 1974 she left her base in the Kentish port of Dover to take up station at Weymouth. Here she is re-opening the Weymouth – Cherbourg route on the 6th April, 1974.

appeared on the Harwich – Zeebrugge run and later that same year on the Fishguard – Rosslare route before returning to the Weymouth – Cherbourg crossing. This remained her main track of operation, except for a brief spell running between Holyhead and Dun Laoghaire in 1979. In 1981, she saw service to the Channel Islands before moving to Newhaven. Her final destination was San Estaban de Pravia in Spain, where she arrived for demolition in 1982.

# SVEA DROTT
# later EARL GODWIN

Completed 1966 by Oresundsvarvet AB, Landskrona. 4,018 gross tons. Length overall: 325 ft / 99.1m. (295 ft. 3$^{ins}$ / 90.0m. between perpendiculars). Beam: 58 ft. 1in / 17.7m. Draught: 14 ft. 5$^{ins}$ / 4.4m. Two V12-cylinder Deutz oil engines. 12,000 bhp. Twin controllable-pitch propellers. Service speed: 20¾ knots. Call sign: SJYE.

Built for Stockholm Rederi AB Svea, this neat ferry served on the Helsingfors – Travemünde route of the Trave Line. In 1974, she was bareboat chartered to Rederi AB Gotland, who then sub-chartered her to Sealink. They put her on their Weymouth – Channel Islands route in place of the *Falaise* which had been taken out of service because of mechanical problems. She must have pleased them as, later that year, they purchased her and renamed her *Earl Godwin* in 1975. On occasion, she was transferred to Portsmouth or even to the Irish Sea.

In 1990, she was sold to Navigazione Arcipelago Maddalenino of Cagliari in Sardinia, whose ferries were for many years famous for the cartoon picture of a whale painted on their sides. Aptly, they called their new purchase *Moby Baby* and they sailed her between Piombino and Portoferraio on the island of Elba. She remains on that route.

A new profile at Weymouth: the *Svea Drott* in August, 1974 (upper) and, after re-naming, the *Earl Godwin* on the 2$^{nd}$ June, 1985 (lower).

# EARL WILLIAM

Completed 1964 by Kaldnes Mekaniske Verksted A/S, Tönsberg. 3,765 gross tons. Length overall: 326 ft. 6$^{ins}$ / 99.5 m. Beam: 58 ft. 2$^{ins}$ / 17.7m. Draught: 14 ft. 6$^{ins}$ / 4.4m. Two V12-cylinder Pielstick oil engines. 10,200 bhp. Twin screw. Service speed: 18½ knots. Call sign: GWIA.

This ultra-modern ferry was built for the Otto Thoresen Shipping Co. A/S of Oslo, who took a prominent part in the Scandinavian invasion of the British ferry scene. Aptly, she was called *Viking II* and placed on Thoresen's newly established services from Southampton to Cherbourg and to Le Havre. Over the years, she was also chartered to the Atlantic Steam Navigation Co., Stena Line and Lion Ferry.

In 1976, she was sold to British Rail/Sealink and ran as *Earl William* on their routes from Portsmouth and Weymouth to the Channel Islands and to Cherbourg. (*Lloyd's Register of Shipping* had her as *Carferry Viking II* for a while in 1977.) 1981 and 1982 were not very good years for her as she collided, firstly, with the quay at St. Helier and, on the second occasion, with a submerged rock.

Eventually laid up at Harwich, she was used as a detention centre for illegal immigrants who must have had a very uncomfortable experience when, during a hurricane, she broke her moorings and was driven aground. Repaired and put back into service, the *Earl William* opened a new route between Liverpool and Dun Laoghaire. This, however, was not a success and she was placed in lay-up in 1990, occasionally appearing on other routes as a relief ship. She was sold in 1992 to Adonis Shipping of Malta and was delivered as *William*. Run by Neptunus Lines, she was renamed *Pearl William*. In 1996, she became *Mar-Julia* of P&L Ferries, Malta and then in 1997, under new owners Lucky Shipping, she was chartered to Stern Lines as the *Cesme Stern*, registered in Kingstown, St. Vincent. That same year, she was arrested and sold, finally sailing as *Windward II* for Windward Lines, also of Kingstown in 2001. When last heard of, she was under arrest at Port of Spain in Trinidad.

# EARL HAROLD

Completed 1971 by Cantieri Navali Breda SpA, Venice. 6,177 gross tons. Length overall: 369 ft. 5ins / 112.6 m. Beam: 57 ft. 3ins / 17.45m. Draught: 12 ft. 0ins / 3.66m. Two Pielstick-Crossley Premier-SEMT V16-cylinder oil engines. 14,560 bhp. Twin screw. Service speed: 19½ knots. Call sign: GOVA.

Launched as *Ailsa Princess*, this ferry went into service on British Rail's Sealink Irish Sea routes. Later, in 1982, she was switched briefly to the Isle of Man service. In that year, she also appeared on the Weymouth to Cherbourg route and she permanently turned to southern shores in 1983.

On the privatisation of Sealink and its purchase by Sea Containers in 1984, the *'Princess'* took on the corporate livery of British Ferries and, in the following year, was renamed *Earl Harold*. She was laid up at Weymouth with the other units of the Channel Islands fleet in 1986 with her crew protesting about the proposed amalgamation with Channel Island Ferries. Sealink finally withdrew her from service after the *Herald of Free Enterprise* disaster of 6thMarch, 1987, probably thinking that it would be too expensive to bring an older ship into line with new safety regulations.

In April, 1989, the *Earl* was chartered to the B&I Line for use on their Pembroke Dock to Rosslare service but questions about her safety were asked in the Dáil Éireann, the lower chamber of the Irish Parliament. The Minister for Marine, Mr. Daly, said that she complied with IMO regulations to which both the UK and Eire were signatories. But, mooted as being unsuitable for the route, the *Earl* was quickly withdrawn and sold to GA Ferries of Greece, becoming their *Dimitra*. Staying in Greek waters, she was sold to Agapitos Lines and, in 1994, after a rebuild, was renamed *Naias Express*. Agapitos became part of Hellas Ferries and, in 1999, the ship was renamed *Express Adonis*. She is still in service, although by now demoted to the company's less important routes.

# CONDOR 9

Completed 1990 by Aluminium Shipbuilders, Ltd., Portchester, near Fareham. 62.13 tonnes deadweight. Length overall: 159 ft. 9ins / 48.7m. Beam: 60 ft. 4ins / 18.4m. Draught: 6 ft. 8ins / 2.04m. Four MWM V16-cylinder oil engines. 9,141 bhp. Four MJP J650R-DD water jet propulsors. 35 knots loaded; 42 knots light. Call sign: MMKX4.

Although Aluminium Shipbuilders, managed by John Davis, were based in the Isle of Wight, they leased Number 3 Shed (originally constructed for building hovercraft) at Vosper Ltd.'s shipyard at Portchester in order to build *Condor 9*. She was a wave-

The paddle-steamer *Princess Elizabeth* reversing in Weymouth Bay in 1983.

piercing catamaran based on an Incat design. Operated by Condor, Ltd., a subsidiary of Commodore Shipping (UK), Ltd., she quickly experienced operational and technical problems which necessitated her drydocking for repairs, as seen in this photograph. In 1994, she was chartered to SF-Line of Mariehamn in the Finnish-owned Aland Islands for Viking Line service between Helsinki and Tallinn, becoming their *Viking Express*. She then went on charter in the Caribbean.

*Condor 9* returned to the South Coast in 1995 but was withdrawn from the Weymouth to Channel Islands high-speed service in March, 2002, being replaced by *Condor 10*. The '9' was subsequently sold to interests in St. Vincent and renamed *Cortez*. In 2003, Commodore Shipping was itself renamed Condor Ferries. The King George V Drydock, seen in this picture, was de-commissioned in 2004 and was scrapped. Its gates had been deemed unsafe.

# From Southampton

## PRINCESS ELIZABETH

Completed 1927 by Day, Summers & Co., Southampton. 388 gross tons. Length overall: 195 ft. 0$^{ins}$ / 59.4m. Beam: 24 ft. 2$^{ins}$ / 7.4m. (48 ft. / 14.6m. over the paddle boxes). Draught: 8 ft. 0$^{ins}$ / 2.4m. Coal-fired diagonal steam engine. Paddles. Service speed: 14½ knots. Call sign: KWLP.

This venerable paddle steamer was built for the line that famously had the longest name in the shipping world, The Southampton, Isle of Wight & South of England Royal Mail Steam Packet Company (better and more manageably known as Red Funnel Steamers). Introduced in 1927, she was an improved version of the company's very successful, but short-lived, *Princess Mary* of 1911. Like that well-known vessel, the *Princess Elizabeth* was designed by Lawrence Pritchard and his team.

The last ship to come from the Southampton yard of Day, Summers & Co., she was built to undertake a variety of rôles, including passenger and car ferry duties between Southampton and Cowes; tendering liners that lay at anchor in The Solent (famously including the French Line ships, including the great *Normandie*); and running summer excursions between various ports and

*Princess Elizabeth* again, this time arriving in the Pool of London on the 4th June, 1970, with Tower Bridge in the background. She is proudly flying the colours she so bravely wore at Dunkirk.

piers along the South Coast. Her foredeck was specially strengthened to carry cars, craned from ship or shore.

Requisitioned by The Admiralty in 1940, she became HMS *Princess Elizabeth* and acted as an anti-aircraft vessel in the 10thMinesweeping Flotilla of the Dover Command. She brought honour to herself, to her crew and to the company that owned her when she took part in the evacuation of the British Expeditionary Force from Dunkirk in May, 1940. She made four trips to the battle-torn beaches, rescuing a total of 1,763 troops and helping to bring succour to the survivors from her sister *Gracie Fields* which sank under tow after being machine-gunned and bombed whilst performing similar duties. As a result of these brave exploits, the *'Princess'* gained the 'Dunkirk 1940' military cross.

In 1944, she was converted from a coal-burner to an oil-burner and some structural rebuilding extended her aft saloon to the full width of the ship. Post-War, she was the first steamer to resume excursion service to Bournemouth, where she was accorded a civic welcome. Having spent five years as the stand-by steamer, she was sold in 1958, when new tonnage appeared on the Southampton – Cowes route in the form of the purpose-built passenger and vehicle ro-ro ferry *Carisbrooke Castle*.

The buyers of the now-redundant *'Princess'* were Torbay Steamers, Ltd., who sent her on excursions to the South Devon coast. For legal reasons, they later restyled themselves Coastal Steamers & Marine Services, Ltd.

Initially running from Bournemouth, she was later transferred to Weymouth. By now, her owners had again restyled themselves, this time as Coastal Steamers (Weymouth), Ltd. During this period, her antique appearance won her rôles in two films - Walt Disney's *The Castaways* of 1961 and *Gordon of Khartoum* of 1965. Her next owners planned to convert her into a floating casino in 1966 but, as this plan did not reach fruition, she was sold for scrap.

In 1968, however, she was saved at the eleventh hour when a Mr. H. Butler bought her and had her towed to Northney Yacht Marina on Hayling Island. The plans for her there fell through and, yet again, she was sold, this time to Mr. D. Hickman, who in 1970 took her to London to become a floating restaurant after having her machinery removed at Husband's shipyard, Marchwood. Various further changes of ownership occurred over the next few years until she was moved again, this time to Paris in 1987. In 2000, this fine little ship was transferred to Dunkirk, where she had distinguished herself sixty years previously during her 'Finest Hour', becoming a fitting memorial to the heroism of those tense and dreadful days of evacuation.

# MARILU, former MEDINA

Completed 1931 by John I. Thornycroft & Co., Ltd., Woolston, Southampton. 347 gross tons. Length over-all: 143 ft. 0$^{ins}$ / 43.6m. Beam: 28 ft. 1in / 8.6m. Draught: 8 ft. 7$^{ins}$ / 2.6m. Originally two 4-cylinder oil engines by L. Gardner & Sons, Ltd., Manchester. 456 bhp. (Later, two Crossley oil engines.) Twin screw. Service speed: 11 knots (later 13 knots). Call sign: MPYS.

Launched on the 6$^{th}$ January, 1931, the *Medina* was the first diesel vessel built for The Southampton, Isle of Wight & South of England Royal Mail Steam Packet Company (Red Funnel Steamers). She made her first voyage only five weeks later, in the regular service from the Royal Pier at Southampton to the Pontoon at Cowes.

She was sometimes also used as a tender to the big liners, such as the *Normandie*, when they anchored out in The Solent and she made excursions to local seaside piers. But she was not suited for this kind of work as the pronounced flair of her bows was vulnerable to damage and her excursion work became more of the non-landing type. For this and other reasons, she was not a success and when the company ordered their next ship, the *Gracie Fields* of 1936, they reverted to paddle propulsion. Nevertheless, *Medina* maintained the ferry run to and from the Isle of Wight throughout the Second World War.

In 1952, she was given a thorough refit by Thornycroft's and, because of her indifferent stability, she was re-ballasted. New diesel engines were fitted, which increased her speed. Ten years later, on the introduction of the new purpose-built car ferry *Osborne Castle*, the *Medina* (which could only carry ten cars) was sold to M. H. Bland & Co., Ltd. of Gibraltar, becoming their *Mons Abyla* and continuing her use as a tender to visiting liners and cruise ships. Blands sold her in 1968 and within three years she passed through the hands of four owners: the Port Department of the Government of Gibraltar; W. J. Havens; Esme Lucas of Gibraltar; and then, in December, 1971, R. Mills of London, who intended to use her as a floating discotheque on the north-west Moroccan coast. However, this plan was abandoned before she could even be put to use.

Sold to Marilu Intermediterranean Transport Shipping, S.A. of Panama in May, 1972, she was renamed *Marilu*. For a time, she became part of a yacht marina in London's Old Albert Dock area but, in the October of the following year, she was returned to The Solent area to become a floating office and washing facility for adjacent berth-users at Lymington Yacht Haven. She now reverted to her old name of *Medina*. It was at the end of 1973 that she was slipped at Husband's shipyard, giving Bob the opportunity to take this photograph.

A transfer to Ramsgate in 1976 saw her being used as a restaurant but in the following year she was moved again, this time to Brighton where she became a floating clubhouse in the newly constructed marina. She did not remain there long, being sold for scrap and towed to breakers at nearby Newhaven. However, the old ship survived, turning up at Rotherhithe in London's dockland and then, in July 1984, at Canary Wharf.

After her lack of success in the South, she was taken to the Tyne, where it was planned to use her as a floating Chinese restaurant. Her funnel was removed and a box-like structure was built amidships, over which a metal framework was erected fore and aft. It was at this point that the money ran out — perhaps mercifully — and 'The Wok', as the shipyard workers had come to call her, was placed in drydock. There she was broken up. Thus, the chequered career of Red Funnel's first motor vessel came to an end.

High and dry at Husband's shipyard, Marchwood in 1973, the *Marilu* subsequently staggered through a series of unsuccessful employments.

# BALMORAL

Completed 1949 by John I. Thornycroft & Co., Ltd., Woolston, Southampton. 688 gross tons. Length overall: 203 ft. 8ins / 62.1m. Beam: 32 ft. 0ins / 9.75m. Draught: 6 ft. 7½ins / 2.0m. Two Newbury Sirron 6-cylinder oil engines, built by Thornycroft. 1,200 bhp. Later replaced by Grenaa engines. Twin screw. Service speed: 15 knots. Call sign: MDMZ.

*Balmoral* was launched on the 27thJune, 1949 by Mrs. C. D. Pinnock, wife of the then chairman of The Southampton, Isle of Wight & South of England Royal Mail Steam Packet Company. Designed primarily as a ferry for the company's Southampton to Cowes (Isle of Wight) service, *Balmoral* could also be used for tendering and excursion duties, in which latter rôle she could be seen, often fully loaded, ploughing westwards down The Solent on a summer Saturday morning in whatever weather the English season could throw at her. In a 'roughie', a dark line of passengers would be lining her Weather Deck and it can only be surmised that they were not there to admire the passing verdant coastline of the Isle of Wight.

She experienced a few mishaps during her career, including a collision with Sandown Pier in 1958 that caused her withdrawal from service for a few days. A more serious accident occurred in November, 1961 when, sailing empty out of Cowes to make room for the regular ferry, she was in collision with the Sitmar liner *Fairsky*. *Balmoral* suffered a wrecked starboard lifeboat and a wound that extended from her Main Deck to the waterline. On another occasion, a grounding in fog off Prince's Green, along the Cowes sea-front, damaged both her rudder and her propellers. Her passengers were ferried ashore in small craft.

It was intended (some say as early as 1963) to rebuild the *Balmoral* as a car ferry, complete with cutaway decks aft, an internal turntable and a new funnel, the style of which foreshadowed that of the later design of the improved *Carisbrooke*-class vessels. But this rebuild did not occur and she was withdrawn in 1968,

Dressed overall, the *Balmoral* is seen at the Silver Jubilee Review, Spithead, on the 27th June, 1977.

when the fourth of the new, dedicated car ferries came on the scene. Slipping quietly out of service, *Balmoral* was chartered by the Bristol firm of P. & A. Campbell (Red Funnel's old adversaries), who gave her their white funnel livery and used her for excursions around the Bristol Channel. She appeared only infrequently in the southern area but one of those rare occasions was the Jubilee Review of 1977, as shown on page 107. Campbell's eventually bought her in 1978 but disposed of her in 1980 to the Landmark Trust's White Funnel Steamers, Ltd. They used her on services to the island of Lundy.

Because of the bane of rising costs, she was sold in 1982 to become a floating public house in Dundee. This venture failed and the old ship was closed down and boarded up. Her salvation came in the form of the Paddle Steamer Preservation Society, who acquired her in 1983 for Waverley Excursions, Ltd., as a successor for the lost *Prince Ivanhoe*, ex-*Shanklin* (ibid). *Balmoral* now became a partner for the paddle steamer *Waverley*. Over the winter of 2002-3, she was given a life extension during an ambitious refit at Avonmouth when new Danish-built engines replaced her old Thornycroft units, which had given such brilliant service and which now went to a private museum in Wales. Unfortunately, the conservation attempt failed and, apparently, they went for scrap.

*Balmoral* has continued in service, but not without incident. On 18thOctober, 2004 she hit rocks off the Gower Peninsula while on a cruise from Penarth. Fortunately, none of her passengers or crew were injured but the *Balmoral* suffered propeller damage. Then, in August, 2005, she began taking in water while lying in Swansea Docks. Divers discovered that her hull had been damaged when she had scraped bottom some time earlier and she had to be taken to Sharpness Dock for repairs.

# NORRIS CASTLE

Completed 1968 by John I. Thornycroft & Co., Ltd., Woolston, Southampton. 734 gross tons (922 gross tons after being rebuilt). Length overall: 188 ft. 3ins / 57.3m. Beam: 40 ft. 0ins / 12.2m. Draught: 7 ft. 0ins / 2.1m. Two Crossley 8-cylinder oil engines. 1,800 bhp. Twin screws. Service speed: 16 knots. Call sign: GZBW.

The *Norris Castle* was one of three similar bow-loading ferries delivered to Red Funnel Steamers for their service from Southampton to Cowes. They were based on the earlier design of the *Carisbrooke Castle* and their funnels were fitted with the distinctive Thornycroft smoke-deflecting cowl.

The navigators of the Red Funnel ferries always had their work cut out during the sailing season, especially during Cowes Week. 'Steam giving way to sail' was not practical in the confined waters of Cowes Harbour as amateur sailors in their dinghies and yachts relied sometimes too literally on the old rule of the road and occasionally a collision would occur as a result. The author recalls at least one set of incautious sails disappearing beneath the bows of a ferry, much like the wings of an ambushed dragonfly being devoured by a large black reptile.

In 1976, the *Norris Castle* was rebuilt as a drive-through ferry, thus considerably altering her profile but improving her car-handling abilities. In 1994, with new tonnage appearing on the route, she was sold to Jadrolinija P.O. of Rijeka in Croatia. She still sails for them on coastal routes under the name *Lovrjenac*.

# RED FALCON

Completed 1994 by Ferguson Shipbuilders, Ltd., Port Glasgow. 2,880 gross tons. Length overall: 274 ft. 0ins / 83.5m. Beam: 59 ft. 0ins. / 18.01m. Draught: 9 ft. 0ins. / 2.74m. Two 8-cylinder Stork-Wärtsilä diesels. 3,249 bhp. Service speed: 14 knots.

Built for Red Funnel to replace the 28-year old *Cowes Castle*, the *Red Falcon* made her maiden crossing of The Solent on the company's Southampton to East Cowes car ferry route on the 25th March, 1994. She was one of three sisters of the 'Raptor' class, the others being the *Red Osprey* and *Red Eagle*. She was involved in a collision in March, 1999.

Making sixteen crossings of The Solent per day, the *Red Falcon* also assists the Global Ocean Observing

The drive-through ferry *Red Falcon* in Southampton Water on the 29th March, 1994, during her first week of service.

System, carrying a 'Ferry Box' which measures salinity, temperature, chlorophyll-fluorescence and other data that assist in the production of maps detailing the location and timing of plankton blooms.

In January, 2004, *Red Falcon* was sent to Remontowa shipyard in Gdansk, in Poland. Like her sisters, she was given an additional car deck, raising her height by 9 ft. 1ins / 2.8 metres. In the process, her passenger and bridge areas were 'sliced' and lifted away enabling the extra section to be inserted. In addition, her hull was lengthened by 31 ft. / 9.66 metres. The first of the 'Raptors' to be so rebuilt, the *Red Osprey*, arrived back in Southampton in time to carry sightseers for the spectacular departure of the *Queen Mary 2* on her maiden voyage. A Norwegian vessel, the *Nordhodland*, was chartered to cover the route while the three sisters were absent in rotation. She was aptly renamed *Bergen Castle* (many previous Red Funnel ferries had a *Castle* suffix).

# HYTHE HOTSPUR

Completed 1974 by James & Stone, Brightlingsea, Essex. 119 gross tons. Length overall: 75 ft. 10ins / 23.1m. Beam: 25 ft. 0ins / 7.65m. Draught: 5 ft. 8ins / 1.7m. Two Gardner 6-cylinder diesel engines. Twin azimuth thrusters. Service speed: 8½ knots. Call sign: GUEL.

Built as the *Southsea Queen* for the Portsmouth Harbour Ferry Company running between the Gosport waterfront and Portsmouth Harbour, this small vessel was bought by General Estates in June, 1978 and renamed *Hythe Hotspur* for a ferry service between Southampton Town Quay and the pierhead at Hythe. She also found employment as an occasional pleasure vessel. For instance, in July 1982, suitably flying a P&O houseflag, she joined the celebrations which marked the return of the *Canberra* (ibid) from her heroic duties in the Falklands War.

By 1994, by which time General Estates had sold the ferry service to Derrick Shipping, Ltd., it was antici-

A crowded *Hythe Hotspur* was one of the hundreds of spectator craft which welcomed the *Canberra* back from the Falklands War on the 11th July, 1982.

pated that *Hythe Hotspur* and her running companion *Hotspur IV* would be replaced by a single catamaran and *Hythe Hotspur* was sold. (In fact, Derrick Shipping later went into liquidation and the service was taken over by White Horse Ferries.) The new owners of *Hythe Hotspur* were Blue Funnel Cruises who run a fleet of sightseeing vessels around the port of Southampton and The Solent. They renamed her *Poole Scene*. She retained this name for only a few years before being sold again, this time to the Clyde Marine Motoring Co. of Greenock who put her on the River Clyde as a pleasure craft. Headlines were not far away, however. On the 27th December, 2000, she set sail from Princes Pier bound for the Kyles of Bute in less than perfect weather. She was carrying 41 passengers and a crew of three. Visibility was poor, less than 0.1 miles. Meanwhile, the 2,579 gross ton cargo and container vessel *Nordsee* was inward bound from Southampton to Greenock. As the *Nordsee* emerged from a fog bank, the *Poole Scene* ran into her starboard side. The *Poole Scene's* bow was crushed almost to the forward windows of her saloon and 16 of her passengers and 1 crewman were injured, although only one needed to be retained in hospital. The skipper was later fined £300.

After repairs, the *Poole Scene* was renamed *Cruiser*. She continues to trade quite happily on the beautiful waters of the Clyde – a small boat with a big history.

# PATRICIA

Completed 1967 by A/B Lindholmens Varv, Gothenburg. 8,897 gross tons. Length overall: 463 ft. 6ins. / 141.2m. Beam: 68 ft. 9ins. / 20.96m. Draught: 18 ft. 3ins. / 5.55m. Four 6-cylinder Pielstick-Lindholmens oil engines. 10,081 bhp. Twin screw. Service speed: 18 knots. Call sign SDYA.

This very smart ferry was built for a new Swedish Lloyd service between Southampton and Bilbao in Spain. She gained an excellent reputation as an elegant, almost luxurious 'ferry-liner' and many passengers took the round voyage as a mini-cruise. But by 1978, the old-established Swedish Lloyd company was in financial difficulties and, consequently, the *Patricia* was sold to another Swedish concern, Stena Line, becoming their *Stena Oceanica*. She was sent to Smith's Dock on the Tyne to have her capacity increased and, in particular, to have the height of her vehicle deck raised so that she could cope with lorry traffic. Her superstructure was heightened and extended and as a result, stability-improving sponsons

Swedish Lloyd was one of several Scandinavian companies who entered the ferry trades out of British ports in the 1960s. Here the *Patricia* is seen at Southampton before sailing on their route to Bilbao.

had to be fitted to her hull to compensate for the change in her centre of gravity. Her gross tonnage rose considerably to 14,131. Relocated to Stena's Frederikshavn to Oslo route, she now appeared as the *Stena Saga* in 1979.

In 1988, she was transferred to Lion Ferry, a Stena subsidiary, to work the Kattegat route between Sweden and Denmark as the *Lion Queen*. 1990 saw her crossing the Atlantic, arriving in British Columbia via the Panama Canal. Renamed *Crown Princess Victoria*, she sailed for Stena Line of Canada's B.C. Ferries in a service between Victoria and Seattle. She was not a success and was laid up after a few months, later becoming *Crown Princess*. There followed a rather complicated chapter in her long career, at first as *Pacific Star* under charter to Starlite Cruises of Piraeus, but she was soon sailing between Florida and the Bahamas as *Sun Fiesta*. Then, after a short period in Greece, she returned to Lion Ferry, again as *Lion Queen* on her old route. However, she was later placed on a new itinerary, between Sweden and Poland. Then, displaced by a larger unit, she was offered for sale.

Her career now began a gradual decline to a somewhat sordid level. At first, she was a casino ship for New Century Cruise Lines of Singapore, who named her *Amusement World* and placed her at anchor off the island of Batam. Gamblers were rushed out to her in high-speed ferries. She disappeared briefly, on charter as – of all things, considering her current employment – the pilgrim ship *Putri Bintan*, before returning as *Amusement World*.

In 2001, she was anchored in the Strait of Singapore, again for the use of gamblers but now calling in at Pasir Gudang (Malaysia) each day to disembark and embark clients. Once a week, she also made a call at the Singapore Cruise Centre and it was during one of these visits that police raided her and arrested the concessionaire of the vessel's 'Pinky Pub' on charges of operating an on-board brothel. It was stated in the press that her facilities also included a transvestite bar. Surely, the ship's fortunes could only improve! In 2002, she was employed in a Singapore – Malaysia – Thailand service but by 2004 she was cruising from Penang.

# DRAGON

Completed 1967 by Ateliers et Chantiers de Bretagne, Nantes but completed by Dubigeon-Normandie. 6,141 gross tons. Length overall: 441 ft. 8ins / 134.6m. (415 ft. 1in / 126.5m. between perpendiculars). Beam: 71 ft. 9ins / 21.9m. Draught: 15 ft. 9¾ins / 4.8m. Two V12-cylinder Pielstick oil engines. 9,467 bhp. Two controllable pitch propellers. Service speed: 19 knots. Call sign: GWXV.

The *Dragon* and her sister *Leopard* were two extremely pretty vessels built for Normandy Ferries, a joint venture between French interests and General Steam Navigation, later a part of P&O. *Dragon* had a British crew, while her sister was French-staffed. In 1976, ownership was taken over by P&O Ferries as a counter to the new 'Viking' drive-through ferries belonging to Townsend-Thoresen.

The P&O ships were the last of the ferries to operate from the Southampton terminal in the Princess Alexandra Dock, with the *Dragon* making the final sailing in December, 1984, as shown in this photograph. A decline in trade had led to several other lines pulling out of the port but it was industrial troubles and the introduction of Townsend's 'Super Viking' class that led to Normandy Ferries switching to Portsmouth, a situation that lasted for only a month as the whole operation, including the ships, was then taken over by Townsend-Thoresen.

The cars in the foreground of this photograph are a reminder that Southampton has for many years had a busy trade in cars being exported and imported. To-day, they mostly arrive in huge and extremely ugly, specially-built car carriers.

Townsend-Thoresen gave the *Dragon* a new name, *Ionic Ferry*, and transferred her to the North Channel service between Cairnryan and Larne. In 1992, she was sold to the Greek company Marlines, becoming their *Viscountess M.* and, in 1995, *Charm M.* (*Leopard* had also been purchased by Marlines and had become the *Countess M.*). 1997 saw the former *Dragon* sold to the Georgian Shipping Company of Tbilisi, who renamed her *Meme Abashidze*.

*Dragon* at her Southampton terminal. In the foreground is a consignment of Triumph and Jaguar cars going for export.

After a slight rebuild, she sailed for this concern until 1999, when Access Ferries of the Cayman Islands bought her for Greek service, temporarily truncating her name to *Med* before finally settling on *Mega* in July, 2000.

She ended up as *Millennium Express II*, registered for Singlewell Shipping.Ltd. of Limassol in Cyprus. It was as such that, whilst sailing empty to re-position on a new Adriatic route in 2002, she suffered a serious engine room fire that spread to engulf her amidships structure. After a lay-up in Eleusis Bay, she was sent to the breakers at Aliaga in Turkey. Although she was rust-streaked and fire-damaged, her fine lines were still recognisable after so many years.

*Eagle* during her short stint on the Southampton to Lisbon and Tangiers route; the year is 1974.

# EAGLE

Completed 1971 by Dubigeon-Normandie S.A., Nantes. 11,609 gross tons. Overall length: 466 ft. 3$^{ins}$. / 142.1m. Beam: 74 ft. 3$^{ins}$ / 22.6m. Draught: 18 ft. 1¼$^{ins}$ / 5.5m. Two V12-cylinder SEMT-Pielstick-Atlantique oil engines. 21,800 bhp. Two controllable pitch propellers. Service speed: 23 knots. Call sign: GOXE.

Built for the newly-formed Southern Ferries, a division of the General Steam Navigation Co., Ltd. (who were later taken over by P&O), this typical product of the Dubigeon-Normandie yard was placed in service from Southampton to Lisbon and Tangier. She hit the headlines in February, 1974 when she was caught in a violent storm and an 8-ton earth-moving machine broke loose and charged about her vehicle deck. *Eagle* lasted on this route for only four years before being sold in 1975 to

the Nouvelle Compagnie de Paquebots of Marseilles, an offshoot of the venerable Paquet Line. They renamed her *Azur* and used her for Mediterranean ferry operations between Toulon and Capri and for cruising. In 1981, she became a full-time cruise ship, for which purpose she was extensively rebuilt with cabins now filling her former car decks. From 1985, Caribbean cruises were included in her itinerary.

Chandris Cruises became her next owners, in 1987, and the ship now had a prefix added to her name, which was expanded to *The Azur*. Five years later, she was sold to Festival Cruises for operation by First European Cruises – sometimes, confusingly, without the definite article prefix. Based in Venice, *(The) Azur* was reportedly the largest ship able to pass through the Corinth Canal.

She sailed into trouble in February, 2004 when she was arrested at Gibraltar at the request of the banks who held mortgages on her. Festival Cruises were beset by financial problems, which eventually overwhelmed them, and obtained approval from a Gibraltar court for their smallest vessels, *The Azur*, *Bolero* and *Flamenco*, to be sold at public auction. Later in 2004, *The Azur* became the Israeli *Eloise* and then *Royal Iris*.

# MONTE TOLEDO

Completed 1974 by Union Naval de Levante, Valencia. 10,851 gross tons. Length overall: 497 ft. 0ins / 151.5m. Beam: 65 ft. 11ins / 20.7m. Draught: 22 ft. 4ins / 6.8m. Two MAN-Bazan 16-cylinder oil engines. 17,800 bhp. Two controllable pitch propellers. Service speed: 21 knots. Call sign: EBTI.

The construction of this large 'cruise-ferry' and her sister *Monte Granada* for the Aznar Line (Naviera Aznar SA of Bilbao in Spain) was a break from company tradition. Previously, the firm had mainly operated cargo-passenger ships between Spain and South America and from the Canary Islands to Liverpool and to London. The main cargo on the Canary Islands routes had been tomatoes and other fruit but, like the rival Fred. Olsen Line, Aznar had also built up a considerable following of British passengers, most of whom took the round voyage as a cruise.

The first of the new vessels was the *Monte Toledo*, which started a new car ferry service between Southampton and Santander in northern Spain. (The *Monte Granada* maintained the popular Liverpool – Canaries sailings in the winter months and switched to an Amsterdam – Southampton – Santander route in the Summer.) But the sisters did not stay long with the Aznar Line, which had run into financial problems as a result of speculation in the tanker and ro-ro markets, and was forced to sell them.

The buyers, in 1977, were the General National Maritime Transport Company of Benghazi in Libya. They renamed the ships *Toletela* and *Garnata* and placed them in service mainly between Libya and Malta. By 2002, both ships were laid up, one in Italy and the other in Libya. However, the publisher of this book saw *Garnata* undergoing repairs in a shipyard in Rijeka, Croatia in August, 2004. She later returned to Tripoli but was then disabled by an engine-room fire. *Toletela* was reported to have been sold to Indian shipbreakers in March, 2005.

The *Stena Normandy* undergoing berthing trials at Empress Dock, Southampton on the 20th January, 1991.

# STENA NORMANDY

Completed 1982, Götaverken Arendal A/B, Gothenburg. 17,043 gross tons. Length overall: 489 ft. 0ins / 149.03m. Beam: 91 ft. 11ins / 28.0m. Draught: 20 ft. 1in / 6.13m. Four V-12-cylinder Nohab-Wärtsilä Vasa oil engines. 20,600 bhp. Two controllable pitch propellers. Service speed: 19 knots. Call sign: C6HU5.

Originally to have been named *Drottning Silvia* (*Queen Silvia*), this ship was eventually called *Prinsessan Birgitta*. She sailed for the Stena-Sessan Line on their Gothenburg to Frederikshavn route but, after modifications in 1983 (which increased her tonnage) she was chartered to Sealink as their *St. Nicholas* for the Harwich – Hook of Holland service. Although Sealink purchased her in 1988, they sold her to Rederi A/B Gotland the following year, and then chartered her back.

The constant changes in the ferry industry in the early 1990s saw ownership pass back to the Stena group of Gothenburg. As the *Stena Normandy*, she inaugurated a new Sealink service between Southampton and Cherbourg in 1991. Then considered a large ferry for Southampton, she often made a splendid sight at night as, brilliantly lit, she would arrive in The Solent en route for the Hampshire port. The service was closed in December, 1996 and she was returned to her Swedish owners, who dropped the *Stena* prefix before chartering her to Estonian operators. In 1998, she was chartered by Irish Ferries, Ltd. and, in 1999, was bought by that company's parent, Irish Continental Line, for the services from Rosslare to Cherbourg and to another French port, Roscoff.

# SES WIGHT KING

Completed 1989 by Brødrene AA Båtbyggeri A/S, Hyen, Norway. 395 gross tons (32 tonnes deadweight). Length overall: 115 ft. 8ins / 35.25m. Beam: 37 ft. 9ins / 11.5m. Draught: 6 ft. 10ins / 2.1m. (off cushion), 2 ft. 4ins / 0.7m (on cushion). Two MWM V16-cylinder oil engines. 4,350 bhp. Two propellers and two KaMeWa waterjet units. Service speed: 46 knots. Call sign: LAQC2.

A CIRR 120-P class Surface Effect Ship, this catamaran hovercraft was designed by Cirrus International of Bergen and was launched as the *Sant'Agata* with a passenger capacity of 280 (at other times variously stated as 300 and 330). Initially, she was chartered for the new Cowes Express service between Southampton and Thetis Wharf, East Cowes. Operations were discontinued in June, 1990 after the craft developed mechanical troubles but were resumed thirteen months later when *Sant'Agata* was renamed, rather more appropriately, *Wight King*. When the Cowes Express service became unviable, *Wight King* was refitted at Poole and became Fred. Olsen's *Bahia Express*. Later again, she became the *Shahrazad Express* of another Norwegian concern, Fekete & Co.

*Ses Wight King* at her Town Quay berth at Southampton on the 31st August, 1991 with the former Red Funnel tug/tender *Calshot* in the background, awaiting restoration.

# From Portsmouth

## BRADING

A moody picture of the
*Brading* off Spithead
during the Silver Jubilee
Fleet review on
the 27th June, 1977.

Completed 1948 by Wm. Denny & Bros., Ltd., Dumbarton. 837 gross tons. Length overall: 200 ft. 0ins / 61.0m. Beam: 46 ft. 1in / 14.0m. Draught: 7 ft. 0ins / 2.1m. Two 8-cylinder Denny-Sulzer oil engines. 1,900 bhp. Twin screw. Service speed: 15 knots. Call sign: MPZR.

This small ferry was one of a pair built to the order of the Southern Railway. However, by the time the sisters were delivered in 1948, the Southern Railway had been nationalised to become part of British Rail. The two ships were intended to replace war losses in the paddler fleet. A third, and slightly modified, near-sister, the *Shanklin* (below), joined them in the Portsmouth Harbour to Ryde Pier Head service in 1951. Built as two-class vessels (First and Third), the *Brading* and her sister *Southsea* were converted into single-class ships when the *Shanklin* was introduced, thus doing away with the near-duplication of services on board, with all the associated costs.

Mechanical problems and her inability to carry cars and other vehicles caused the withdrawal of the *Brading* in 1985. Although not a paddler, she was nearly bought by the Paddle Steamer Preservation Society but, cannibalised for various fittings, she went to John Pound's scrapyard at Hilsea Creek in Portsmouth. Demolition had started on the gridiron when, in the autumn of 1994, she caught fire. Because the smoke did not drift onto the nearby M27 road, the hapless vessel was left to burn herself out.

*Shanklin* was one of the many Denny-built ships which sailed out of South Coast ports. Here she is departing Portsmouth in 1977 with the Round Tower receding astern.

# SHANKLIN

Completed 1951 by Wm. Denny & Bros., Ltd., Dumbarton.   833 gross tons.  Length overall: 200 ft. 3$^{ins}$ / 61.0m.  Beam: 47 ft. 8$^{ins}$  14.5m.  Draught: 7 ft. 0$^{ins}$ /2.1m.  Two 8-cylinder Denny-Sulzer oil engines. 1,900 bhp.  Twin screw.  Service speed: 14 knots.  Call sign: GNJZ.

The broad-beamed *Shanklin* was the third of the three sisters built for the Portsmouth Harbour Station to Ryde Pier Head (Isle of Wight) service.  She differed from the other two in certain respects, notably her engine arrangement.  She also had a taller funnel and, unlike her sisters, she was a one-class vessel.   The other two ships were subsequently converted to carry a single class also.  However, *Shanklin* proved to be the least reliable of the trio and was apparently less popular with her crew.

Her machinery let her down on occasion and she was relegated to being the stand-by vessel.  She was revitalised in 1979 but was again laid-up the following year because of her continuing engine problems.  Although screw-driven, she was soon sold to the Paddle Steamer Preservation Society who were, in principle, reluctant to see yet another fine little coastal passenger ship disappear into oblivion.

She returned north to her native Clyde and, renamed *Prince Ivanhoe*, ran excursions with the Society's paddle steamer *Waverley* (ibid).  *Prince Ivanhoe* was just establishing herself as a popular vessel, not only on the Clyde but in the Bristol Channel, when in August, 1981 she struck an uncharted underwater object off Port Eynon on the Gower Peninsula and was holed and beached.  Her funnel is still visible at high tide.  The only casualty resulting from this accident was a member of the Society who unfortunately collapsed and died.

# ST. CECILIA

Completed 1987 by Cochrane & Sons Shipyard, Selby, Yorkshire.  2,968 gross tons.  Length overall: 262 ft. 6$^{ins}$ / 80m.  Beam: 55ft. 3$^{ins}$ / 16.8m.  Draught: 8 ft. 0$^{ins}$ / 2.4m.  Three 6-cylinder MAN-B&W oil engines. 3,267 bhp.  Service speed: 13 knots.  Call sign: GIFU.

*St. Cecilia* on her way to the King George V Dry Dock, Southampton for a 'wash and brush-up', 24th January, 1989.

*Viking Victory* departing Portsmouth harbour in June, 1977. Some of the handsome Georgian buildings of the Royal Naval Hospital at Haslar can be seen in the distance.

*St. Cecilia* was built for the Isle of Wight service of Sealink, then a Sea Containers subsidiary. She is a multi-purpose passenger/vehicle ferry and operates between Fishbourne on the Island and Portsmouth Harbour, along with her sisters in the 'Saint' class – *St. Catherine*, *St. Helen* and *St. Faith*. In 1990, after Sealink's acquisition by Stena AB of Sweden, the route and the ships were purchased by Wightlink (until then previously known as Passro (Shipping) Co., Ltd. – a dormant company in the Sea Containers group) and the ferries were consequently repainted in their new owners' livery.

# VIKING VICTORY

Completed 1964 by Kaldnes Mekaniske Verksted A/S, Tonsberg, Norway. 3,608 gross tons. Length overall: 326 ft. 6$^{ins}$ / 99.5m. Beam: 59 ft. 9$^{ins}$ / 18.2m. Draught: 14 ft. 6$^{ins}$ / 4.43m. Two 12-cylinder Pielstick-Lindholmens oil engines. 10,200 bhp. Twin screw. Service speed: 20 knots. Call sign: JXYO.

Built as *Car Ferry Viking* but soon renamed *Viking I*, this pioneering ship was a member of the Norwegian-owned Thoresen Car Ferries' 'Viking' class. She was intended for her owners' new service between Southampton and either Le Havre or Cherbourg. Revolutionary in being a drive-through ferry (rather than solely a side, stern or bow loader), she made the competition obsolete overnight. However, she never

seemed to go for more than a couple of years without being chartered to other companies that, perhaps, wished to experiment with this new type of car ferry. In 1965, she went to the Atlantic Steam Navigation Company to work on the Tilbury to Antwerp route. Later that same year, she returned to them to run in their Felixstowe to Rotterdam and Belfast to Larne services.

In 1968, Thoresen merged with Townsend (with their 'Free Enterprise' class ships) but *Viking I* retained her name and carried on with her charter work. After a 1969 charter to O/Y Siljarederiet A/B of Finland, she transferred to her owners' Dover to Zeebrugge service before moving back to her old Southampton base. For a short while in 1973, she plied the Trelleborg to Travemünde trade for T-T Lines and 1975 found her sailing between Harwich and Hamburg for Lion Ferry A/B, who operated the route under the trade name Prinzen Line.

Townsend Thoresen decided to move their Southampton-based operations to Portsmouth – an hour's less sailing time and fuel – and so, in 1976, *Viking I* was renamed *Viking Victory* in honour of the maritime jewel of her new homeport. As such, she made a striking debut in Portsmouth harbour on a dull, grey day to trial the use of Flathouse Quay as a potential cross-Channel ferry terminal. (The port up to that time had mainly been used as a major naval port and for small cargo vessels bringing in such materials as timber.) As she passed the Round Tower at the port's mouth, her red hull and green funnels represented an alien splash of colour – almost a heresy in a port generally used to shades of grey.

Although her main occupation was sailing between Portsmouth and either Le Havre or Cherbourg, this plucky little ship's wanderings were not yet over. Charters to Sealink on various routes and transfers within her own company continued in quick succession.

With the introduction of larger ships, the *Viking Victory* was sold in 1983 to Happiness Maritime Co. of Piraeus and renamed *Sun Boat*. Further disposals, often to short-lived companies, came at rapid intervals – Red Sea Line called her *Caravan* in 1985; she was *Vasmed* for Bluebird Shipping of Cyprus in 1986; and that same year she became *Sunny Boat* of Sharo Shipping, back in mainland Greece. Four years later, and still based in Greece, she sailed under the name *European Glory* on charter to European Seaways and then as *Neptunia* for an associate of Hellenic Mediterranean Lines. That historic company eventually purchased her and called her *Media II* in 1992.

Ten years later, in 2002, she was bought by Mediterranean Freedom Marine of Cyprus for their fledgling Palmier Line's service between Viora in Albania and Brindisi on the Adriatic coast of the heel of Italy. Her name was slightly modified to *Media V*. Although she is tiny in comparison with most modern ferries, this hard-working little ship is still sailing but she is reportedly looking very tired and ready, it seems, for retirement.

# PRIDE OF WINCHESTER

Completed 1975 by Aalborg Vaerft A/S. Aalborg. 6,387 gross tons. Length overall: 422 ft. 7$^{ins}$ / 128.8m. Beam: 66 ft. 3$^{ins}$ / 20.2m. Draught: 14 ft. 9$^{ins}$ / 4.5m. Three Stork-Werkspoor oil engines (one 9-cylinder and two 8-cylinder). 13,800 bhp. Three propellers. Service speed: 19 knots. Call sign: GVES.

The *Pride* class, as it developed through successive versions, produced, in the author's opinion, some of the most unfortunate 'designed-by-committee' vessels to be seen on the routes between Britain and the Continent – a far cry from the grace and elegance of the ferries of only a few years previously, but undoubtedly very efficient. *Pride of Winchester* had been launched as the *Viking Viscount* for Townsend-Thoresen's Felixstowe - Zeebrugge service. 1983 saw Townsend-Thoresen being acquired by the newly-formed P&O European Ferries and in 1985 *Viking Viscount* was moved to Portsmouth and placed on the routes to Le Havre and Cherbourg.

In 1989, she was renamed *Pride of Winchester* and, as such, would make the news at least once when, towards the end of her career with P&O, a davit broke during lifeboat practice with a resultant fatality. Replaced by a larger ship in 1994, she was sold to Lane Sea Lines of Greece, becoming their *Vitsentzos Kornaros* and running on the Piraeus – Crete and Piraeus – Rhodes routes.

# PRIDE OF LE HAVRE

Completed 1975 by Aalborg Vaerft A/S, Aalborg, Denmark. 6,386 gross tons as built, 14,760 gross tons after rebuild. Length overall: 422 ft. 6ins / 122.8m. Beam: 66 ft. 3ins / 20.2m. Draught: 14 ft. 10ins / 4.6m. (see text for dimensions after rebuilding) One 9-cylinder and two 8-cylinder Stork-Werkspoor oil engines. 13,450 bhp. Centre propeller and two wings. Service speed: 19 knots.

Designed to carry 1,200 passengers and 320 cars and built for Thoresen Car Ferries, soon to become Townsend Thoresen Ferries, the *Viking Valiant* at first sailed briefly between Felixstowe and Zeebrugge before transferring to the South Coast route between Southampton and Le Havre in 1976. During the Silver Jubilee celebrations in 1977, she took visitors round the assembled fleet of warships.

In 1986, before her U.K. departure port was due to be changed to Portsmouth, the *Viking Valiant* was sent to the Schichau-Unterweser yard in Bremerhaven in West Germany. There, extensive alterations were made, including a heightening of her superstructure by the addition of an extra vehicle deck and the fitting of a new bow. Her length and beam increased to 143.7m. and 23.4m. respectively and her tonnage rose to 14,760 gross tons. The result can only be described as one of the worst-looking ships ever to ply between the U.K. and the Continent.

P&O acquired the European Ferries group in 1987 – soon becoming embroiled in the *Herald of Free Enterprise* disaster inquiry – and the line became known as P&O European Ferries (Portsmouth). A renaming of the ship occurred in 1989 when she became *Pride* (a misnomer if ever there was one!) *of Le Havre*. In 1994, her continental destination was changed to Cherbourg and, accordingly, her name became *Pride of Cherbourg*. She kept this name until 2002, when a new *Pride of Cherbourg* appeared on the scene. The former *Viking Valiant* now became *Pride of Cherbourg A*.

*Pride of Winchester* (left) in Portsmouth harbour on the 29th June, 1993 and *Pride of Le Havre* (right) also in Portsmouth harbour on the 13th July, 1993.

However, within a year, with Brittany Ferries proving to be fierce competitors, she was sold out of the fleet, going to Egyptian owners. She now became *Pride of Al Salam I* of El Salam Maritime Transport and was placed on the Panamanian register. A charter followed in 2003 to the Moroccan state shipping company Comanav (Compagnie Marocaine de Navigation) for their service between Nador and Almeria. This was renewed in 2004 and the ship was renamed *Nador*. In May, 2005 a further change of name saw her become *Mogador*.

# NORMANDIE

Completed 1992 by Kvaerner Masa Yards, Inc., Turku, Finland. 27,541 gross tons. Length overall: 529 ft. 6$^{ins}$ / 161.4 m. over bulbous bow. Beam: 87 ft. 3$^{ins}$ / 26.6m. Draught: 18 ft. 6$^{ins}$ / 5.65m. Four Wärtsilä V12-cylinder oil engines. 24,150 bhp. Twin controllable-pitch propellers. Service speed: 21 knots. Call sign: FNNO.

On her appearance in the Brittany Ferries (Bretagne-Angleterre-Irelande S.A.) fleet, the *Normandie* was the largest vessel so far to use the Portsmouth ferry berths. She could carry up to 2,160 passengers, a figure which only a few years earlier would have been almost inconceivable and was a measure of the extent to which ferry traffic had grown. She made a considerable impression with her handsome lines – and because she brought her evocative and honourable name back to these southern waters. After a brief 'shake-down cruise', she entered service on the Portsmouth to Caen route on the 18$^{th}$May, 1992.

Perhaps her most notable voyage occurred on the 5$^{th}$ June, 2004 when, fittingly, she was one of the leading ships in the flotilla which crossed the Channel as part of the 60$^{th}$ Anniversary celebrations of the Normandy landings. Her passengers were veterans of that momentous event.

*Normandie* and *Pride of Cherbourg* outward bound from Portsmouth on the 13$^{th}$ July, 1994. Also in the picture, the Gosport – Portsmouth ferry.

# PRIDE OF BILBAO

Completed 1983 by O/Y Wärtsilä A/B, Turku, Finland.  37,583 gross tons.  Length overall: 580 ft. 0ins / 176.8m.  Beam: 93 ft. 2ins / 28.4m.  Draught: 22 ft. 0ins / 6.72m.  Four 12-cylinder Wärtsila-SEMT-Pielstick oil engines.  31,280 bhp.  Twin screw.  Service speed: 26 knots.  Call sign: SLOV.

Launched as the *Olympia* for Rederi A/B Slite, one of the partners in the Viking Line consortium, this large ferry entered service on the Stockholm – Helsinki route.  She was a notable member of a new generation of Baltic ferries which became famous not only for their size and speed but for the facilities which they offered their passengers.  In 1993, she was chartered to P&O European Ferries, who renamed her *Pride of Bilbao*, aptly since that May she started running on the Portsmouth – Bilbao route.  During the peak season, she also made weekend sailings between Portsmouth and Cherbourg.

Later in 1993, Rederi Slite went into bankruptcy and the ship was offered for sale.  Surprisingly, although she was still under long-term charter to P&O, she was bought by the Irish Continental group.  Briefly, she was registered at Nassau in the Bahamas but later she was re-registered in the U.K.  Tax concessions by the British government, intended to strengthen the Red Ensign, encouraged P&O to re-flag many of its ships.

The *Pride of Bilbao*'s amenities and appointments are highly regarded and she is now the sole P&O ferry operating out of Portsmouth.  Not only is she a successful ferry but her round voyages have proved popular as five-star 'mini-cruises' of three days' duration.  She also acts as an aid to scientific research: in 2002, she was fitted with data-collecting equipment (as part of a Global Ocean Observing System called 'FerryBox') that records information from the surrounding ocean, such as temperature and salinity.  These data are then analysed by the Bay of Biscay Dolphin Research Programme.   They are used in the study of the whale and dolphin populations of the Bay of Biscay and the English Channel and also enable a better assessment to be made of how the sea affects carbon dioxide levels in the atmosphere.  P&O have been keen supporters of this project since 1995 and even run 'Whale Watch' cruises.  Some 15,000 individual whales and dolphins have been recorded over the past five years.

*Pride of Bilbao* leaving Portsmouth on the 29th June, 1993.  The inward-bound Portsmouth to Ryde ferry *Our Lady Patricia* can also be seen. In the distance is one of the three forts at Spithead that constituted part of the naval base's seaward defences, known as 'Palmerston's Follies'.

# Tugs, Tenders, Lifeboats and a Sludge Boat

## GEORGE V

Completed 1915 by J. P. Rennoldson & Sons, South Shields. 224 gross tons. Overall length: 106 ft. 1ins / 32.3m. Beam: 24 ft. 5ins / 7.4m. Draught: 12 ft. 4ins / 3.8m. Originally, one 3-cylinder steam reciprocating engine. 850 ihp. Later, one 12-cylinder oil engine. 1,086 bhp. Single screw. Call sign: MFVW.

Immediately on completion, *George V* was chartered by her owners, Robert Redhead, to the Royal Navy for six months and soon afterwards she was chartered to them again for two more years. Returned to Redhead's in 1919, she worked for them until 1929, when she was transferred to Redhead & Dry's Tugs, Ltd.

France, Fenwick Tyne & Wear Company, Ltd. took her over in May, 1944 and, ten years later, she was re-engined by P. K. Harris & Sons of Appledore. Now diesel-powered, she became the most powerful tug on the Tyne. In the process, however, her classic steam tug profile had been compromised by the substitution of a squat funnel typical of a motor vessel.

Tyne Tugs took her on charter in 1959 and that, same year, *George V* assisted in towing three British Petroleum (BP) tankers from lay-up on the River Fal to the Tyne, where they were to be refitted. 1958 had also been an eventful year for her as, along with another British and two Dutch tugs, she had salvaged the Swiss cargo ship *Nyon*, which had grounded off St. Abbs Head and broken in half.

In 1977, the old tug was again transferred, this time to Lawson-Batey Tugs, Ltd. of Newcastle, and then, a year later (at the grand old age of 63!), she was sold to Coastal Marine Services of Plymouth. On the 25th January, 1980, she signalled that she had been in collision, possibly with the West Shambles Buoy in the eastern approaches to Weymouth Bay, and had damaged her propeller. She had been en route to Weymouth to pick up a tow but, because of the damage she had sustained, she was laid up in Weymouth harbour, as seen in this photograph.

She departed on the 19th March, 1980, it was assumed for the breakers. But, in 1981, the old craft was sold to the Bankside Shipping & Towage Co., Ltd. of Queenborough for further service. She then passed to N.E. Murray, also of Queenborough, before Estuary Tugs of Sark bought her early in 1984. Just over two years later, she was sold to Lavington International of Gibraltar. However, she eventually returned to Queenborough and was seen there as recently as August, 2003. De-engined, derelict and 88 years old, she was apparently being offered for sale for £1!

The venerable *George V*, damaged and awaiting sale, lies at Weymouth on the 26th February, 1980.

# GALWAY BAY

Completed 1930 as the *Calshot* by John I. Thornycroft & Co., Ltd., Woolston, Southampton.  684 gross tons. Length overall: 157 ft. 0ins / 47.9m.  Beam: 33 ft. 1in / 10.1m.  Draught: 12 ft. 0ins / 3.7m.  Originally triple expansion steam engines developing 1,500 ihp, but by now two 8-cylinder diesel engines.  800 bhp.  Twin screw.  Call sign: GSJX.

Launched as the *Calshot* for Red Funnel, this tug/tender went down the 'ways and into the River Itchen on the 4th November, 1929.  She was the largest such vessel to be built for the Southampton company and attended the World's biggest liners either within the Port's boundaries or when they were at anchor in The Solent.  She could often be seen in the company of giants such as the *Queen Mary, Queen Elizabeth, Bremen, Europa* or the fabled *Normandie* which would lie at the Motherbank anchorage off Ryde – this famous French Line ship never came into Southampton Docks.  Sometimes *Calshot* acted as a relief excursion vessel but was not, apparently, popular with the staff at the various piers that she visited as she had wire hawsers in lieu of rope.

In the Second World War, she followed two of her massive wards to Scotland, disembarking and embarking servicemen and women and civilian personnel by the thousand during the *Queen Mary*'s and *Queen Elizabeth*'s visits to the Tail o' the Bank on the River Clyde.  Returning to Southampton after the end of hostilities, *Calshot* resumed her peacetime duties, carrying the rich, the famous and the ordinary to or from their ships.

In 1964, she was sold to Port and Liner Services (Ireland), Ltd., a subsidiary of the Holland America Line, and was sent to Galway for tendering purposes and for excursion work.  At the time, Holland America passenger ships were frequent callers at the port and *Calshot* was aptly re-named *Galway Bay*.  Re-engined with diesels and with her funnel subsequently shortened by 15 feet, she was sold in 1971 to Galway Ferries for operation between Galway and the Aran Islands.  A proposed sale to a German company fell through in 1984 and she continued to work in Irish waters.

Eventually, Southampton City Council acquired her for preservation and display.  A team from the city's museums, led by Nigel Overton of Southampton Maritime Museum, brought her back to her home port.  In the years following her return, the *Calshot* (as she is again called) has been shunted from berth to berth and currently lies alongside Berth 42 at the entrance to the Ocean Dock (formerly the White Star Dock).  A funnel extension replacement (donated by Vosper Thornycroft (UK), Ltd.) which would bring her funnel back to its original height, still lies on the quayside in readiness for fitting.

The old ship is now under the auspices of Tug Tender *Calshot* Trust but is in dire need of repair, with leaking decks urgently requiring attention.  The original intention was to complete restoration in time for her 75th Anniversary but, with only limited resources available, that has not been possible.  A hoped-for Lottery grant seems to be the only hope of survival for this important and distinguished little ship.  In complete contrast, the ex-White Star tender *Nomadic* has had a speedy rescue financed by Belfast City Council.

# ROMSEY

Completed 1964 by Richard Dunston (Hessle), Ltd., Hessle.  173 gross tons. Length overall: 103 ft.0ins / 31.4m. Beam: 27 ft. 0ins / 8.2m.  Draught: 12 ft. 6ins / 3.8m.  One 8-cylinder Crossley oil engine.  Call sign: GDXZ.

Built for the Alexandra Towing Co., Ltd., the *Romsey* (locally pronounced 'Rumsey') is shown here against a typical Bob Bruce Grice sunlit backdrop.  The *Romsey*, along with two sisters, represented a break in tradition for the tug company as the orders were placed with the Hessle yard of Richard Dunston.  The new vessels would incorporate all the modern equipment that had become essential to craft of their type – radar, echosounder and VHF radio. *Romsey* also carried a large supply of detergent should she ever be called upon for use in oil dispersal work. Accommodation for officers and crew was to a very high standard.

The tug was launched on the 14th April, 1964 and, after various trials including a static bollard pull in which she achieved a pull of 18 tons, she was delivered to her owners' Southampton fleet that July. During her career, she assisted with the berthing and sailing of many ocean giants along with lesser craft of all types. Most unusual was the nuclear-driven *U.S.S. Savannah*, which she assisted during this space-age vessel's call into Southampton. In 1990, the *Romsey* was sold to become the *Caribe II* of Oil Transport Co. S.A. in the Dominican Republic.

The very modern *Romsey* in action off Dockhead, Southampton, on the 16thAugust, 1968.

*Galway Bay*, soon to regain her original name of *Calshot*, lies in dry dock at Southampton on the 19th May, 1988.

# BROCKLEBANK

Completed 1965 by W. J. Yarwood & Sons, Ltd., Northwich, Cheshire.  172 gross tons.  Length overall: 102 ft. 11$^{ins}$ / 31.4m.  Beam: 25 ft. 6$^{ins}$ / 7.8m.  Draught: 12 ft. 6$^{ins}$ / 3.81m.  One 8-cylinder Crossley oil engine. Single screw.  Service speed: 12 knots.  Call sign: GQGE.

This fine little tug was built for the Alexandra Towing Co., Ltd. and was mainly based in Liverpool.  She not only performed towage duties but also served as a pollution control vessel and sometimes voyaged to Barrow-in-Furness to assist at the launching of ships built there.  Since 1988, she has belonged to the Merseyside Maritime Museum, where she is a floating exhibit in the Albert Dock.  Maintained by a group of enthusiastic volunteers, she is a worthy representative of the important fleets of tugs that have served that port over many decades.  However, *Brocklebank* also travels to other ports for various festivals, such as the D-Day Commemorations in Southampton.

(Facing page.) *Romsey* with her fleetmate *Victoria* and with *Völkerfreundschaft* in the background.

*Brocklebank* seen during the early morning in Ocean Dock, Southampton on the 4$^{th}$ June, 1994, the day of the D-Day celebrations.  Also in the picture are *Queen Elizabeth 2* , USS *Guam*, *Jeremiah O'Brien*, *State of Maine* and the US Army tug *Champagne Mame*.

*Calshot (II)* photographed at Netley as she closed in on the *Norway* which was proceeding up Southampton Water towards her berth, 7th May, 1980.

# CALSHOT (II)

Completed 1964 by John I. Thornycroft & Co., Ltd., Woolston, Southampton. 494 gross tons. Length overall: 139 ft. 0ins / 42.4m. Beam: 35 ft. 1in / 10.7m. Draught: 14 ft. 6ins / 4.4m. Two 8-cylinder Crossley oil engines. 1,800 bhp. Twin screw. Call sign: GMYA.

A dual purpose tug/tender capable of carrying 200 persons, this second Red Funnel *Calshot* was built to replace her famous namesake. (Her sister, *Gatcombe*, was in turn built to succeed the *Paladin* which had attended both Cunard *Queens* at their launchings and had later become a film star in the Peter Sellers movie *The Mouse That Roared*.) However, with the number of liners coming into The Solent falling inexorably, demand for the services of tenders diminished and *Calshot* was increasingly used in her towing rôle. During the Silver Jubilee Review in 1977, however, she did serve as a tender for the B.P. Tanker Company's *British Respect* (ibid) at her anchorage in The Solent.

She was also used as an oil-dispersal vessel, attending wherever an oil slick occurred around the coast and carrying supplies of dispersant for other vessels. She was involved in the aftermath of many major oil spills from Norfolk to Milford Haven, assisting in cleaning up after the *Pacific Glory* and *Eleni V* incidents, among others. She was also recruited for oil dispersing exercises as far north as Scotland and was chartered for a few weeks to an oil company operating in the North Sea, acting as a support and supply vessel and, in the process, calling at Norwegian and Dutch ports.

*Calshot* was sold in 1989 to Dublin Bay Cruises, becoming the *Tara II*, and then, in 1992, to Remolques del Mediterraneo S.A., who renamed her *Boluda Abrego*. She currently operates as a supply/tender out of Burriana, about 50 km. to the north of Valencia.

# CLAUSENTUM

Completed 1980 by Richards (Shipbuilders), Ltd., Lowestoft. 334 gross tons. Length overall: 109 ft. 0¼ ins / 33.2m. Beam: 33 ft. 9ins / 10.3m. Draught: 13 ft. 8ins / 4.2m. Two 6-cylinder Paxman Ruston oil engines. 2,820 bhp. Twin controllable pitch propellers. Service speed: 12½ knots. Call sign: GBDU.

Another photograph taken on the 7th May, 1980 when the *Norway* arrived in Southampton Water. The Red Funnel tug *Clausentum* is running alongside her.

The *Clausentum* was one of Red Funnel's (then new) twin-funneled tugs. She was fitted with Kort nozzles in which controllable-pitch propellers turned. She also had a pair of water/foam high-pressure nozzles for fire-fighting, in addition to oil-dispersing capacity. She remained with Red Funnel until 1993 when she was acquired by the Londonderry Port & Harbour Commissioners, for whom she served as the tug and fire-fighting vessel *Strathfoyle*. While mainly employed in Londonderry, she also went out for charter work in South Wales, on the Clyde and in Norway. In 2002, she became the *Westsund* after being purchased by Svendborg Bugsier A/S of Denmark.

# PHAROS

Completed 1955 by the Caledon Shipbuilding & Engineering Co., Ltd., Dundee. 1,712 gross tons. Length overall: 258 ft. 10$^{ins}$ / 78.9m. Beam: 40 ft. 5$^{ins}$ / 12.3m. Draught: 12 ft. 7¼$^{ins}$ / 3.8m. Two 7-cylinder British Polar oil engines. 2,620 bhp. Twin screw. Service speed: 14 knots. Call sign: MWBK.

The suitably named *Pharos*, a Scottish lighthouse tender, came south for for the Silver Jubilee Fleet Review of June, 1977.

Built for the Commissioners of Northern Lighthouses (the Scottish equivalent of Trinity House) as a tender to supply lighthouses and maintain buoys round the Scottish coasts, this sturdy vessel was also sometimes used for the Commissioners' management committee meetings at Oban. Princess Anne, the Princess Royal, the Board's Patron, attended on occasion. *Pharos* was a very smart ship, with her wheelhouse painted in an imitation of wood. In later years a helipad was fitted to her after deck. She has gone on to lead a second career with Windjammer Barefoot Cruises, who have a fleet of sailing vessels taking adventurous passengers round the Caribbean. Renamed *Amazing Grace*, she acts as a supply vessel for her fleetmates but also carries cruise passengers herself.

# ILT GRANUAILE

Completed 1970 by Ferguson Brothers, Ltd., Port Glasgow. 2,003 gross tons. Length overall: 264 ft. 8$^{ins}$ / 80.68m. Beam: 42 ft. 6$^{ins}$ / 12.96m. Draught: 13 ft. 2$^{ins}$ / 4.0m. Two 8-cylinder oil engines. 3,200 bhp. Twin controllable pitch propellers. Service speed: 13.5 knots. Call sign: EICQ.

This buoy and lighthouse tender, built for the Commissioners of Irish Lights, was named after a remarkable 16th century Irishwoman, Grace O'Malley, who became the female counterpart of Drake, apparently comparing favourably in both stamina and bravery. In fact, she became known as 'The Queen of the Pirates'.

The ship that bore her name was built with passive roll stabilising tanks, controllable pitch propellers and twin rudders that, combined with the fitting of bow thrusters and buoy-handling cranes a few years later, made her particularly suitable for her work. She was also the first ILT to be provided with a helicopter facility.

After the introduction into service of a new ship in 1999, the *Granuaile* acquired the suffix *II* (much as her predecessor of 1948 had done), thus releasing her original name for the new vessel. She was sold in May, 2000 to Gardline Shipping of Great Yarmouth, who renamed her *Ocean Seeker* and had her converted into a hydrographic vessel operating in UK waters.

The sophisticated *Granuaile* represented the Commissioners of Irish Lights at the Silver Jubilee Fleet Review.

# RNLI JOY AND JOHN WADE

The lifeboat *Joy and John Wade* making her way towards the Fleet Review on the 27th June, 1977.

Completed 1977 by Halmatic, Havant, Hampshire. 31 tons displacement. Length overall: 52 ft. 0ins / 15.8m. Beam: 17 ft. 6ins / 5.3m. Draught: 3 ft. 10ins / 1.2m. (for'd) and 5 ft. 0ins / 1.5m (aft). Two Caterpillar D343 oil engines. 460 bhp. Twin screw. Speed: 18 knots. Pennant number: 52-08. Official number: 1053.

The British lifeboat service is not a government-operated organisation but is run by a charity, The Royal National Lifeboat Institution, which is financed by voluntary contributions. The Institution has its headquarters at Poole, housed in a new, purpose-built complex which was opened by Her Majesty the Queen.

The *Joy and John Wade* was built to the design of Messrs. G. L. Watson and is a member of the *Arun* class of lifeboats, which appeared in at least ten variants. The prototype of the class was introduced into service in 1971 and was built of wood, with a higher sheerline than the subsequent vessels. The *Joy and John Wade*, on the other hand, was constructed of GRP (Glass Reinforced Plastic – now called Fibre Reinforced Plastic). Until 1985 the following three series of boats were given aluminium superstructures as it was found that too much radio interference and weight resulted from the use of GRP. The *Joy and John Wade* (named by H.R.H., the Duke of Kent) re-introduced the transom stern to the series. Her pennant number, 52-08, derived from her being the eighth member of the class and one of the 52-footers (those with a rounded stern were 54 feet long.) The '52's carried a crew of six. Typically of the *Arun*s, she would lie afloat in the idyllic surrounds of Yarmouth Harbour, Isle of Wight, in readiness for the call to action.

The proximity of the famed Needles peninsula provided many casualties requiring the attendance of the lifeboats. A notably gallant effort by her crew took place during the hurricane of October, 1987, when she stood by the *Union Mars* in 100 mph winds and horrific seas. In 1994, she and other RNLI boats from the area stood by P&O's *Canberra* (ibid) after the liner experienced engine failure south of the Wight and started to drift dangerously close to the shore.

In her years of service the *Joy and John Wade* was called out 737 times and saved 256 lives. She was withdrawn from the Yarmouth station in February, 2001 and went into reserve at Poole. She was replaced by a *Severn* class boat, the *Eric and Susan Hiscock*.

When this photograph was taken, the *Joy and John Wade* was making her debut in The Solent. She had just arrived at her station at Yarmouth and was making her way to represent the RNLI in the Silver Jubilee Fleet Review, together with two lifeboats from other stations.

*Shieldhall* and the paddle steamer *Waverley* while proceeding in a 'Parade of Steam' down Southampton Water, on the 31st August, 1991.

# SHIELDHALL

Completed 1955 by Lobnitz & Co., Ltd., Renfrew.  1,792 gross tons.  Length overall: 288 ft. 0ins / 87.8m.  Beam: 44 ft. 7ins / 13.6m.  Draught: 13 ft. 4ins / 4.1m.  Two 6-cylinder triple-expansion steam engines.  1,600 ihp.  Single screw.  Service speed: 9 knots.  Call sign: GNGE.

A sludge-carrier of a distinctly 'retro' design harking back to the 1920s, *Shieldhall* was built for Glasgow Corporation to transport her odorous cargo away from the city's sewage works, from whose location she took her name, for dumping at sea.  Besides her designated purpose, she also had a passenger-carrying certificate and could, in the summer months, carry eighty passengers on day trips out to sea.  This practice stemmed from the days of the Great War when similar craft (euphemistically called 'banana boats') would take convalescing soldiers out of the city in order to give them some bracing and curative sea air.  A panelled lounge was therefore included in *Shieldhall*'s design.

Laid up in 1977, she was purchased the following year by the Southern Water Authority, given some minor modifications and began carrying sludge from Southampton to the grounds south of the Isle of Wight.  This phase of her career lasted seven years.  Rising fuel costs then sent her into a period of idleness but she had caught the eye of the Southampton City Museum Services and a preservation society was formed.  As a result, *Shieldhall* was purchased from her owners for £20,000.  The Solent Steam Packet, Ltd. was formed and a volunteer workforce has, amongst other projects, restored her lounge to its former glory.  Her bridge and engine room, also a source of pride to those who operate her, have appeared in several films and television programmes.

Now delicately described as a 'retired cargo(!) carrier' and manfully crewed by volunteers, *Shieldhall* can still be seen steaming around The Solent on various excursions and corporate outings.  She has participated in important international events such as Cowes Week and has steamed as far afield as Holland, where she has joined in the Maritime Steam Festival at Dordrecht.  She has also been present at historic occasions, such as the final return to Southampton of the liner *Canberra* (ibid) and the arrival of the new *Queen Mary 2* (ibid) from her builders.

The steam-powered sludge boat *Shieldall* sailing up Southampton Water, still under the flag of the Southern Water Authority, 18th March 1985.

# SPECIAL VISITORS

## R.R.S. DISCOVERY (II)

Completed 1929 by Ferguson Brothers, Ltd., Port Glasgow. 1,062 gross tons. Length overall: 221 ft. 2$^{ins}$ / 67.4m. Beam: 36 ft. 2$^{ins}$ / 11.0m. Draught: 16 ft. 7$^{ins}$ / 5.1m. Steam turbines by the builders. Single screw. Call sign: GWVM.

In her first ten years, the scientific research vessel *Discovery* carried out five commissions in the oceans around Antarctica for Britain's 'Discovery' Committee. Years later, in 1950-51, she returned to those waters. Named after Captain Scott's *Discovery* (now preserved at Dundee), she was highly regarded and was described as 'singularly successful and happy' – except for an incident in May, 1933 when Captain Peter Carey was lost overboard. Previously, during a voyage in 1931, Sir Douglas Mawson had flown from her to explore 2,500 miles of the coastline of Antarctica.

During the Second World War, she was used by the Royal Navy as an armed patrol vessel. In the post-War years, between 1947 and 1948, Trinity House loaned her to the Commissioners of Irish Lights. After that, she was employed mostly by the National Institute of Oceanography, being used in the Antarctic region. The information gleaned by the ship's scientists proved invaluable in the understanding of the sea's biology and hydrography, increasing the knowledge of ocean currents and of the ecosystem of the southern polar seas. It also helped in the formation of international control bodies for fisheries and whale stocks. Another research vessel called *Discovery* was completed in 1962.

In 1950, with his camera ever present, Bob was in a group that visited *Discovery* (II). In those pre-Health and Safety days, the party had been told to keep together and to take care. This instruction did not deter Bob, who proceeded to climb a crane to take this shot, a wonderfully detailed period piece – note *Discovery*'s wooden bridge front, for instance.

## F.B.S. CAMPANIA

Completed 1943 by Harland & Wolff, Ltd., Belfast. 12,450 tons standard; 15,970 tons deep load. Length overall: 583 ft. 3$^{ins}$ / 177.8m. (512 ft. 0$^{ins}$ / 156.1m. between perpendiculars). Beam: 70 ft. 0$^{ins}$ / 21.3m. (95 ft. 0$^{ins}$ / 28.9m. breadth extreme). Draught: 23 ft. 11$^{ins}$ / 7.3m. Two oil engines. 10,700 bhp. Twin screw. Service speed: 18 knots. Pennant Number: D48. Call sign as F.B.S. *Campania*: GKFG.

The exhibition vessel F.B.S. *Campania* had been laid down as a refrigerated cargo ship for Shaw, Savill & Albion but, after launching, was completed as an escort carrier for the Royal Navy. One of her 'sisters' in what was known as the *Activity* class was the former Union-Castle liner *Pretoria Castle*. (HMS *Campania* was called after an early aircraft carrier which had started life as the famous Cunard liner *Campania* of 1893. She had held the Blue Riband and had been reprieved from scrapping at the outbreak of the First World War. In 1915, she had been converted into an aircraft carrier but met her end during a gale in 1918, drifting onto the ram bow of HMS *Revenge*, anchored nearby, and subsequently sinking.)

The second HMS *Campania* saw duty escorting convoys in several areas. In September, 1944, her embarked aircraft sank the German submarine *U921* and three months later, while guarding one of the heroic Russian convoys, the *U365*. She was laid up in Gareloch in 1946.

(Facing page). R.R.S. *Discovery* photographed on the 4$^{th}$ May, 1950 in Devonport Dockyard – rather outside the geographical scope of this book, but well worth including.

However, in 1950 she was loaned to become a travelling exhibition ship during the Festival of Britain the following year. As such, she visited ten ports around the British coast, the first being Southampton where she arrived on the 4th May, 1951, departing ten days later. She carried displays portraying 'Land of Britain', 'Discovery' and 'People at Home', helping to ensure that the excitement of the Festival was not confined to London.

Bob Bruce Grice was commissioned by the Admiralty to photograph the interior details of the ship (pipe runs, etc.) to enable designers and draughtsmen to complete drawings for her conversion into the Festival showboat. On being met on the quayside by a petty officer, who was to boat him to the vessel, he was told that the *Campania* was a 'dead ship' without power. With the aid of a torch, Bob was able to crawl around the vessel and take his flash photographs 'blind'. Much to his relief, the resultant images (the quality of which was unknown until he returned to London to develop them) drew praise from those who required them.

F.B.S. *Campania* on the 21st April, 1951 being towed out of the Mersey following her conversion – again, not a local picture but interesting nonetheless.

F.B.S. (i.e. Festival of Britain Ship) *Campania* played host to 893,095 visitors during her tour. Dundee was her final call and, after leaving there on the 6th October, she was put into reserve before again being re-activated, this time to carry equipment to Monte Bello Island for the British atomic bomb tests in October, 1952. Paid off in Portsmouth in December, she was laid up in Chatham before arriving at Blyth on Armistice Day, 1955 to be broken up.

# HMS CAVALIER

Completed 1944 by J. Samuel White & Co., Ltd., Cowes. 2,106 displacement tons. Length overall: 362 ft. 9ins / 110.6m. (339 ft. 6ins / 103.5m. between perpendiculars). Beam: 35 ft. 8ins / 10.9m. Draught: 12 ft. 6ins / 3.8m. forward and 15 ft. 11ins. / 4.6m. aft. Geared steam turbines. 40,000 shp. Twin screw. Service speed: 36 knots. Pennant number: R73 (later D73).

Originally to have been built as HMS *Pelew* by Cammell Laird on the River Mersey, the 'C'-class destroyer HMS *Cavalier* was in fact laid down locally on the Isle of Wight at the famous but now-defunct shipyard of J. Samuel White in February, 1943. Launched fourteen months later, she was one of 96 emergency destroyers then being built in wartime Britain. German planes had targeted and bombed the yard in 1942 and part of Whites' subsequent rebuilding involved the inclusion of a welding facility. The *Cavalier* was therefore amongst the first warships to have a hull that partly used this developing technology.

Joining the 6th Destroyer Flotilla, she saw action off Norway; did convoy escort duty; and, exploiting her high speed, accompanied the two Cunard *Queens* from the Bloody Foreland to their anchorage at Tail o' the Bank in the River Clyde when they made their arrivals from New York full of American troops en route for training in Britain, in readiness for the invasion of occupied Europe.

The *Cavalier* was programmed to take part in the Pacific War against Japan after Nazi Germany had fallen, but her refit was not completed in time. However, she was stationed in the East Indies for a while. On her return, she was placed in reserve.

In the mid-'50s, she was sent to Portsmouth Dockyard for a refit and later to the Southampton yard of John I. Thornycroft for modernisation. Stationed 'out east' again, in 1962 she assisted in the defence of the Kingdom of Brunei against armed rebels. In 1970, by now a member of the Home Fleet, she was involved in a dramatic rescue involving a Scottish coaster in the Bristol Channel. When the decision was taken to phase out the old fleet destroyers, a race was arranged in July, 1971 between HMS *Cavalier* and HMS *Rapid*. The *Cavalier* won, but only by the merest margin, after steaming at 31.8 knots over a course of 64 miles. In 1972, she was placed in reserve at Chatham in readiness for disposal.

She was eventually saved from the breakers and, in a five-year campaign led by Lord Louis Mountbatten, purchased for £65,000 by the *Cavalier* Trust and brought to Southampton, as seen in this photograph. Her rôle as a museum ship alongside 45 Berth failed as she did not attract the numbers of visitors envisaged and she was moved, firstly, to a new marina at Brighton and then to another museum rôle in Newcastle-on-Tyne. However, in 1999, and in the face of foreign competition, she was acquired by the Historic Dockyard at Chatham and, after resting in No. 2 Drydock whilst restoration work was undertaken, she was refloated and opened to the public – initially only externally but, from July, 2001, internally as well. Under the care of the HMS *Cavalier* (Chatham) Trust, Ltd., the old destroyer received a grant from The Heritage Lottery Fund in July, 2002. Although long decommissioned, she still has the distinction of being permitted to fly the White Ensign and to retain the prefix HMS.

# H.M.Y. BRITANNIA

Completed 1953 by John Brown & Co. (Clydebank), Ltd., Clydebank. 5,769 gross tons. Length overall: 412 ft. 3$^{ins}$ / 125.7m. Beam: 55 ft. 0$^{ins}$ / 16.8m. Draught: 17 ft. 0$^{ins}$ / 5.2m. Two sets of single-reduction geared steam turbines. 12,000 shp. Twin screw. Service speed: 20 knots. Pennant Number: A00.

H.M.Y. *Britannia* photographed 4$^{th}$ August, 1977, flying the flag of H.R.H. the Duke of Edinburgh while sailing up the River Test to the Western Docks to embark Her Majesty prior to the Royal Family's annual cruise around Great Britain.

The Royal Yacht *Britannia* was launched by the youthful Queen Elizabeth II on the 16$^{th}$ April, 1953, as a replacement for the retired *Victoria and Albert*. The designers had been instructed to produce a vessel which could, if necessary, act as a medium-sized hospital ship. (She fulfilled this rôle in early 1986, when she was called upon to serve as a humanitarian rescue vessel whilst off the South Yemeni coast during the civil strife in Aden.) *Britannia* performed magnificently as a Royal Yacht and quite often, in her own right, as an elegant and popular ambassador for Great Britain in both cultural and business exchanges.

Each August, the Duke of Edinburgh would use her as his base while he enjoyed the excitement and the glitter – both sporting and social – of Cowes Week, the great yachting festival held off the Isle of Wight (balls, dinners and the late-night enjoyment of pickled onions with his sailing mentor, Uffa Fox). She would then take the Royal Family on their annual round-Britain cruise. The author remembers that, as a young pupil at Primary School at Gurnard, near Cowes, he was given a portion of a large painting to complete by the headmistress (Miss Trask). It was a picture of the Royal Yacht when still new and yet to make her debut at Cowes Week. His section was mostly dark blue!

In a refit in 1958, the radio aerial on *Britannia*'s foremast and the top 20 feet of her mainmast were pivoted to enable her to pass under the bridges of the St. Lawrence Seaway. A million ocean miles; eighty-five State visits; eight fleet reviews; nearly five hundred other uses by the Queen; and dozens of commercial events to promote Britain's overseas trade earned *Britannia* a beloved place in the lives of both the Royal Family and her crew, the 'Yachties'. She was an excellent ambassador.

Of the many tales told about her, one story concerns a test of the air-conditioning in the royal apartments. A young sailor, dressed in a wet shirt, had to stand beneath the vents. If he felt too chilly, the airflow was adjusted to a more comfortable setting! All her crew would wear plimsolls (soft shoes) in order to keep her decks clean and the royal apartments quiet. A retired U.S. Navy captain who had come over on the *Jeremiah O'Brien* (ibid) when she took part in the D-Day celebrations, visited the *Britannia*. He subsequently told the publisher of this book that he had never seen such an immaculately clean engine room.

Because of perhaps misguided economies, the Royal Yacht was retired on the 22nd November, 1997 (to the obvious distress of the Queen, who was visibly moved at the decommissioning ceremony in Portsmouth). The ship was taken to Leith in Scotland, where she is now open to the public.

# WAVERLEY

Completed 1947 by A. & J. Inglis, Ltd., Glasgow. 693 gross tons. Length overall: 239 ft. 7ins / 73.0m. Beam: 30 ft. 3ins / 9.2m. Draught: 6 ft. 6ins / 2.0m. 3-cylinder triple expansion steam engine by Rankin & Blackmore, Ltd., Greenock. Paddles. Service speed: 14 knots. Call sign: GRPM.

The *Waverley* is one of the great survivors. Launched on the 2nd October, 1947, she was built for the London & North Eastern Railway for sailings out of Craigendoran on the River Clyde to Arrochar. After the nationalisation of the railways in 1948, she passed to the British Transport Commission and was given their buff funnels. In 1951, she was transferred into the ownership of BTC's Scottish shipping subsidiary, the Caledonian Steam Packet Co., Ltd. (Caledonian MacBrayne from 1973), sailing in various services around the Clyde area.

By 1973, with falling passenger numbers (more people having become car owners) and with her machinery requiring ever-increasing and costly maintenance, the *Waverley* was withdrawn from service. For the token fee of £1, she was sold in 1974 to the Paddle Steamer Preservation Society, which has since managed (with a great deal of hard work) to keep the paddler operational, splendidly repainted in her old L&NER livery.

Under the auspices of the PSPS subsidiary Waverley Steam Navigation Company, Ltd., the PS *Waverley* is marketed as 'The last ocean-going paddle steamer in the World'. A boiler renewal in 1980-81 and a major £3½ million renovation during the winter of 2001-02 have kept the old ship sailing. The renovation, which among much else included 'straightening' one of the funnels which had been set at a slight angle to its companion, was undertaken by the Great Yarmouth yard of George Prior Engineering, Ltd. The ship continues her annual programmes of sailings around the British coast: 'doon the watter' on the Clyde; around the Bristol Channel; and from the South Coast to the Thames.

*Waverley* at
Bournemouth, 15th May,
1978. This was a notable
occasion. Not only was
it *Waverley*'s first call at
the pier – possibly the co-
author of this book was
on board – but it was also
the first visit by a paddler
since 1966.

# RAINBOW WARRIOR

*Rainbow Warrior* at Town Quay, Southampton, 4th March, 1981. Customs officers can be seen on deck, conducting a search operation.

Completed 1955 by Hall, Russell & Co., Ltd., Aberdeen. 418 gross tons. Length overall: 131 ft. 0ins / 40.0m. Beam: 27 ft. 6ins / 8.4m. Diesel-electric, with four engines. 600 bhp. Single screw. Service speed: 11 knots. Call sign: GSZY.

Built as the R.V. (Research Vessel) *Sir William Hardy* for the Department of Scientific and Industrial Research, this sturdy ship was the first diesel-electric trawler on the North Sea. In 1977, by then laid up, she was bought by Greenpeace, the international environmental pressure group, to take their activists to wherever they thought the natural world and its resources were under threat. They renamed her *Rainbow Warrior*.

Her first two-year campaign was spent actively protesting against Spanish, Norwegian and Icelandic whaling and sealing interests. Under arrest in 1980, she had parts of her engine removed by the Spanish authorities who wished to immobilise her but she managed to escape under cover of darkness after her crew repaired the machinery, using spare parts clandestinely brought in by sympathisers.

Oil exploitation, toxic waste disposal and the destruction of dolphins all came within *Rainbow Warrior*'s broad protective horizon but her protests against the nuclear tests in French Polynesia proved to be her undoing. En route to the French nuclear bomb test site of Muroroa Atoll, she called in at Auckland, New Zealand. Three days later, just before midnight on the 10th June, 1985, two explosive devices detonated on board, not only sinking the little vessel but also killing a photographer. A later enquiry found that an agent of the French office of External Security had set the bombs. The French Defence Minister later resigned as a result.

# R.V. BENJAMIN BOWRING

Completed 1952 by Aalborg Vaerft, Aalborg, Denmark.  1,250 gross tons.  Length overall: 212 ft. 11$^{ins}$ / 64.89m.  Breadth: 36 ft. 9$^{ins}$ / 11.2m.  Draught: 19 ft. 7$^{ins}$ / 5.96m.  Single screw.  6-cylinder Burmeister & Wain type 635-VF-62 oil engine.  1,560 ihp.  Service speed: 12 knots.

R.V. *Benjamin Bowring* at Berth 46, Southampton, in 1982, being prepared for another leg of the Transglobe Expedition.

Launched as *Kista Dan* for the famous Danish firm of J. Lauritzen and intended for operation to the Antarctic, this sturdy vessel had a hull strengthened for navigation through ice, an ice-breaker bow and protection around her rudder and propeller.  She was the first vessel of her type to be painted with the now-familiar red hull of ships operating in polar areas.  Among her exploits were several voyages with Sir Vivian Fuchs, the leader of the Trans-Antarctic Expedition of 1956.  She also appeared in the film *Hell Below Zero*.

In 1967, she was sold to the Karlsen Shipping Co. of Halifax, Nova Scotia, who renamed her *Martin Karlsen*.  In 1979, she was sold again, this time to the Bowring Steamship Co., Ltd., who called her *Benjamin Bowring* and transferred her to their subsidiary, The Bearcreek Oil and Shipping Co.  They chartered her to the Transglobe Expedition, which set out to achieve the first-ever longitudinal circumnavigation of the World across sea, land and both ice caps.  Bob's photograph presents an unusual view of her whilst she was being stored and equipped for her voyage to Spitsbergen to rendezvous with the expedition's Sir Ranulph Fiennes and Dr. Charles Burton.  She is wearing the famous Bowring funnel colours.

In 1983, she was sold again, this time to Halba Shipping of London, and renamed *Arctic Gael*.  However, she was not used as intended but remained laid-up until purchased by Freighters & Tankers, Ltd. of Hamilton, Bermuda, who named her *Olimpiakos*.  They had plans to convert her into a private yacht but the work was never completed.  In 1997, she was sold to Polar Ventures, Ltd but was now in a poor state of repair, particularly after suffering storm damage and colliding with a harbour wall.  Disposed of in 1998, she ended her days in a Turkish breaker's yard.

# DOULOS

Completed 1914 by the Newport News Shipbuilding & Drydock Co. 6,804 gross tons. Length overall: 410 ft. 0ins /125.0m (406 ft. 0ins /123.75m. between perpendiculars). Beam: 54 ft. 0ins / 16.5m. Draught: 18 ft. 2ins / 5.5m. Originally one triple expansion steam engine. Now one 18-cylinder FIAT oil engine. 8,100 bhp. Single screw. Service speed: 14 knots. Call sign: 9HKF.

This remarkable survivor was launched as yard no. 176 in August, 1914. She was then the cargo steamer *Medina* of the Mallory Steamship Company, who employed her in their service along the U.S. East Coast to the Gulf ports. With the entry of the United States into the Great War, she was requisitioned as a naval supply ship. In 1922, some years after her return to civilian service, her furnaces were converted to burn oil. For much of the Second World War she continued in commercial service, but with some voyages to Iceland and Greenland under charter to the U.S. War Shipping Administration.

Having survived the War, the *Medina* was sold in 1948 to the Italian-owned but Panamanian-registered Cia. San Miguel SA, who had her rebuilt as the 6,549 gross ton emigrant ship *Roma*. With accommodation for 287 in first class and 694 in an extremely stark third class, she now had an enlarged superstructure and a new funnel and bow. Before entering the migrant trade, she made several voyages taking American

The ancient *Doulos* in Southampton on the 14th March, 1985. She has travelled the World as a Christian missionary ship. Note the vans on her foredeck.

(Facing page). S.T.A. *Lord Nelson* with her yards manned as she approaches the Queen Elizabeth II Terminal, Southampton on the 3rd April, 1989.

Catholic pilgrims to Italy during Holy Year, 1950. Later that year, a single voyage to Australia ended in disaster, with the ship suffering engine problems and her owners collapsing into bankruptcy. In 1952, she was sold by auction to the ambitious Costa Line of Genoa, who renamed her *Franca C.* and sent her for a further refit, during which she was given an ex-naval FIAT-Grandi Motori 6-cylinder diesel engine and had her passenger quarters improved. Costa used her to start a new service between Italy, Venezuela and the Caribbean.

In 1959, this very ordinary little liner was transformed into a quite luxurious cruise ship with stylish Italian décor, including works by famous artists. Costa used her to enter the American cruise market, at first from Fort Lauderdale but later from San Juan. It was for these *Franca C.* cruises that they devised the concept of the 'fly-cruise', with passengers being flown out to join the ship already in the Caribbean. They were so successful that before long almost every other cruise line was doing the same. Although she was now a very old ship, Costa continued to spend heavily on improving her, notably by fitting another new engine in 1970, this time an 18-cylinder FIAT unit.

In 1977, however, she was sold to Operation Mobilization for use by GBA (Gute Bücher für Alle – Good Books for All), a Christian missionary organisation based in Germany. Now called *Doulos* (an ancient Greek word meaning servant or slave), she was refitted as a floating mission centre, carrying half-a-million books to all parts of the globe. Her hold and her swimming pool and lido areas were converted into covered bookshops and exhibition spaces and her other public rooms could be used for conferences. Manned entirely by volunteers, she has since travelled all over the World, occasionally arousing opposition, as in Malta where the government refused to allow her people to give away Bibles and other religious books in return for donations to the Mission. She visited Southampton in 1980 and in 1985, as seen here, and again in 2004.

A further refit in 1993, giving her new diesel alternators and electrical switchboards, extended her life. She is perhaps the oldest ocean-going passenger ship still sailing and, with her ancient but elegant counter stern, is a wonderful reminder of a bygone age. She bids fair to sail for some years to come – a very remarkable ship indeed!

# S.T.A. LORD NELSON

Built 1986 by J. W. Cook & Co. (Wivenhoe), Ltd., Wivenhoe, Essex. 400 tons displacement. Length overall: 171 ft. 3ins / 52.2m. (141 ft. / 43.0m. at the water-line). Beam: 28 ft. 0ins / 8.5m. Draught: 13ft. 6ins / 4.1m. Sail area: 10,755 square feet.

The Jubilee Sailing Trust was formed with the help of donations from the Queen's Silver Jubilee Fund and their first ship was designed by Colin Mudie as the *Lord Nelson*. This sail training ship was built of steel and was designed to be partly manned by people with disabilities. Accordingly, she has wide, flat decks and many other special features. Her original builders went bankrupt because of losses on a different contract and the *Lord Nelson* was taken to the Vosper Thornycroft yard at Woolston for the majority of the remaining work, and then to E. Cole & Sons on the River Medina, Isle of Wight for completion. Harry Spencer's yard at Cowes then rigged her.

Tens of thousands of disabled people have worked with her professional crew, who are often delighted with the physical and mental effects of a sailing voyage on their charges. In this photograph, the *Lord Nelson* is returning from a 5 month, 11,000 mile voyage around the Caribbean. In the Trafalgar 200 Commemorations in 2005, she played the part of HMS *Picket* which raced back to England with the news of the famous victory and of the death of Nelson.

# JEREMIAH O'BRIEN

Completed 1943 by New England Shipbuilding Corporation, Portland, Maine. 7,176 gross tons. Length overall: 441 ft. 6ins / 134.6m. Beam: 57 ft. 0ins / 17.4m. Draught: 27 ft. 9ins / 8.5m. 3-cylinder triple-expansion steam engine. 2,500 ihp. Single screw. Service speed: 11 knots. Call sign: KXCH.

The *Jeremiah O'Brien* was a Class EC2-S-C1 'Liberty' Ship, one of no less than 2,710 similar vessels built in America during the Second World War to replace the millions of valuable tons of Allied shipping being sunk by German 'U-Boats' and surface raiders. Based on a British standard design, the 'Liberty' Ships were assembled on a production line basis. One, indeed, was completed in only eight days. Eventually, production outpaced the rate at which ships were being lost. The 'Liberties' had a cargo capacity of 10,500 tons and performed heroically, bringing supplies to hard-pressed Britain and to the Allied forces in Europe and elsewhere. Although built to last for only a few voyages, many 'Liberties' later survived in commercial service for many years, playing an important part in the revival of the merchant fleets of the Allied countries after the War.

The *Jeremiah O'Brien* saw war service on both the Atlantic and Pacific Oceans and took part in the D-Day landings on the 6th June, 1944. After the War, she spent thirty-four years laid up ('mothballed') with scores of other ships as part of the U.S. Maritime Administration (MARAD)'s reserve fleet in Suisan Bay, near Benicia, California. Fortunately, a MARAD officer determined to save at least one of the 'Liberties' from the scrap yard and preserve her for future generations. It was decided that she should be taken out of reserve and given a thorough refit. Amazingly, she steamed out of the reserve fleet under her own power.

Based at Pier 45 on the famed Fisherman's Wharf in San Francisco, this venerable vessel is a floating museum, maintained by dedicated volunteers. She regularly makes trips around the Bay and her engine room, with reduced-scale handrails fitted around access platforms, was used in the 1997 blockbuster film *Titanic*. Most notably, however, in 1994 she crossed the Atlantic, under her own steam and with a volunteer crew whose average age was probably over 70, to take part in the D-Day celebrations in Britain and France.

*Jeremiah O'Brien* at Southampton in early June, 1994, arriving in readiness for the spectacular 50th Anniversary of D-Day.

# STATE OF MAINE

Completed 1951 by the New York Shipbuilding Company, Camden, New Jersey. 12,600 gross tons. Length overall: 533 ft. 6ins / 162.6m. Beam: 73 ft. 3ins / 22.3m. Draught: 27 ft. 1in / 6.22m. Two sets of General Electric geared steam turbines. 13,750 shp. 21 knots (maximum). Single screw.

The training vessel *State of Maine* was laid down in 1949 as the *President Hayes*, one of three passenger-cargo liners for American President Lines. However, in September, 1950, before they could be completed, they were all re-assigned to the American government's MSTS (Military Sea Transportation Service). The Korean War had broken out that June and the sisters were needed as troop transports. Now called *Upshur* (after Abel P. Upshur, who had been Secretary of State in the days of President Tyler) and designated *T-AP-198*, the former *President Hayes* was launched on the 19th January, 1951.

She and her sisters were the work of George G. Sharp, an American naval architect noted for his adventurous designs, who gave them a distinctive, modernistic profile with a rounded front to the superstructure and two slender side-by-side funnels. The *Upshur* was commissioned on the 20th December, 1952. She had accommodation for 400 officers and 1,500 troops. Mainly employed on the U.S.A. to Northern Europe and Mediterranean routes, she was a regular visitor to Southampton in the 1950s, as were her sisters *Barrett* and *Geiger*. They were retired in 1971-73 and the *Upshur* was handed over to the Maine Maritime Academy for use as a training vessel. They called her *State of Maine*. In 1995, she was returned to the American government's Marine Administration (MARAD), who at first intended to lay her up as part of the National Defense Reserve Fleet but instead handed her over to the U.S. Coast Guard's Research and Development Center at Mobile, Alabama for use as a fire-training vessel. Controlled fires are lit aboard her, hopefully to be extinguished by the trainees.

The stylish *State of Maine* at Southampton on the 1st June, 1994 being refuelled by the oiler *Solent Raider* in readiness for the celebrations of the 50th Anniversary of the D-Day Landings. In the foreground is the tug *Flying Kestrel*.

# CARGO SHIPS

## BENREOCH

The Scottish freighter *Benreoch* is seen working cargo at Berth 41, Eastern Docks, Southampton on the 23rd October, 1968.

Completed 1952 by Charles Connell & Co., Ltd., Glasgow. 10,142 gross tons. Length overall: 503 ft. 6ins / 153.5m. Beam: 64 ft. 1in / 19.5m. Draught: 30 ft. 0ins / 9.1m. Two sets of steam turbines. 9,359 shp. Single screw. Service speed: 17 knots. Call sign: GPVB.

Belonging to an old-established Scottish company, Ben Line Steamers, Ltd., the *Benreoch* was a fine example of a type which has now virtually disappeared from the seas, the 'breakbulk' cargo liner. Speedy for her day and the first Ben Line ship to exceed 10,000 tons, she was employed in the company's regular trade between British ports and the Far East. In February, 1955, she initiated a direct service between London and Singapore.

In 1976, superseded by the new generation of container ships and with her steam turbines much more fuel-thirsty than diesels, the *Benreoch* was 'sold Greek', like so many other British cargo liners at that time. Her new owners were Tudis Navigation Co., SA and, appropriately, they renamed her *Tudis*. She did not last long, however, being delivered for breaking at Kaohsiung in Taiwan in 1979.

# KINPURNIE CASTLE

Completed 1966 by the Greenock Dockyard Co., Ltd., Greenock. 7,955 gross tons. Length overall: 529 ft. 4ins / 161.3m. (485 ft. 4ins. / 147.9 m. between perpendiculars) Beam: 68 ft. 11ns / 21.0m. Draught: 28 ft. 3ins / 8.6m. Two oil engines. 10,350 bhp. Twin screws. Service speed: 17½ knots. Call sign: GQNE.

This sturdy refrigerated cargo liner was originally *Clan Ross*. Despite her typical Clan Line name, she was allotted to another member of the British & Commonwealth group, the Houston Line. However, in 1976 she and several sisters were transferred within the group to the Union-Castle Mail Steamship Co., Ltd. Now named *Kinpurnie Castle* after the Scottish home of the Cayzer family who controlled British & Commonwealth, she joined the cargo service from Southampton to South Africa, now in its declining phase.

In 1979, she was renamed *Kinpurnie Universal* following the integration of the Union-Castle refrigerated fleet with that of the associated Safmarine company under the title Universal Reefers. Now modified to carry frozen meat, *Kinpurnie Universal* sailed on for three more years before being sold in 1982 to Greek owners who called her *Syros Reefer*. However, in 1984 she ran aground off Port Stanley in the Falkland Islands and, although she managed to refloat herself, was deemed a total loss and was sent to Indian shipbreakers.

The Union-Castle cargo liner *Kinpurnie Castle* departing Southampton on a misty day, 21st October, 1977.

# CHUSCAL

Completed 1961 by Alexander Stephen & Sons, Ltd., Linthouse, Glasgow. 6,282 gross tons. Length overall: 411 ft. 3$^{ins}$ / 125.3m. Beam: 56 ft. 7$^{ins}$ / 17.2m. Draught: 25 ft. 1¼$^{ins}$ / 7.7m. Two sets of steam turbines by the builders. 9,000 shp. Single screw. Service speed: 17¾ knots. Call sign: GHJS.

'Banana boats' were traditionally good-looking ships and the *Chuscal* and her three sisters were no exception. Built for Elders & Fyffes by one of their favourite shipbuilders, Alexander Stephen, she was intended to carry fruit from the Cameroons. She had capacious refrigerated holds which were partly loaded through side ports (the outlines of which can be seen in the hull). Later, when Fyffes withdrew from the Cameroons trade, she was used on other banana routes. In 1972, she was sold to Homeric Shipping of Panama, who renamed her *Mardinia Packer*. However, like many other turbine-powered ships at that time, she soon went for scrap, being sold to breakers at Inverkeithing in 1974 after a career of only 13 years.

In this 'period' photograph, it can be seen that Southampton docks were still owned by the B.T.D.B. (the nationalised British Transport Docks Board) and that the cranes were products of the famous Stoddart & Pitt company of Bath. Also note the Hillman Husky car.

*Chuscal* at the banana terminal, Southampton in the 1960s.

# OPALIA

Completed 1963 by Cammell Laird & Co. (Shipbuilding & Engineering) Ltd., Birkenhead. 32,122 gross tons. Length overall: 748 ft. 1in / 228.0m. Beam: 102 ft. 9$^{ins}$ / 31.3m. Draught: 40 ft. 2$^{ins}$ / 12.2m. Two sets of steam turbines. 16,000 shp. Single screw. Call sign: GLQA.

As with many other vessels in the fleet of Shell Tankers (UK) Ltd. of London, *Opalia* was named after a shell, in this case after the gastropoda class of the heterogastropoda order in the architectonicacea superfamily (epitoniidae family)! On her funnels, she carried the company's appropriate shell logo.

*Opalia* was a modern-looking ship, with twin funnels similar to those of the *Canberra*, but she did not remain with Shell for too many years. Already out-classed in terms of size, she was sold and renamed *Lady T* in 1984. A year later, she was hit by an Iraqi missile when south of Kharg Island. The wreckage was sold to breakers and arrived at Gadani Beach for demolition in May, 1985.

A number of merchant ships took part in the Silver Jubilee Fleet Review of 1977, including the elegant Shell tanker *Opalia*.

# MAHOUT

Completed 1963 by Alexander Stephen & Sons, Ltd., Linthouse, Glasgow. 6,178 gross tons. Length overall: 480 ft. 11$^{ins}$ / 146.6m. Beam: 63 ft. 4$^{ins}$ / 19.3m. Draught: 26 ft. 0$^{ins}$ / 7.9m. One 7-cylinder Sulzer-type oil engine. 10,000 bhp. Single screw. Call sign: GHZU.

# SHONGA

Completed 1973 by Stocznia Szczecińska, Szczecin, Poland. 9,235 gross tons. Length overall (including bulbous bow): 478 ft. 2$^{ins}$ / 145.73m. Beam: 70 ft. 6$^{ins}$ / 21.52m. Draught: 23 ft. / 7.04m. Two 6-cylinder oil engines. 9,900 bhp. Single controllable pitch propeller. Service speed: 16 knots. Call sign: GTEF.

Photographed at the Ocean Dock, Southampton on the 4$^{th}$ August, 1977, the *Shonga* is astern of the *Mahout*. In the foreground is the sight-seeing pleasure launch *Skylark*. The two cargo ships are dressed overall to mark Her Majesty the Queen's departure on the Royal Yacht *Britannia*, which had come from Cowes where H.R.H. the Duke of Edinburgh had been enjoying Cowes Week, the annual yachting festival. The Queen and Prince Philip would now set off on the traditional Royal holiday of a round-Britain cruise.

*Mahout* was built for the Brocklebank cargo service to Calcutta. At the time, T. & J. Brocklebank, a Cunard subsidiary, were one of the oldest shipping companies still active. When sold in 1978, the *Mahout* became the *Aglaos* and then, in 1980, the *Evaelia S*. As such, she was reported to have been severely damaged on the 12$^{th}$ September, 1982 during the Iraq/Iran war.

*Shonga* was one of several modern cargo ships built as a speculation by a Polish yard. On completion, they found their way into the fleets of Elder Dempster and other companies within the Alfred Holt group (Ocean Transport & Trading Co., Ltd.). Notable for her heavy cargo gear, the *Shonga* ran in Elder Dempster's services to West Africa. In 1983, after only ten years, she was briefly laid up in the River Fal in Cornwall and, although soon re-commissioned, was sold in 1984 to Hayden, Inc. and registered under the Liberian flag as the *Aroma*, and later *Dona*. Further sales and renamings followed in the next few years – *Mariocean*, *Grand Liberty*, *Lotus Dawn* and, in 1992, *Excelsior Luck*, belonging to Taiwanese owners. But her luck seems to have run out as she disappeared from the register in 1998-9.

# MARIYOS CITY

Completed 1967 by N.V. Boewes Scheeps-bouw, Martenshoek, The Netherlands. 499 gross tons. Length overall: 202 ft. 1in / 61.6m. Beam: 33 ft. 10ins / 10.3m. Draught: 12ft. 6ins / 3.8m. One 6-cylinder oil engine by Atlas-MaK Maschinenbau, Kiel. 760 bhp. Single screw. Service speed: 11 knots. Call sign: OVOW.

Many small short-sea vessels brought cargoes such as grain and wine into Southampton and the *Mariyos City* was just one of them. Here she is seen after delivering a consignment of maize from Rotterdam to the Rank Hovis flourmills in the Western Docks. Ahead and looming over her is the Union-Castle Line's beautiful *Windsor Castle* and beyond that, but barely seen, is a Clan Line vessel.

The *Mariyos City* had been built as the *Grimaldi* for D/S Solnæs A/S of Copenhagen, becom-ing the *Brigit* in 1973. In 1975, she passed to Marpro Ltd. of Singapore, where she was reg-istered under the name we see here. In about 1980, she was sold to United Coastal Services of Sendirian (Penang, Malaysia) and renamed *Hamida*. She was still sailing as such in 2003.

# DART EUROPE

Completed 1970 by S. A. Cockerill, Hoboken, Antwerp. 31,036 gross tons. Length overall: 759 ft. 8ins / 231.55m. Beam: 100 ft. 0ins / 30.48m. Draught: 28 ft. 3ins / 8.6m. One Sulzer oil engine. 29,000 bhp. Single screw. Service speed: 23 knots. Call sign: ONDA.

For four decades, Southampton has been one of the country's most important container ports. The third of three sisters (the other two being products of Swan, Hunter on the Tyne), the *Dart Europe* was at first the largest container ship in the World. She was built to the order of CMB (Cie. Maritime Belge), who placed her in the Dart Container Line service between Europe and Canada, in which they were partners together with several other well-known shipping companies. She reverted to CMB con-trol in 1984 and was renamed *CMB Europe*.

The following year, she was sold to Canadian Maritime Services (Canadian Pacific, Ltd.), becoming the *Canmar Europe*. In August, 1995, she was involved in a collision with the containership *Cast Bear* (23,761 gross tons, CAST Line, also owned by Canadian Pacific) while transiting Lac St. Pierre on the St. Lawrence in foggy conditions. The impact was not even felt on the smaller vessel, whose officers

*Mariyos City* is dwarfed by the *Windsor Castle* at Southampton on the 19th September, 1975.

received the information by radiotelephone!  On being sold in 1996, the *Canmar Europe* was again renamed, this time somewhat surprisingly as *Folly*.  In 1999, she became *Zim Colombo*, presumably for a charter to Zim Israel Navigation.  By now, she belonged to Costamare Shipping of Piraeus but was soon sold for scrap.

# CHILTERN PRINCE

Completed 1970 by Clelands Shipbuilding Co., Ltd., Wallsend-on-Tyne.  1,499 gross tons.  Length overall: 285 ft. 0ins / 86.9m.  Beam: 47 ft. 4ins / 14.4m.  Draught: 6 ft. 6ins / 2.0m.  Single 9-cylinder oil engine.  2,460 bhp.  Single screw.  Service speed: 13½ knots.  Call sign: GNAV.

*Dart Europe* (below, left) inward bound from New York, 30th October, 1975, photographed from the bridge of the Alexander Towing tug *North Loch*.

*Chiltern Prince* (below, right) going astern in Ocean Dock, Southampton in March, 1972.

The Furness Withy group's small cargo vessel *Chiltern Prince* was one of a pair, her sister being the *Malvern Prince*.  Looking handsome in her historic Prince Line livery (with Prince of Wales feathers on the funnel), she was used in the Mediterranean trades.  She is here seen during a call at Southampton to off-load two large launches and various stores which she had brought from Malta following the reduction of the British military presence on that island.

In 1981, she was sold to the Vietnam Sea Transport & Chartering Co., owned by the Vietnamese government, becoming the *Friendship* under the management of an associated Panamanian company, Vina-Club Shipping.  In 1986, she was again renamed, this time as *Thang Loi 2*.  According to *Lloyd's Register*, she is still a member of the Vietnamese fleet.

# NIKOLAY KOPERNICK

Completed 1974 by Stocznia Gdanska, Gdansk, Poland. 6,400 gross tons. Length overall: 458 ft. 8$^{ins}$ / 139.8m. (including bulbous bow). Beam: 59 ft. 2$^{ins}$ / 18.04m. Draught: 25 ft. 6$^{ins}$ / 7.78m. One 8-cylinder Sulzer-type oil engine by Cegielski Zaklady. 13,200 bhp. Single screw. Service speed: 20½ knots. Call sign: UWPU.

Vessels from the republics of the former Soviet Union have often called at Southampton. The *Nikolay Kopernick* belonged to the Latvian Shipping Co. of Riga, who de-Russianised her name to *Nikolajs Koperniks* after Latvia gained its independence from the Soviet Union.

She was one of a class of speedy freighters with ice-strengthened hulls and refrigerated capacity which were supplied to various Eastern Bloc countries by the Gdansk shipyards (later famous as the birthplace of the Solidarity movement and of Polish independence). In recent years, the Latvian Shipping Co. has had a troubled career, with massive financial losses and a lengthy courtroom battle with the Gdansk shipyard.

There was even an appeal to the House of Lords over this dispute. The *Nikolay Kopernick* is here seen bringing bananas into Southampton.

*Nikolay Kopernick* arriving in the Empress Dock, Southampton on the 20$^{th}$ December, 1980.

(Previous pages).
*British Respect* at the
Silver Jubilee Fleet
Review, 1977.

# BRITISH RESPECT

Completed 1974 by Kawasaki Heavy Industries, Sakaide, Japan. 136,601 gross tons. Length overall: 1,102 ft. 6[ins] / 336.03m. including bulbous bow. Beam: 181 ft. 4[ins] / 55.28m. Draught: 88ft. 8[ins] / 27.01m. Two Kawasaki steam turbine units. 36,000 shp. Single screw. Service speed: 17 knots. Call sign: GTUX.

Built for British Petroleum as one of a class of VLCCs (Very Large Crude Carriers), the *British Respect* was, as it turned out, aptly named for a ship which took part in the Royal Review by Her Majesty the Queen. A huge vessel (although as much as 100,000 gross tons smaller than the Ultra Large Crude Carriers of the day), this tanker was sold in 1992 to E.N.E. Delos, Limited of Piraeus, renamed *Delos* and registered under the Greek flag. By 2000, she was laid up and was eventually scrapped.

# BURMAH ENDEAVOUR

Completed 1977 by China Shipbuilding Corporation, Kaohsiung. 231,629 gross tons (459,000 deadweight tons). Length overall: 1,215 ft. 3[ins] / 370.42m. Beam: 223 ft. 4[ins] / 68.06m. Draught: 82 ft. 2[ins] / 25.04m. Two sets of steam turbines by I.H.I., 45,000 shp. Single screw. Service speed: 15¼ knots. Call sign: GXVE.

Built for Burmah Endeavour, Ltd., part of the Burmah Oil group, this huge tanker was British-registered. It was estimated at the time that she could carry enough oil to fuel the entire United Kingdom for two days. She was, in fact, the third largest vessel in the World. Unfortunately, over-commitment to the tanker market was to bring Burmah, one of the biggest of the British oil companies, crashing down.

In 1983, with a world glut of VLCC (Very Large Crude Carrier) and ULCC (Ultra Large Crude Carrier) tonnage, the *Burmah Endeavour* had to be laid up. (At one time, seventeen of these enormous tankers were idle in the Norwegian Fjords alone.) The *Burmah Endeavour* lay at Berths 101/102 in Southampton's Western Docks from the 6th April, 1983 until the 2nd June, 1986. When she finally left the port, it took eight tugs and up to 2½ hours to manoeuvre her to the top Swinging Ground. She had left her berth at low tide so that, in case of an emergency such as grounding, there would be six hours in which to refloat her.

Now registered in Bermuda, she later found employment as a storage vessel at the Hormuz Terminal at Larak Island in the Gulf. While there, she was attacked by Iraqi aircraft. Fortunately, although a fire broke out, it was soon extinguished and she suffered only minor damage. In 1988, she was renamed *Stena Queen*, being by now under charter to the Stena group of Sweden. Four years later, she became the *Folk 1*, being used for storage at Juaymah, an offshore sub-port of Ra's Tannurah in Saudi Arabia.

In mid-2003, she was sold to China for demolition. It may be that in the process, the Chinese learned valuable lessons about the construction of a ULCC. By 2015, the China State Shipbuilding Corporation plans to have built a £3 billion shipyard that will be able to produce similarly large vessels. With this and other huge yards, China will have become the World's biggest shipbuilding nation.

*Burmah Endeavour* on the 2nd June, 1986 at Southampton after being successfully turned, ready to leave after a long lay-up.

# ASHINGTON

Completed 1979 by Clelands Shipbuilding Co., Ltd., Wallsend. 4,334 gross tons. Length overall: 339 ft. 11ins / 103.61m. Beam: 52 ft. 9ins / 16.08m. Draught: 23 ft. 1in / 7.03m. One 8-cylinder Mirrlees oil engine. 4,800 bhp. Single controllable-pitch propeller. Call sign: GXOG.

The *Ashington* had been built for Stephenson Clarke Shipping, Ltd., who for many years specialised in carrying coal, particularly from the ports on the North East coast. Her builders, Clelands, were part of the small ships division of the Swan Hunter group. In 1986, she was experimentally fitted with 'Walker Wing Sails', new devices claimed to reduce fuel consumption. She was now described as a wind-assisted bulk carrier. By 1991, however, the sails had been removed. In 1997, she was sold to a Norwegian-owned company, Ashington K/S, reverting to her original description of a general cargo vessel. Later, she was renamed *Fjord Pearl* and as such is still in service.

# NYK ALTAIR

Completed 1994 by Ishakawajima-Harima Heavy Industries Co. (known as IHI), Kure, Japan. 60,117 gross tons. Length overall: 984 ft. 1in / 299.95m. (including bulbous bow). Beam: 121 ft. 9ins / 37.10m. Draught: 71 ft. 6ins / 21.8m. One V12-cylinder Sulzer-type oil engine. 59,400 bhp. Single screw. Service speed: 23½ knots. Call sign: 3FRS4.

The Japanese NYK company (Nippon Yusen Kaisha) is one of the very largest shipping lines. The famous black funnels with double red stripes on a broad white band have been a familiar sight in ports all over the World since the 1880s. The *NYK Altair* was built with a capacity for 4,743 TEUs for the Japan and Far East to Northern Europe container service and was a product of the IHI yard, famous for its mass-production methods of ship construction. In 2001, she became the *Sandra Azul* of Tama Shipping of Panama, under which name she still sails.

*Ashington* leaving the King George V drydock, Southampton for trials, 13th June, 1986.

NYK *Altai* (see previous page) arriving at Southampton on the 14th January, 1995 with *Netley Castle* inward-bound from Cowes.

*S.A. Waterberg* outward bound from Southampton in July, 1986 photographed from the bridge of the *Shieldhall*.

# S.A. WATERBERG

Completed 1979 by Chantiers Navals de La Ciotat, La Ciotat, France. 53,050 gross tons. Length overall: 848 ft. 1in / 258.5m. (including bulbous bow). Beam: 106 ft. 0ins / 32.31m. Draught: 43 ft. 2ins / 13.15m. Two 8-cylinder Sulzer oil engines. 53,600 bhp. Twin screw. Service speed: 20 knots. Call sign: ZRCS.

Constructed for the South African Marine Corporation, Ltd., usually called Safmarine, the *S. A. Waterberg* and her three sisters were known as the 'Big Whites'. Each of these substantial ships was capable of carrying 2,464 TEUs (containers) but by the turn of the 21st Century, a new generation of container ships was coming into service that could carry 8,000. Even bigger, 10,000 TEU vessels were on order and 13,000 TEU ships were considered feasible. As already noted, Southampton is one of Britain's major container ports but in April, 1992 the Safmarine operation was transferred to Tilbury. In 2001, the *S. A. Waterberg* was sold to the huge A. P. Møller group of Copenhagen, becoming their *Maersk Constantia*.

# THE SILVER JUBILEE REVIEW, JUNE 1977

The Silver Jubilee Review of the Fleet was held at Spithead and in The Solent on Tuesday, 28th June, 1977, in celebration of the 25th Anniversary of the Coronation of Her Majesty, Queen Elizabeth II. Spread over an area of almost 30 square miles, more than 180 ships were present, including 100 from the Royal Navy and 22 from Commonwealth and foreign navies together with representatives of the Merchant Navy and the fishing fleet, the Royal Navy Auxiliary, Trinity House, the Royal National Lifeboat Institution and many other organisations. In addition, dozens of spectator craft helped to swell the numbers afloat.

The Royal Yacht *Britannia*, with Her Majesty, The Queen and members of the Royal Family embarked, passes the anchorage reserved for a flotilla of pleasure yachts.

# Naval Vessels present at The Review

A selection of Bob Bruce Grice's photographs of some of the naval vessels which took part in that famous occasion

# HMS ARK ROYAL

Completed 1955 by Cammell Laird & Co., Ltd., Birkenhead.  43,000 tons displacement.  Length overall: 845 ft. 0ins / 257.5m (720 ft. 0ins / 219.5m. between perpendiculars).  Beam: 112 ft. 9ins / 34.4m. (168 ft. / 51.2m. wide over the flight deck).  Draught: 36 ft. 0ins / 11.0m.  Three sets of Parsons single-reduction geared turbines.  Eight Admiralty-type three-drum boilers.  152,000 shp.  Quadruple screw. 31½ knots.  Pennant Number: R09.

One of four *Audacious*-class Fleet Carriers, of which two were cancelled, *Ark Royal* was laid down on the 3rd May, 1943 as HMS *Irresistible*.  She was given the famous name *Ark Royal* in 1945.  By then, changes in the design of the class were underway to suit the ships to post-War requirements and it was not until the 3rd May, 1950 that *Ark Royal* was launched – after exactly seven years, building having been suspended for a while. She was commissioned on the 28th February, 1955.  She was the first British aircraft carrier to be fitted with steam catapults, of which she had two types.

She was decommissioned in 1966 and was given a lengthy refit, which was completed in February, 1970.  She now had an angled flight deck and a new catapult system.  She was re-commissioned in 1972.  During their service careers, both *Ark Royal* and her sister HMS *Eagle* suffered from maintenance problems.  *Ark Royal* became a television star when she featured in the BBC series *Sailor*, best remembered now for Rod Stewart's throaty rendering of *We Are Sailing*.  She also had the honour of being the largest ship to take part in the Silver Jubilee Review in 1977.

Although she was due to be de-commissioned in 1975, the *Ark* was reprieved and given a further refit in 1973-74, finally being scrapped in 1978 as part of one of those occasional 'Defence Economies'.  In the meantime, *Eagle* was cannibalised to maintain her sister.  Plans to preserve the *Ark Royal* unfortunately came to naught.

# HMS HERMES

Completed 1959 by Vickers-Armstrongs (Shipbuilding), Ltd., Barrow-in-Furness.  23,900 tons displacement.  Length overall: 744 ft. 4ins / 226.9m. (650 ft. 0ins / 198.1m. between perpendiculars).  Beam: 90 ft. 0ins / 27.4m. (160 ft. 0ins / 48.8m. over flight deck).  Draught: 28 ft. 6ins / 8.7m.  Three sets of Parsons geared steam turbines.  Four Admiralty-type drum boilers.  76,000 shp.  Twin screw.  28 knots.  Pennant Number: R12.

A *Centaur*-class Light Fleet Carrier, this ship was laid down on the 21st June, 1944 as HMS *Elephant*.  She was, however, launched as the *Hermes* on the 16th February, 1953 (named after a carrier sunk off Ceylon in 1942) and was commissioned on the 18th November, 1959.  During a rebuild at Devonport Dockyard from 1971 to 1973, she was converted into a Commando Carrier.  Another rebuild, in 1976, turned her into an Anti-Submarine Warfare Carrier and yet a third, in 1981, enabled her to carry Sea Harriers.  For this rôle, she was given a 12º 'ski jump'. She was due to be decommissioned in 1982 after yet another Defence Review, but was quickly refitted at the outbreak of the Falklands War in April of that year and became the British flagship, carrying Royal Marines and a detachment of the SAS in addition to her Sea Harrier jets and Sea King helicopters.  During the campaign, one of her helicopters was lost with all its crew while carrying out a 'Vertrep' exercise – Vertical Replenishment at Sea – during heavy weather.

The *Hermes* would have been scrapped when the delayed *Invincible* class of what were colloquially known in their early years as 'Through Deck Cruisers' came into service but she was sold to the Indian Navy in 1986, becoming their INS *Viraat*.

# HMS FEARLESS

Completed 1963 by Harland & Wolff, Ltd., Belfast. 11,060 tons displacement. Length overall: 520 ft. 0ins /
158.5m. (500 ft. 0ins / 152.4m. between perpendiculars). Beam: 80 ft. 0ins / 24.4m. Draught: 20 ft. 6ins / 6.2m.
Two English Electric steam turbines. Two Babcock & Wilcox boilers. 22,000 shp. Twin screw. 21 knots. Pennant
Number: L10 (originally L3004). Call sign: GKYQ.

Designated an Amphibious Assault Ship (or LPD – Landing Platform Dock), *Fearless* carried four LCU (Landing
Craft Utilities) that could be floated into her stern dock and four LCVP (Landing Craft Vehicle and Personnel
carriers) that were stowed in davits. She also incorporated personnel and vehicle and landing abilities and an
operational helicopter facility. She was commissioned in 1965.

In 1968, she was used as a conference centre during the talks between representatives of the British government
and of Rhodesia, which had recently declared U.D.I. (Unilateral Declaration of Independence). She later served
in the Falklands Campaign of 1982, acting as the flagship of COMAW (Commodore of Amphibious Warfare) and
was the command platform for the Brigadier in Charge of Troops. Major General Moore had his headquarters
on board and the *Fearless* had the distinction of hosting the initial negotiations leading to the surrender of the
Argentine forces.

*Fearless* – and her sister *Intrepid* – were the last steam-driven ships in the Royal Navy and she was paid off in
March, 2002 and decommissioned that August. She is currently laid-up in Portsmouth naval base, being 'cannibalised' for the maintenance of her sister. The ships are due to be replaced by HMS *Albion* and HMS *Bulwark* when
these latter two warships come into service. It is anticipated that *Fearless* will then replace the old *Rame Head* as
the Royal Marines' training ship in Portsmouth Harbour but, at the time of writing, this has not yet happened.

# HMS RECLAIM

Completed 1948 by William Simons & Co., Ltd., Renfrew. 1,360 gross tons. Length overall: 217 ft. 10ins / 66.4m.
(200 ft. / 60.9m. between perpendiculars). Beam: 38 ft. 0ins / 11.6m. Draught: 15 ft. 6ins / 4.7m. Triple-expansion steam engines. 1,500 ihp. Twin screws. (also sail-assisted, when required.) Service speed: 12 knots.
Pennant number: A231.

Laid down in 1946, launched on the 12th March, 1948
and completed in October that same year, this vessel
was originally to have been called *Salverdent*. She
was completed as a dual-purpose deep diving and
submarine rescue ship, complete with underwater television and echo-sounding and sonar equipment. She
had a crew of ninety-two, including twelve divers.

Attached to the land-based diving establishment
HMS *Vernon* (now the commercial Gun Wharf
Quays) at Portsmouth, she was temporarily sent to
HMS *Lochinvar* to act as a mine counter-measure
support ship at Port Edgar before returning to her
allotted rôle in the South. By the time she was
towed to a Belgian scrapyard in May, 1982, she was
the oldest active ship in the Royal Navy.

# HMS SEALION

Completed 1959 by Cammell Laird & Co., Ltd., Birkenhead. 1,610 displacement tons (standard) and 2,030 displacement tons (surfaced). Length overall: 295 ft. 3$^{ins}$ / 90.0m. (241 ft. 0$^{ins}$ / 73.5m. between perpendiculars). Beam: 28 ft. 6$^{ins}$ / 8.7m. Draught: 18 ft. 0$^{ins}$ / 5.5m. Two Admiralty Standard Range VMS diesels (3,680 bhp) and two electric motors (6,000 shp). Twin screw. 12 knots surfaced. 17 knots submerged. Pennant Number S07.

A *Porpoise*-class submarine, *Sealion* was laid down in June, 1958, launched in September, 1959 and commissioned in February, 1961.

The *Porpoise* and *Oberon* classes together made up the so-called 'P&O' class, all of similar dimensions, tonnages and weaponry.

The *Porpoises* were the first British submarines to be designed and built after the War. They were fitted with eight 21-$^{ins}$ torpedo tubes and were armed with 24 torpedoes.

*Sealion* paid off in December, 1987 and, despite hopes that she might be preserved, was broken up at Blyth in March, 1990.

# RMAS AGILE

Completed 1959 by Goole Shipbuilding Co., Ltd.  760 displacement tons.  Length overall: 154 ft. 9$^{ins}$ / 47.2m. (140 ft. 0$^{ins}$ / 42.7m. between perpendiculars).  Beam: 35 ft. 0$^{ins}$ / 10.7m.  Draught: 11 ft. 0$^{ins}$ / 3.4m.  Four Davey Paxman HAXM diesels.  1,800 bhp.  Twin screw (KaMeWa controllable pitch propellers). 13 knots.  Pennant Number: A88.  Call sign: GXKK.

Of a group of five tugs built for the Admiralty, *Agile* was the only one to come from Goole Shipbuilding, the other four being products of A. & J. Inglis, Ltd. of Glasgow.  They were in two groups, of three and two, very similar, and all, after 1971, known as the *Confiance* class.

They were fitted for, but not with, a single 40mm gun.  Originally rated as a dockyard tug, *Agile* became an ocean towing tug with the Royal Maritime Auxiliary Service in 1971.  As such, her duties included not

only attending berthing movements of naval vessels within Portsmouth Dockyard, but also towing decommissioned warships to the breakers' yards.

She worked hard during the Silver Jubilee Review, carrying both Service and civilian personnel to and from the ships involved and taking 'gash' (rubbish) for disposal on shore. Groups of Admiralty employees were given sightseeing opportunities on these journeys to and from the fleet.

In the picture on the previous page we see her with other units of the Royal Maritime Auxiliary Service, while in the photograph below there is her sister, the Scottish-built *Confiance*.

# HMS HERMIONE

Completed 1967 by Alexander Stephen & Sons, Ltd., Linthouse, Glasgow. 2,962 displacement tons (full load). Length overall: 372 ft. 0$^{ins}$ / 113.4m. (360 ft. 0$^{ins}$ / 109.7m. at waterline). Beam: 43 ft. 0$^{ins}$ / 13.1m.. Draught: 18 ft. 6$^{ins}$ / 5.6m. Two sets of double reduction geared turbines. 30,000 shp. Twin screw. 29 knots. Pennant Number F58.

The *Leander* class of frigates was a development of the earlier Type 12 and consisted of 26 vessels built over a period of 13 years and divided into three distinct types. *Hermione* was one of ten members of the third batch, known as the 'Broad-beamed *Leander*s'. Although she was built and launched at Linthouse, she was fitted out and completed by Yarrows at Scotstoun. She was commissioned in July, 1969.

In the 1970s and 1980s, the *Leander*s were the mainstay of the Royal Navy, performing varied duties. *Hermione* had originally been fitted for the Seacat missile system but between July, 1980 and October, 1983 she was converted to carry Seawolf weapons. In 1987, she saw service escorting non-belligerent merchant vessels through the Straits of Hormuz during the prolonged and bloody Iran-Iraq War.

As a result of the 'Peace Dividend' brought about by the collapse of the Soviet Union and the following 'downsizing' of the Royal Navy in the government's optimistically called Options for Change, she was sold for breaking, sharing the same tow Out East as the *Jupiter*. *Hermione* was delivered to breakers in Bombay but *Jupiter* kept her appointment with the cutting torches at Hong Kong.

# HMS SHEFFIELD

Completed 1972 by Vickers-Armstrongs (Shipbuilders), Ltd., Barrow-in-Furness. 3,560 tons displacement. Length overall: 412 ft. 6ins / 125.4m (392 ft. 0ins / 119.5m. between perpendiculars). Beam: 46 ft. 9ins / 14.2m. Draught: 19 ft. 0ins / 5.8m. Two Rolls Royce 'Olympus' TM3B gas turbines and two Rolls Royce 'Tyne' RM1A gas turbines. Two controllable-pitch propellers. 18 knots when running on the 'Tynes', 29 knots on the 'Olympuses'. Range: 4,500 nautical miles at 18 knots. Pennant Number D80.

This ill-fated vessel was laid down on the 15th January, 1970 and launched on the 10th June, 1971. She was commissioned on the 16th February, 1975. She was the first of the Type 42 destroyers and was the name ship of the class that followed. The Sheffield class, in fact, appeared in two forms: six ships in Batch 1 and four in Batch 2, which were similar to the original ships but with improved sensors. There followed a further four in a third batch, which was known as the Manchester class - described as Stretched 42s, they were 7 metres longer. Like her sisters, HMS Sheffield had twin launchers for Sea Dart guided missiles. With the combination of two types of gas turbines, one for cruising and one for high speed, the ships were referred to as 'COGOG' – Combined Gas On Gas.

Because of structural problems amidships, which caused hogging when the 42s were sailing in rough seas, box girders were eventually fitted externally to provide stiffening, somewhat marring the gentle sheer of their rather graceful hulls.

In 1982, HMS Sheffield and four sisterships headed south as the dispute between Great Britain and Argentina over the sovereignty of the Falkland Islands escalated. Ironically, Britain had earlier sold two Type 42s to Argentina and, to avoid any confusion should the two fleets be engaged in action, the British vessels now had black stripes painted vertically down their sides amidships for ease of identification.

On the 4th May, 1982, the Sheffield was hit by an Exocet air-to-surface missile. Because essential pipelines, for Avcat aviation fuel, for instance, ran along the ship's side through the outboard passageways and pierced the main transverse bulkheads, the resultant blaze spread quickly from compartment to compartment. Twenty officers and men were lost and the ship was abandoned, eventually sinking on the 9th May.

Of the other 42s on duty in the South Atlantic, HMS Coventry was hit be two 1,000-lb bombs and subsequently capsized, sinking with the loss of nineteen men.

# USSN BILLFISH

Completed 1970 by General Dynamics (Electric Boat). 3,640 tons displacement (4,640 when submerged). Length overall: 292 ft. 3$^{ins}$ / 89.1m. Beam: 31 ft. 8$^{ins}$ / 9.7m. Draught: 26 ft. 0$^{ins}$ / 7.9m. One Westinghouse pressurised water reactor (S5W) and two steam turbines. 15,000 shp. Single screw. 20 knots (surfaced) and more than 30 knots (submerged). Pennant Number SSN676.

One of the foreign representatives at the Review was the American nuclear submarine *Billfish*. She had been laid down in 1968 and was launched in May 1970, being commissioned in March, 1971. She was one of thirty-seven *Sturgeon*-class SSNs (Submarine Nuclear Propulsion), based on the design of the smaller *Thresher* class. She carried Harpoon missiles and was fitted with four torpedo tubes.

# USS CALIFORNIA

(with the local cross-Solent cargo vessel *Riverclose* sailing by, packed with spectators) Completed 1972 by the Newport News Shipbuilding & Dry Dock Co., Newport News, Virginia. 9,561 tons displacement. Length overall: 596 ft. 0$^{ins}$ / 181.7m. Beam: 61 ft. 0in / 18.6m. Draught: 31 ft. 6$^{ins}$ / 9.6m. Two D26 General Electric pressurised water nuclear reactors. Twin screw. Over 30 knots. Pennant Number: CGN36.

Another American naval vessel present at the Review was this nuclear-powered cruiser (originally classed as a guided missile frigate). She had been launched by Mrs. Richard Nixon, the wife of President Nixon, on the 22$^{nd}$ September, 1971, twenty months after construction started. The *California* was commissioned in February, 1974. She was manned by 40 officers and 544 enlisted men. Armament consisted of two Mk14 Harpoon missile launchers, two 20mm Phalanx CIWS (Close In Weapon Systems), one ASROC missile launcher, two Mk13 missile launchers and Mk46 torpedos. Her apparent lack of a funnel gave her a particularly contemporary air of stealth and concealed power.

Known as the 'Golden Grizzly' after her Californian grizzly bear badge, the ship was based in Norfolk, Virginia and cruised the Atlantic, the Mediterranean and the Indian Ocean. In later years, she sailed 12,000 miles in eighteen days as part of an all-nuclear Task Group providing a presence following the Islamic fundamentalist coup that overthrew the Shah of Iran. In 1980, she became the second nuclear warship to circumnavigate the World, the first having been the *USS Enterprise* in 1964.

Relocated to the Pacific in 1983, the *California* participated in many operations and underwent lengthy periods in dockyard hands having improvements made to her propulsion system. In 1988, she became part of an anti-drug smuggling squadron in the Eastern Pacific and the Caribbean. The same year saw her de-activated at the Puget Sound Naval Shipyard.

# OTHER NAVAL VESSELS
# ON OTHER OCCASIONS

## HMS VICTORY

completed 1765 at Chatham Dockyard. 3,500 tons displacement. Length overall 226 ft. 0$^{ins}$ (186ft. long on the Lower Gun Deck). Beam: 51 ft. 0$^{ins}$. Sail area: 6,510 sq. yards. 8 – 9 knots. (Somehow, it seems inappropriate to quote the dimensions of the *Victory* in metres – Publisher.)

Classed as a 104-gun First rate Ship of the Line, HMS*Victory* was armed with thirty 32-pounder cannon, twenty-eight 24-pounders, forty-four 12-pounders and two 68-pounder carronades. Her mainmast rises 226 ft. above the waterline.

This famous vessel was designed by Thomas Slade, Snr. and her keel was laid down in 1759. After a prolonged build, she was launched in 1765 but her entry into His Majesty's Navy had to wait, as she was not commissioned until 1778. She achieved immortal fame as Nelson's flagship at the Battle of Trafalgar but, with her good sailing qualities, she had been a popular ship with the admirals she had served before Nelson. Even after her outstanding performance at Trafalgar in 1805, she continued to give good service until November, 1812.

For the following hundred years, the still-venerated *Victory* was moored in Portsmouth Harbour, acting in several rôles until 1921. By then, she was in desperate need of repair but the Society of Nautical Research decided that she should be saved not only in homage to Vice-Admiral Lord Nelson and the others who fought at Trafalgar but also as a fitting memorial to the hard days of sail in which the Royal Navy attained its supremacy on the oceans of the World. Included among the eminent names supporting the project was that of the renowned Portsmouth marine artist W. L. Wyllie, who took a very personal interest in the restoration and preservation of the old battleship. HMS *Victory* entered No. 2 Dry Dock at Portsmouth on the 12th January, 1922, where preservation was undertaken. She has remained there as the monument she was intended to be. She is now a part of what has become known as the Portsmouth Historic Dockyard, her companions now including the Tudor warship *Mary Rose* and the Victorian battleship *Warrior* (ibid). Against the background of the Georgian architecture of the surrounding buildings, these glorious warships provide an elegant and fascinating outing of great

nautical interest. *Victory* is open to the public throughout the year – except Christmas Day – and almost 40,000 eager tourists tread her hallowed decks every year.

A few years ago, BBC Television South made an announcement that the *Victory* was to be completely restored to sailing order – an intriguing plan until one realised the timing of the statement – April the 1st! HMS *Victory* is the oldest commissioned warship in the World and is still operated by Royal Navy personnel. Although sitting serenely in her dock (originally built for the navy of Henry VIII and, fittingly for its present tenant, the World's oldest dry dock) she remains the Flagship of the Second Sea Lord and Commander-in-Chief Home Command. In 2005, she was, of course, the focus of the Trafalgar 200 celebrations, during which a simulated 'rippling' broadside was fired in the presence of Her Majesty The Queen.

# HMS WARRIOR

Completed 1861 by Thames Ironworks & Shipbuilding Co., Blackwall, London. 9,210 displacement tons. Length overall: 418 ft. 0ins / 127.4m. Beam: 58 ft. 5ins / 17.8m. Draught: 26 ft. 0ins / 7.9m. Penn's double-acting single-expansion, horizontal trunk steam engines. 5,267 ihp. Single screw. 14½ knots.

The *Warrior* was intended to outclass anything that the French could offer and was the product of many talents. She was designed by the Royal Navy's Chief Constructor, Isaac Watts, and his assistant Thomas Lloyd, aided by the famous shipbuilder John Scott Russell working on the strategic plan of First Sea Lord Sir John Parkington and an initial design by the Surveyor of the Navy, Admiral Sir Baldwin Wake.

In 1858, the French had ordered the *Gloire*, a wooden ship sheathed in iron –an 'ironclad' – but the *Warrior* was to be the first all-iron warship (drawing on the latest technology as exemplified by the *Great Eastern* (ibid.)). She had armour $4\frac{1}{2}^{ins}$ thick and inboard of that was a $14^{ins}$ 'sub-armour' of teak intended to absorb any residue shock from impacts on the iron shell. She also incorporated the new breach-loading cannons. On completion, she was revolutionary – the World's first true battleship, the largest, most powerful, most heavily-armoured warship, rendering obsolete every other afloat. She carried a formidable armament: twenty-six 68 pound muzzle-loaders; ten 100 pound breach loading cannons; plus four 40-pounders, two 20-pounders, one 12-pounder and one 6-pounder.

The ill fortune which had attended the launch of the *Great Eastern* seemed to have followed John Scott Russell when he attempted to launch the *Warrior* on the 29th December, 1860. She refused to budge. But this time it was due to the grease on the 'ways freezing. It was only when hot braziers were brought into close proximity and men on the ship were instructed to shift their weight backwards and forwards from one side to the other that the bond between slip and ship was broken.

The *Warrior*'s first captain, the Hon. Arthur Cochrane (son of the inspirational, swashbuckling adventurer Thomas Cochrane, Lord Dundonald) described her as 'a black snake amongst the rabbits' and she became known as 'The Black Snake of the Channel'. In 1864-67, she was given a refit in Portsmouth Dockyard and was re-armed. In July, 1869, she and her sister *Black Prince*, along with HMS *Terrible*, towed a floating dock to Bermuda.

Refitted again in 1872-75, the *Warrior* remained in service until 1883 when, re-classed as an armoured cruiser but by now obsolete, she was declared redundant. She remained in lay-up until 1900. The following year, stricken from the List, she became a storage hulk and in 1904 was attached as a depôt ship to HMS *Vernon*, the R.N. Torpedo School. She was called *Vernon III* when the name *Warrior* was given to an armoured cruiser which was subsequently sunk as a result of damage suffered at the Battle of Jutland. In 1923, the old ship was given back her original illustrious title but she lost it again when an aircraft carrier assumed it in 1942. She now became the uninspiringly-named *Oil Fuel Hulk C77* following her adaptation as a floating oil jetty at Llanion Cove at Pembroke Dock. By then, it seemed that not even scrap dealers were interested in her! Hundreds of ships refuelled alongside her each year and an occasional dry-docking and an applied layer of concrete on her upper deck kept her preserved below decks over the ensuing decades.

Public interest in the *Warrior* as an important historic vessel began in the 1960s and gained momentum in 1978 when the Royal Navy decided that they no longer required her services. So, in September, 1979, after she had been towed to Hartlepool, restoration of this epoch-making vessel began at last. At first, the work was done under the auspices of the Maritime Trust but later it was transferred to The Warrior Preservation Trust. Unemployed but skilled men were taken on to perform the work of restoring the old ship to her former glory.

Finally, in 1987, the magnificent and revolutionary Victorian warship was brought to Portsmouth Harbour to be given a permanent mooring. In Bob Bruce Grice's photograph, she is seen after passing the Round Tower, the ancient fortification that guards the entrance to the harbour. At this point in the gala occasion, hundreds of balloons were released to celebrate the grand old ship's arrival. In October, 2004, she was drydocked at Portsmouth, returning to her jetty the following month.

Years later, during the construction of the Millennium Spinnaker Tower, the local newspaper reported that a company involved with the tower's steelwork had supplied some of the original heavy iron beams which went into the *Warrior* all those years ago.

(Facing page).
The *Foudroyant* in No.5
Dry Dock at Southampton
for repairs and hull main-
tenance by Harland &
Wolff.

# TS FOUDROYANT

Completed 1817 at the Honourable East India Company's shipyard, Wadia, Bombay.  1,066 gross tons.  1,447 displacement tons.  Length overall: 180 ft. 0$^{ins}$ / 54.9m.  Beam: 40 ft. 3$^{ins}$ / 12.3m.  Draught: 13 ft. 6$^{ins}$ / 4.1m.

This sturdy veteran was originally known as HMS *Trincomalee*.  Because of a shortage of adequate oak in England, she was built of the superior teak in an Indian yard under the supervision of the highly regarded Jamsetjee Bomanjee.  She was one of thirty-two *Leda*-class sixth rate frigates of 38 guns.  By the time she was delivered to Their Lordships of the Admiralty in Great Britain, the Napoleonic Wars, for which she had been built, had come to an end and for nearly three decades she was placed 'in ordinary' (in reserve) with a temporary roof covering her upper decks to protect her from the weather.

In 1845, she was de-rated, partially rebuilt and cut down to a 20-gun corvette.  At last, she was commissioned and finally saw service, being stationed in the North Atlantic, in the West Indies and latterly at Vancouver as a member of the Pacific Squadron.  She was also involved in the Crimean War before returning briefly to the Pacific.  In 1857, she was paid off at Chatham and was then successively used at Sunderland as a tender to HM Drill Ship *Castor*; at West Hartlepool in training command; and as a District Drill Ship at Southampton.  At each station, she was modified to enable her to receive the latest types of armament for training purposes.

In 1897, although scheduled for scrapping at Reed's yard in Portsmouth, she was bought by a philanthropist, Mr. Wheatley Cobb, as a replacement for his privately-owned training ship *Foudroyant*, one of Nelson's old flagships, which had been wrecked off Blackpool Pier during a storm.  Mr. Cobb had his new acquisition taken to Cowes for repairs (between 1897 and 1902) prior to sending her to Falmouth for final fitting out as a training ship.  She was now called *Foudroyant* in honour of her lost predecessor.  In 1927, she was moved to Milford Haven, where she had once been stationed.

In 1932, following Wheatley Cobb's death, the former frigate was presented by his widow to the Society for Nautical Research and transferred to the Foudroyant Trust.  She joined HMS *Implacable* (later scuttled after being deemed unsafe) in Portsmouth Harbour to continue the training of cadets.  During the locally very dangerous years of the Second World War, she was used as an accommodation ship and storage vessel but the training of cadets recommenced after the War.  At one stage, the *Foudroyant* suffered a fire between her side timbers that was finally brought under control by a team of Royal Navy firefighters from the cruiser HMS *Birmingham*.

In 1987, the bold decision was made to have her fully restored and she was taken on a barge to Hartlepool, where HMS *Warrior* (ibid) had earlier been restored.  Again, the work was done by skilled local craftsmen, bringing welcome employment to a very depressed area.  The task was completed in the early summer of 2001.  Once again bearing her original name of *Trincomalee*, the old ship remains resplendent in the town of her rebirth and restoration.  She is second only to the USS *Constitution*, the oldest warship still afloat.

TS *Foudroyant* in
Portsmouth Harbour in
February 1972.

# HMS BELFAST

Completed 1939 by Harland & Wolff, Ltd., Belfast. 11,553 tons displacement. Length overall: 613 ft. 6$^{ins}$ / 187.0m. Beam: 69 ft. 0$^{ins}$ / 21.0m. Draught: 19 ft. 9$^{ins}$ / 6.0m. Four Parsons-type turbines, single-reduction geared, and four Admiralty-type 3-drum boilers. 80,000 shp. Quadruple screw. 32 knots. Pennant number: C35.

This famous warship is an *Edinburgh*-class cruiser, a modification of the *Southampton* class. Very suitably, the *Belfast* was named after her birthplace and, equally appropriately, she was launched on St. Patrick's Day, the 17th March, 1938, by the wife of the then Prime Minister, Neville Chamberlain. The *Belfast* had a complement of 750 – or 850 when acting as flagship. Her keel had been laid on the 10th December, 1936 and the ship was commissioned into the Royal Navy on the 5th August, 1939, less than a month before the outbreak of the Second World War.

Within a month, while off Iceland she intercepted and captured the German liner *Cap Norte*, which later became the well-known British troopship *Empire Trooper*. Five weeks later, *Belfast* herself became a victim when she activated a magnetic mine. Her back was broken and it took three years to effect the necessary repairs. With her displacement increased as a result of the incorporation of additional anti-torpedo bulges, she was re-commissioned in November, 1942 as an escort to the vital convoys taking war materials to Russia. However, in November, 1943 she joined the chase hunting the German battle cruiser *Scharnhorst* which had been attacking Allied convoys. The pursuers finally located their quarry on Boxing Day, 1943 and, just as *Belfast* fired her torpedoes, the *Scharnhorst* sank with huge loss of life after receiving hits from British destroyers. March, 1944 saw *Belfast* escorting the task force that would ultimately sink the enemy battleship *Tirpitz*, anchored in a Norwegian fjord. The 6th June, 1944 added another glorious chapter to *Belfast*'s career when she supported the D-Day landings in

HMS *Belfast* photographed against the sun on the 2nd September, 1971 as she left Portsmouth Harbour for the last time, bound for a working retirement in the Pool of London.

Normandy, an action which marked the last time her guns would be fired in anger in the Second World War since her subsequent arrival in Far Eastern waters came too late to help in the fighting. However, she was in time to give succour to released Allied Prisoners of War.

After the War, she was involved in peace-keeping duties during the final Communist advance through China and later bombarded North Korean positions during that country's attempts to invade South Korea. Various peacetime deployments followed in both Far Eastern and African waters and then, in August, 1963, she was paid off.

In 1971, avoiding the fate that awaited many of her heroic contemporaries at the ever-hungry breakers' yards, she was saved and put on permanent display just upstream of Tower Bridge in London. Appropriately, she was opened to the public on the 21st October – Trafalgar Day – 1971. She returned to Portsmouth in June, 1999 for essential dry-docking and at the same time was repainted in her D-Day livery before returning to her moorings in the capital city to resume her position as a popular tourist attraction and an important survivor of a great generation of British warships.

HMS *Amazon* photographed during her commissioning ceremony at the Ocean Terminal, Southampton in the presence of HRH, The Princess Anne, 11th May, 1974.

# HMS AMAZON

Completed 1971 by John I. Thornycroft & Co., Ltd, Woolston, Southampton. 2,750 displacement tons. Length overall: 384 ft. 0ins (360 ft. 0ins at waterline). Beam: 41 ft. 10ins. COGOG – two Rolls Royce 'Olympus' TM38 gas turbines (56,000 bhp) and two Rolls Royce RM1C gas turbines (for cruising – 9,900 hp). Twin screw (controllable pitch propellers). 30 knots over 1,200 miles, 18 knots over 3,500 miles. Pennant Number: F169.

The name ship of the Type *21* frigates, HMS *Amazon* was built locally by John I. Thornycroft at their Woolston yard. They not only constructed three of the eight ships of this type (the remainder being built

by Yarrows at Scotstoun) but were mainly responsible for designing the vessels. The *Amazon* class were the first wholly commercially-designed British warships for many years and also the first to be planned entirely as gas turbine driven. Armament included four Exocet SSMS (Surface to Surface Missile Systems), one quadruple Sea Cat SAM (Surface Air Missile) launcher, one 4.5ins Mk8 automatic gun, four 20mm anti-aircraft guns and two triple torpedo tubes.

The *Amazon* was launched on the 26th April, 1971 by HRH Princess Anne. Although the *Amazon* was adopted by Southampton, the city of her birth, she was based at Plymouth. She and her sisters were generally popular with those who served on them but their design was regarded as too commercially orientated for Their Lordships.

HMS *Amazon* suffered a fire whilst stationed in the Far East in 1977 and two of her sisters, the *Ardent* and the *Antelope*, would ultimately be sunk during the 1982 Falklands campaign. *Ardent*, the first to be lost, was hit by bombs and rockets on the 21st May. Abandoned after catching fire with the loss of 27 men, she sank twelve hours later. The following day *Antelope* was attacked three times after entering the Total Exclusion Zone and joining other ships in San Carlos Sound. One young sailor was killed. An attempt was made to de-fuse two unexploded 1,000-pound bombs but one blew up, killing a member of the two-man disposal team. The ship was abandoned and the next day a spectacular explosion occurred, possibly caused by the second bomb. With her back broken, *Antelope* sank in two pieces, with bow and stern both protruding above the water. Both *Ardent* and *Antelope* are now designated as Military Maritime Graves. *Amazon* was not involved in the Falklands campaign, being in the Persian Gulf at the time.

After the Falklands, the remaining Type *21*s had additional stiffening built into them as their weather decks had developed cracks in the severe conditions encountered in the South Atlantic. They were eventually sold to Pakistan, being transferred in 1993. After a refit and an update of weaponry and surveillance equipment, the restyled *21*s became the *Tariq* class. *Amazon* herself became *Babur* with the former HMS *Ambuscade* being named the lead ship of the new class.

# RFA SIR PERCIVALE

Completed 1968 by Swan, Hunter & Tyne Shipbuilders, Ltd. (Hawthorn Leslie), Hebburn-on-Tyne. 3,270 displacement tons (5,674 full load). Length overall: 412 ft. 2ins (366 ft. 4ins between perpendiculars). Beam: 59 ft. 10ins. Draught: 13 ft. 0ins. Two Mirrlees oil engines. 9,400 bhp. Twin shafts. 17 knots. Call sign: GVTA. Pennant Number: 3036.

Built as a Logistic Landing Ship and manned by the Royal Fleet Auxiliary Service, the RFA *Sir Percivale* was one of a class of six ships, the *Sir Bedivere*, *Sir Galahad*, *Sir Geraint*, *Sir Lancelot* and *Sir Tristram* being the others. They were equipped for bow- and stern-loading and had drive-through facilities. *Sir Percivale* was laid down in April, 1966, launched in October, 1967 and commissioned in March, 1968.

She was called to the Falklands Campaign in 1982 to land troops and tanks. In one of the most tragic episodes of the conflict, her sister *Sir Galahad* was hit and set ablaze. She had been disembarking men of the 1st Welsh Guards, of whom forty-eight were killed in the explosions and fire that followed. Later, the hulk was towed out to sea and sunk.

On the 8th June, the *Sir Tristram* and the *Sir Lancelot* were also bombed and set alight and were eventually abandoned. However, *Sir Tristram* was salvaged, towed to Port Stanley and used there as an accommoda-tion vessel. In 1984, she was brought back to the UK – 'piggy back' on a heavy-lift ship – for a three-year refit on Tyneside. During this time, she was lengthened by 29 feet and her aluminium superstructure was replaced with steel. Similar modifications would later be made to her remaining sisters.

In September, 2002, Sir Percivale was anchored off Freetown, Sierra Leone to take off six soldiers who had been held hostage by rebel forces and ultimately rescued by members of the 1st Battalion of the Parachute Regiment. In 2003, she delivered humanitarian aid to Umm Qasar following the Iraqi War.

Re-engined in 1996, Sir Bedivere was also given an extended refit and she emerged as a practically new ship. She took part in Exercise Saif Sareea II (Swift Sword II) in Oman towards the end of 2001, which demonstrated the U.K.'s ability to deploy ground forces to the Middle East and was the largest single such operation since the Gulf War. In 2003, along with other Royal Navy and RFA units including her sisters, she was again in the region in her rôle as a Landing Ship Logistic. From 10th September, 2003 she was involved in the first Iraqi conflict, initially as a member of the Maritime Counter Measures Group and then as a support vessel until the termination of hostilities in May, 2004. Sir Percivale has lately been given an ESRP (extended survey and repair period) by A&P Tyne and it is hoped that this will prolong her life for a few more years. This might also, perhaps, delay the then-rumoured building of four Bay class replacements – both Sir Percivale and Sir Geraint were due to be retired in 2003/4. (The first of the replacements, Largs Bay, is currently fitting out on the Tyne.) Sir Geraint is presently laid up awaiting disposal and both Sir Tristram and the 16-year old replacement for the original Sir Galahad are currently awaiting re-activation.

The RFA Sir Percivale leaving the Marchwood Military Base on the western shore of the River Test on the 4th August, 1977. The ships of the Royal Fleet Auxiliary Service have been familiar sights in The Solent for many years.

## Locomotive SIR LAMIEL with the USS GUAM

This magnificently restored "King Arthur"-class 4-6-0 steam locomotive, designed by R. E. L. Maunsell, was built in 1925, her original number being E777. A product of the North British Locomotive Co., Ltd., she was built to the order of the Southern Railway and weighed nearly 139 tons. She is now preserved as part of the National Railway Museum Collection at York. In this view, she is passing alongside the American Interim Control ship USS *Guam*, which is lying at Berth 44 during the commemorations of the 50th Anniversary of D-Day. An attendant guard walks in front of the locomotive. As part of the celebrations, a special train service was run from Salisbury to the Eastern Docks.

## Memories of the GREAT EASTERN

Completed in 1858 by John Scott Russell, Napier Works, Isle of Dogs, Millwall, London. 18,915 gross tons. Length overall: 692 ft. 0[ins]. Beam: 83 ft. 0[ins] (118 ft. over the paddleboxes). Draught: 50 ft. 0[ins]. One paddle-engine by John Scott Russell, with four cylinders of 6ft. 2[ins]. x 14 ft. 1,000 nhp. And one screw engine by James Watt & Co. with four cylinders of 7 ft. diameter. 1,600 nhp. Eight boilers. Paddle wheels: 56 ft. diameter and a single four-bladed screw of 24 ft. diameter. 13½ knots.

The *Sir Lamiel* and the USS *Guam* together at Southampton on the 4th June, 1994.

The great Victorian engineer Isambard Kingdom Brunel (born in Portsmouth) conceived and designed three innovative ships, many years ahead of their time – *Great Western*, *Great Britain* and *Great Eastern*. (At one

SITE OF BUILDING & LAUNCHING OF STEAMSHIP "GREAT EASTERN" 1853-8. LENGTH 692 FEET. 27,384 TONS.

stage in her building, the latter was to have been called *Leviathan*. She was at first intended for the Indian route – hence her final name – but, in fact, she never ran in that service.) Her detailed design and building were undertaken by John Scott Russell at his Isle of Dogs shipyard on the banks of the River Thames.

The *Great Eastern* was of unprecedented size – five times the tonnage of her nearest contemporary – and she was not exceeded in length until the White Star Line's *Oceanic* of 1899 and in tonnage until the same company's *Celtic* of 1901. She was the first all-iron ship; had five funnels; six masts carrying 6,500 square yards of sail; had both paddle wheels and a propeller; and was designed to carry 3,000 passengers. She was laid down in February, 1854. Several attempts were made to launch her broadside into the Thames over a period of four months but they proved ineffective and it was not until the 30th January, 1858 that the continued labours were rewarded with success. During her build, she bankrupted her original backers and did the same to others during her operational life.

On the 12th September, 1859, while the mighty *Great Eastern* was en route from her builders to Holyhead and watched from the shore by hundreds of eager spectators, she suffered a disastrous explosion. This was caused by the closure of a steam safety valve and blew the 30-feet high forward funnel right out of its casing, turning the celebrations into a wake for those on board as four men were killed and many more were horribly injured by escaping steam. An eye-witness on board later wrote: 'We had dined. It was 6 o'clock and we were off Hastings, at about seven miles from the shore. Suddenly, the verberation of a tremendous explosion was heard. The reverberations followed. There came a tremendous crash, then

A photograph taken on the 4th June, 1950 at the site of the launch of Brunel's huge liner *Great Eastern*, Isle of Dogs, London.

One of the last remaining fragments of the *Great Eastern*, the forward funnel which was being used for a quite different purpose at the Sutton Poyntz Pumping Station, Weymouth, when Bob Bruce Grice took this photograph on the 15th April, 1985.

a sweeping, rolling, rumbling sound, as of cannon-balls scudding around along the deck above." This was caused by wreckage from the grand, gilded and mirrored saloon raining down onto the Weather Deck.

The news of the tragedy was given to the already seriously ill Brunel. It proved to be the final blow that culminated in his death a week later.

Astoundingly, in spite of this major disaster, which would have brought about the demise of a lesser vessel, the great ship was able to resume her voyage. She spent three weeks being repaired in Weymouth Bay and twenty thousand people paid to tread her decks. From the Dorset town she went to Holyhead, where she survived a particularly violent storm. Later, she sought a more sheltered winter anchorage in Southampton Water, where tragedy struck again when her captain was drowned whilst being rowed ashore in his skiff. After several periods of employment (including an extremely successful spell laying the first transatlantic cable but also with inglorious bouts as a showboat and a floating funfair), this fantastic and truly innovative vessel, sadly denied the success of her original intended employment, was broken up at Rock Ferry, Birkenhead in 1888. One of her masts is still used as a flagpole at a Liverpool football ground. For a long time, it was generally thought that that this was the only surviving piece of this great ship but, in fact, there is another.

While she was being repaired in Weymouth Bay following the explosion, the forward funnel was salvaged and brought ashore. It was bought by the Weymouth Waterworks Company and sunk into the spring basin at the Sutton Poyntz Pumping Station as a strainer shaft. Six feet of the half-inch thick wrought iron funnel protruded above the basin's floor where it screened the chlorine injection point. 2¼ million gallons of water were filtered through it every day before being piped to the Weymouth area. The funnel's daily use ceased in the mid-1980s but it remained there in a good state of preservation, a testament to the quality of the iron from which the *Great Eastern* had been built. In 2005, this precious fragment of the great ship was donated by Wessex Water to the Trust which rescued, restored and now exhibits Brunel's second epoch-making ocean liner, the *Great Britain*, which is open to the public at Bristol.

# CUTTY SARK

In this photograph the famous tea (and later wool) clipper *Cutty Sark* seems ready to set sail but in fact this iconic ship is in her dry dock at Greenwich where she has lain for half a century.

Completed 1869 by Denny Bros., Dumbarton, Scotland after the bankruptcy of her builders Scott & Linton, Ltd. 963 gross tons (2,100 displacement tons). Length overall: 280 ft. (hull 224 ft.; length at the waterline 212 ft. 6$^{ins}$). Beam: 36 ft. Draught: 20 ft. Sail area: 32,800 sq. ft. Official number: 63557. Signal Code: JKWS.

One of the classic, most famous ships of all time, the *Cutty Sark* was designed by Hercules Linton and was built as a composite vessel (i.e.: wood outer planking on iron frames) for John Willis of London. Uniting beauty with utility, she was launched into the River Clyde on the 12$^{th}$ November, 1869.

*Cutty Sark* was named after the witch Nannie in Scottish myth, immortalised in Robert Burns' poem *Tam O'Shanter*. Wearing only a short shift (a 'cutty sark') and in hot pursuit of Tam, Nannie grabbed his horse's tail, which came away in her hand. The ship's figurehead shows her holding it (a length of rope would be frayed

out and placed in her hand when the ship was in port). The *Cutty Sark* was completed as a three-masted full-rigged ship (clipper with stuns'ls). The word 'clipper' was apparently used to describe these vessels because their speed enabled them to 'clip the wind' as well as to clip times off passages.

For a brief period, the *Cutty Sark* was sensationally successful. In eagerly followed races to bring the first of the season's tea in the 16,000-mile dash from Shanghai to London, she made record passages (110 days). Each year, the first cargo to arrive in London would fetch premium prices. Her arch-rival, both on the tea run and later on the wool run, was the equally legendary *Thermopylae* of the Aberdeen White Star Line.

However, these record-breaking ships were quickly rendered obsolete by the increased carrying capacity of larger but slower sailing vessels and, particularly, by the technological rise to supremacy of the steamship. The *Cutty Sark* also happened to appear in the year that the Suez Canal was opened, an event that helped to destroy the competitiveness of the sailing ship. When the tea trade diverted to the steamers sailing the more direct route via Suez, the clippers turned to the carriage of Australian wool, sailing 12,000 miles from Sydney to London.

In mid-November, 1877, the *Cutty Sark* encountered a severe gale as she was heading towards London. While she was riding out the storm at an anchorage in the Downs, off Deal, her cables parted, leaving her adrift. As a result, she collided with two other vessels, also at anchor. Distress flairs attracted the attention of two tugs and the first to arrive, the *McGregor*, took her in tow before she could ground on a mud bank. She was ultimately repaired in London.

By 1880, the *Cutty Sark* had come down in the world: she was trading in coal and her spars were much reduced. However, she continued under the British flag until 1895, when she was sold to a Portuguese owner for £2,100 as a general cargo vessel, being renamed *Ferreira*. The *Thermopylae* did not fare so well – similarly sold to the Portuguese, she was wantonly sunk as a torpedo practice target off the mouth of the River Tagus. In 1916, after the *Ferreira* was dismasted off the Cape of Good Hope, she was sold, re-rigged and renamed *Maria do Amparo*.

But salvation was at hand when, in 1922, Captain Wilfred Dowman recognised her as the speedy clipper which had impressed him when he had seen her race by his own ship many years previously. He subsequently bought her for £3,750 and had her restored at Falmouth – the roadstead made famous in the old sailing ship days as a landfall after many thousands of miles of hazardous voyaging without communication: hence 'Falmouth for orders'. Captain Dowman died in 1936 and two years later his widow gave the still beautiful and beloved ship to the Incorporated Thames Nautical Training College. The old vessel was towed to the River Thames to become a tender – albeit a thoroughbred one! – to the 'mother ship', HMS *Worcester*, moored off Greenhithe.

In 1952, the *Cutty Sark* was donated to the newly formed Cutty Sark Preservation Society and, after much strenuous effort, this 'great and gracious lady', which now lay in a specially-built dry dock at Greenwich, was opened to the public by the Queen on the 25th June, 1957. A notorious but splendid gaff occurred when the renowned BBC commentator Richard Dimbleby referred to the ship as the 'Sutty Kark'. The *Cutty Sark* has given her name, correctly, to a Scotch whisky and to a series of international races for tall ships to promote 'understanding between the nations'. The competing crews are of various ages, abilities and nationalities.

As this is written, the state of this fine and important vessel is a cause for immediate and very urgent concern. During a survey in 1998, it was estimated that if nothing were done to conserve her she would become unsafe within ten years. As a result, a project was launched under the auspices of The Cutty Sark Trust which will, hopefully, prevent further deterioration, especially of her wrought iron hull, and preserve her for many years to come. Combined electrolysis and mechanical cleaning will preserve much of her original fabric, of which approximately 95% remains. Her weakened frames will be strengthened and her keel will be replaced.

It is proposed that, once this work has been completed, the ship should be enclosed at her waterline with a canopy that would represent the passing ocean as well as give protection from the real elements. This major restoration project is expected to last until 2009, but much work and money is still required.

# THE CUTTY SARK TALL SHIPS' RACE

What is now known as the Cutty Sark Tall Ships' Race began in 1956 when twenty-one sail training vessels from eleven nations raced each other from Torbay to Lisbon in an event to mark, it was thought, the passing of sail. However, the event proved so popular that two years later it was staged again. The term Tall Ships was used to describe the fleet and the organisers, The Sail Training-Ship International Race Committee (later to become The Sail Training Association) realised that this could be the start of something which would eventually become an annual event. The purpose of the race was to bring together the youth of many nations. The qualifications required of the competing ships were that they must have a waterline length of least 30 feet; their principal means of propulsion had to be sail; and half the ship's crew must be between the ages of 16 and 25. Since 1972, the event has been sponsored by Cutty Sark Scotch Whisky, thus uniting the race and the brand name under one prestigious icon. The Sail Training Association changed its name in 2003 and is now known as The Tall Ships Youth Trust and can proudly claim to have trained over 65,000 young people since its inception in 1956.

The races depicted here started at Portsmouth (4th August, 1974), Southampton (photographed 20-25th August, 1982) and Weymouth (20th July, 1994). The days leading up to the 1982 race were particularly spectacular as the participating vessels and the surrounding dock areas were opened to the public. In addition, a superb collection of passenger ship models was assembled in the famous Ocean Terminal. It was not realised at the time that this would be one of the last times the public would be allowed access to this Art Deco showpiece.

## DAR PORMORZA

Completed 1909 by Blohm & Voss, Hamburg. 1,566 gross tons (1,784 tons Thames measurement). Length overall: 310 ft. (230 ft. 4ins at the waterline). Beam: 41 ft. Draught: 19 ft. Sail area: 24,000 square feet.

The magnificent Polish sail training ship *Dar Pormorza* heads out of Portsmouth in 1974.

This beautiful vessel was built as the *Prinzess Eitel Friedrich* for the Deutscher Schulschiff Verein (German Schoolship Association) of Bremen. She was ceded to the French as war reparations in 1919, passing to the Société des Armateurs Français (Society of French Shipowners) in 1922 and to the Société de Navigation 'Les Navires Écoles Français' (Society of French Schoolships) in 1925. She was now renamed *Colbert* but never sailed as such. A proposal by Baron de Forest to convert her into a private yacht came to nothing.

In 1929, she was purchased by the people of the northern Polish town of Pormorze, who presented her to the Polish State Sea Training School. Now called *Dar Pormorza* ('Gift of Pormorze'), she was based at Gdynia, replacing the country's Nautical Sailing College's barque *Lwow* of 1869.

During the violent and brutal upheaval of the Second World War, which was particularly cruel to Poland, the *Dar Pormorza* was laid up in Sweden. In 1946, following the cessation of hostilities, she was returned to her sail training duties under the control of Wyzsza Skill Morska. She has been preserved as a museum ship since 1981, her rôle as an active sail trainer being taken by the *DarMlodziezy* (ibid.) in 1982.

# AMERIGO VESPUCCI

Completed 1930 at Castellamare di Stabia, Naples. 2,686 tons Thames measurement (3,543 tons displacement; 4,150 full load). Length overall: 330 ft. (229 ft. 6ins between perpendiculars). Beam: 56 ft. 3ins. Draught: 24 ft. Sail area: 32,300 square feet. Pennant Number A5312.

Designed by Francesco Rotondi for the Accademia Navale in Livorno, this sail training ship was completed in 1930. She was named after the Florentine explorer Amerigo Vespucci (1454-1512) who 'discovered' America and gave his name to that country. His image is represented by the ship's figurehead. The gilded

The Italian sail training ship *Amerigo Vespucci*, here showing off her highly decorated stern with its Admiral's Walk, is handled by a tug as she approaches Southampton on the 31st August, 1989.

decoration ('gingerbread') around her stern is particularly opulent and is shown in eloquent detail in this photograph taken from the tug *Sir Bevois*.

*Amerigo Vespucci* stands quite high out of the water in order to house as many cadets as possible. She is an enlarged version of the *Cristoforo Colombo* (named after the other 'discoverer' of America) which was taken by the Soviets after the War, in 1945, and renamed *Danuy*. She was broken up at Odessa in 1971.

The newly-built *Dar Mlodziezy* berthing at the Ocean Dock, Southampton, in August, 1982.

# DAR MLODZIEZY

Completed 1982 by Stocznia Gdanska im Lenina, Gdansk. 2,385 gross tons (2,791 tons displacement). Length overall: 357 ft. (260 ft. at the waterline). Beam: 45 ft. 11$^{ins}$. Draught: 21 ft. 8$^{ins}$. Sail area: 32,453 square ft. Call sign: SQLZ.

Many maiden voyages have begun or finished at Southampton but, in modern times, that of a sailing vessel was an unusual occurrence. This fine Polish full-rigger was the first of a class of no less than six purpose-built sail training ships designed by Zygmunt Chloren. *Dar Mlodziezy*'s name translates as 'Gift of the Children'.

(Previous pages). A fine view of the magnificent Russian *Kruzhenstern* as she beats through Spithead, all sails set, in 1974.

# KRUZHENSTERN

Completed 1926 by Joh. C. Tecklenborg at Wesermünde, Germany. 3,543 gross tons (5,725 tons Thames measurement). Length overall: 375 ft. 6$^{ins}$ (hull: 342 ft., length at the waterline: 320 ft. 6$^{ins}$.) Beam: 46 ft. 2$^{ins}$. Draught: 25 ft. 5$^{ins}$. Sail area: nearly 37,000 square feet. Call sign: RFVQ.

Designed and built as a steel four-masted barque and launched as the *Padua*, this impressive vessel was constructed to the order of Ferdinand Laeisz of Hamburg, who owned the famous 'Flying P' fleet of sailing ships. She was employed in the nitrate trade, bringing guano from the west coast of South America. However, for a time in the 1930s, she was transferred to the Australian grain trade before re-entering the nitrate trade in 1936.

In 1946, after the defeat of Hitler's Germany, she was seized as reparations by the Soviets while she lay at Flensburg. They renamed her *Kruzhenstern* after Admiral Ivan Kruzhenstern, the Soviet Union's Chief Hydrographer, and have since used her as a sail-training vessel for the Ministry of Fisheries.

# SIR WINSTON CHURCHILL

Completed 1966 by Richard Dunston, Hessle, Hull. 219 gross tons. Length overall: 150 ft. 4$^{ins}$ / 45.8 metres. Waterline length: 105 ft. / 32 metres. Beam: 26 ft. 9$^{ins}$ / 8.15 metres. Draught: 15 ft. 9$^{ins}$ / 4.8 metres. Two 135 bhp Perkins oil engines. Sail area: 8,805 sq. ft. / 818 sq. metres.

# MALCOLM MILLER

Completed 1967 by John Lewis & Sons, Ltd., Aberdeen. 218 gross tons. Length overall: 149 ft. 9$^{ins}$ / 45.7 metres. Waterline length: 105 ft. / 32 metres. Beam: 26 ft. 9$^{ins}$ / 8.15 metres. Draught: 15 ft. 9$^{ins}$ / 4.8 metres. Two 135 bhp Perkins oil engines. Sail area: 8,794 sq. ft. / 817 sq. metres.

The *Sir Winston Churchill* and the *Malcolm Miller* seen together in Southampton Water during the Parade of Sail, which preceded the 1982 Tall Ships' Race.

The two British participants in the Parade of Sail in Southampton Water before the 1982 race were designed by Camper & Nicholson. They were both operated by the Sail Training Association. The *Malcolm Miller* was named after the son of the late Sir James Miller, a former Lord Mayor of London. Although the two vessels were of very similar appearance, the *Churchill* could be distinguished from her sister by her square-cornered deckhouse, which contrasted with the more rounded look of the *Miller*.

An ex-trainee recalls a 'character-building' late season rough weather voyage where the majority of the crew consisted of borstal boys: the time 'served' afloat for one trip counted against their sentence. Both vessels served the STA extremely well but were eventually replaced by the *Prince William* and the *Stavros Niarchos* in 2001 and 2002 respectively. The original vessels were sold to private owners in 2001, with the *Winston Churchill* retaining her distinguished name and the *Malcolm Miller* becoming the *Helena C.* and being converted at Marchwood on Southampton Water into a luxury charter yacht for Caribbean sailing. In 2003, The Sail Training Association was restyled The Tall Ships Youth Trust.

# SEDOV

Completed 1921 by Friedrich Krupp Germania Werft AG, Kiel. 3,476 gross tons (5,300 tons displacement). Length overall: 385 ft. 7ins (328 ft. 6ins at the waterline). Beam: 47ft. 11ins. Draught: 28 ft 7ins. Sail area: 45,000 square ft.

This four-masted steel barque was built as *Magdalene Vinnen* for the Bremen firm of F. A. Vinnen, which had lost all of its pre-Great War fleet as reparations to the Allies. This large new ship was intended for the Chilean nitrate and Australian wool trades. In 1936, she was sold to the famed steamship company Norddeutscher Lloyd (NDL) and acted dually as a grain-carrier and a sail training ship. She was now called *Kommodore Johnsen* in honour of the captain of the crack NDL liner *Europa*. She was nearly lost in heavy weather off the Azores in 1937 but fortunately survived. Throughout the Second World War, she continued carrying wheat in the Baltic.

Passed to Great Britain as a war reparation in December, 1945, she was in turn given to the Russians and laid up in the Soviet port of Liepaya. For a time, she remained idle and neglected. However, her potential was finally realised and she was rebuilt in 1952 for the Soviet Ministry of Fisheries and given her present name. She was put to work as a sail training vessel. She was given a further badly-needed refit at Kronstadt between 1975 and 1981 and was much improved. Looking lovely, she has taken part in every subsequent Cutty Sark Tall Ships Race.

The Russian *Sedov* is just underway in this photograph taken off Weymouth in 1994.

Reminders of previous
ages, the sailing barge
*Beric* and the steamship
*Shieldhall* together at
Ocean Village, Eastern
Docks, Southampton, on
the 7th September, 1989.

# OTHER SAILING SHIPS

## BERIC

Completed 1896 at Cann's Boatyard, Harwich.  63 gross tons.  Official number: 105421.

Sail persisted in some of the coasting trades for a surprisingly long time.  Many sailing barges were largely employed carrying grain from ports, particularly on the Thames, to flour mills along the coast or further up-river.  One such was the *Beric*, which had been built for Groom's and later passed into the hands of Cranfield Brothers, Ltd.  For many years, her main employment was between Tilbury and the Rochford Flour Mills.  Here, however, we see her at Southampton.  In 1957, she was converted from a purely sailing vessel to an auxiliary motor barge.

## KATHLEEN & MAY

Completed 1900 by Ferguson & Baird, Connah's Quay.  136 gross tons.  Length overall: 98 ft. 5[ins].  Beam: 23 ft. 3[ins].  Draught: 10 ft. 1in.  Sail area: 4,550 sq. feet.  Call sign: QHBG.

Built on the Dee Estuary, this well-known three-masted topsail schooner was completed as the *Lizzie May* for Captain John Coppack of the local firm of Coppack Brothers & Co.  She was named after his two daughters.  Of wooden construction, she was used for general coastal cargo and carried typically firebricks, cement, fertiliser, china clay, iron and coal.  Up to 226 tons of cargo could be stowed in her holds.

Later, she was sold to the Irish owner Martin J. Fleming and sailed out of Youghal as the *Kathleen & May*, now named after the Fleming daughters. In 1931, Captain William Jewel of Appledore in North Devon acquired her and had her fitted with a small engine. She continued under the captain's ownership, and that of his son, sailing for them thoughout the War and then until as late as 1960, when she was retired after sixty years of excellent service. It was intended to convert her for passenger use but this did not materialise. She lay on a mud berth at Marvin's Yard in Cowes for a while before being taken to Chichester Harbour, where she spent several weeks frozen into the thick harbour ice during the severe winter of 1962-63. (She had previously survived a grounding on the Goodwin Sands and three collisions.) *Kathleen & May* was then taken back to Appledore but nothing more was done to maintain her.

It was not until 1970 that her true worth was recognised when it was realised that she was the last of the British wooden schooners. The Maritime Trust paid for a major refit. She first opened to the public in Plymouth and was then taken to become part of the Historic Ship Collection at St. Katherine's Dock in London. When it was found that she was too expensive to keep, she was moved to Gloucester Docks. It was not until 1998 that an entrepreneur, Steve Clarke, attracted by her port of registry, Bideford, decided to buy her. She was returned to Bideford and her almost rotted hull was rebuilt in a £1 million rescue operation which included replacing the 3-inch oak planking of her outer shell and the entire deck with ballau, an African timber with similar characteristics to the more expensive teak. She made her maiden voyage after restoration in July, 2002 – suitably to the Irish port of Youghal, from which, earlier in her career, she had sailed for many years. Fortunately, thanks to the rescue bid, *Kathleen & May* will be around and enjoyed for many years to come.

*Kathleen & May*, laid up and open to the public at Guy's Quay, Barbican, Plymouth, on the 13th June, 1974.

# Colour by R. Bruce Grice

Bob Bruce Grice is not only a fine photographer in black and white, he has also taken some very atmospheric pictures in colour.  Some of the most evocative of these appear in this final section of the book.

The small Greek cruise ship *Argonaut*, built as long ago as 1929 as a private yacht for a vastly wealthy American industrialist, leans gently as she is pulled away from her berth by the Red Funnel tug *Gurnard* at the end of a visit to Southampton.

Union-Castle Line's *Reina del Mar* was one of Southampton's regulars in the 'Sixties and early 'Seventies.  Note the forward extension of her superstructure, added during her conversion into a cruise ship.

The Red Ensign makes a splash of colour in this stern view of the *Canberra* in dry dock. Although technically flawed, she was a striking example of 'Sixties style and by the end of her career had become a hugely popular cruise ship.

(Below, left.) After her triumphant return from gallant service as a troopship in the Falklands War, the rust streaked *Canberra*, known to some of her soldier passengers as the 'Great White Whale', rests at her Southampton berth in July, 1982.

(Below, right.) The sun shines on the righteous during this visit to Southampton of the widely-travelled missionary ship *Doulos*. A vessel of many careers and much altered since her completion as long ago as 1914, she is entirely manned by Christian volunteers.

(Previous page.) A striking view of *Canberra*, dated November 1984, at Southampton with the new *Royal Princess* in the distance.

Built as an express liner able to cope with rough North Atlantic conditions, the *Queen Elizabeth 2* has a particularly strong and shapely hull. This made her very suitable for troopship duties in the Falklands campaign of 1982. As she returns to Southampton, she is crowded with combatants.

The *France*, the last - and one of the greatest - of the distinguished line of French transatlantic ships, looks massive as she lies at her berth at Southampton with those distinctive funnels which became her trade mark feature.

Arriving in April, 1982 to take up her new rôle in the British cruise market, P&O's *Sea Princess* is assisted by the Red Funnel tug *Calshot* (II).

A 1984 view of the P&O group's new *Royal Princess*. She was regarded as an innovative ship and her layout was subsequently copied quite widely.

Tthe little *St. Helena* lies at Southampton in 1978 before the start of her passenger-cargo service linking the British islands in the South Atlantic with the mother country and with South Africa.

The preserved paddle steamer *Waverley* still continues the tradition of day-cruising in British coastal waters. She is here seen during a visit to Weymouth in 1979. In the foreground, the local lifeboat races out to answer a distress call.

Once a Red Funnel excursion ship and ferry, the *Medina* went on to have an extremely varied career as a tender in Gibraltar and later in stationary rôles in various ports around the English coast.

(Following page.) Sealink's elegant *Falaise*, here seen during a brief stint at Weymouth in 1973-74 towards the end of her career, had been built in 1947 by Denny Bros. as a classic Southern Railway passenger ferry but was later converted to carry motor vehicles as well as passengers.

Two generations of
Townsend Thoresen
ferries, a sleek-looking
*Viking* (left) and a
utilitarian *Free Enterprise*
(right), sport contrasting
liveries and remind us
that the company
had mixed Norwegian
and British origins.

How times have changed
on the Channel: Condor
Ferries run services from
Weymouth, Poole and
Portsmouth to the Channel
Islands and to French ports
using speedy catamarans
such as the *Condor 10*.

A varied fleet of naval and merchant ships gathered for the Silver Jubilee Review at Spithead in June, 1977. Among them was the tug *Roysterer*, A361 (above) belonging to the Royal Maritime Auxiliary Service and also the commercial tug *Lady Vera* (below) representing the British Tug Owners' Association. Naval vessels and a fleet auxiliary can be seen in the background.

Bearing a suitably Royal name, the modern trawler *Princess Anne* belonging to Deep Sea Fisheries, Ltd. was a flag-bedecked representative of the British fishing fleet at the Silver Jubilee Review in 1977.

Looking, perhaps, uncharacteristically immaculate, the Colne Fishing Company's *St. Patrick* from Lowestoft was another participant in the Silver Jubilee Review. Since 1977, of course, the British fishing fleet has shrunk beyond recognition.

(Following page.) Glamorous passenger ships tend to be the most noticed callers at Southampton but the port also has a vast cargo trade. Here the lightly-loaded German freighter *Gabriele Kögel* lies high in the water alongside the landmark cranes.

# SOURCES

## Author's note

As far as possible, I have tried to use technical data from *Lloyd's Register*. Where a vessel has been subsequently modified and, in many cases, renamed, the details are 'as built'. Historical detail has been gleaned from many sources (see also **Acknowledgements**), including the mighty 'web' which, even to this technophobe, has proved to be almost as invaluable as the written word. My thanks go to the often anonymous authors of these web-sites, a select few of which I have included in a 'wwwebography'.

## Selected Bibliography

303-Arts, Recherches et Créations. 303, La Revue des Pays de la Loire (undated).

Adams, Ron: Red Funnel – and Before. Kingfisher Railway Productions, Southampton, 1986.

Beaver, Paul: The Big Ship. Hugh Evelyn, Ltd., London, undated.

Clammer, Richard: Cosens of Weymouth. Twelveheads Press, Truro, 2001.

Clegg and Styring: Steamers of British Railways. T. Stephenson & Sons, Ltd., Prescot, Lancashire, 1962.

Cooke, Anthony: Emigrant Ships. Carmania Press, London, 1991.

Cooke, Anthony: Liners & Cruise Ships, Vols. 1, 2 and 3. Carmania Press, London, 1996 – 2003.

De Kerbrech, Richard: Shaw, Savill & Albion: The Post-War Fortunes of a Shipping Empire. Conway Maritime Press, London, 1986.

Duggan, James: The Great Iron Ship. Hamish Hamilton, London, 1955.

Dunn, Laurence: Mediterranean Shipping. Carmania Press, London, 1999.

Dunn, Laurence: Passenger Liners. Adlard Coles, Ltd., London, 1961.

Harvey, Clive: The *Saxonia* Sisters. Carmania Press, London, 2001.

Hutchings, David F.: Pride of the North Atlantic. Kingfisher Publications, 2003.

Hutchings, David F.: *QE2*: A Ship for All Seasons. Kingfisher Publications, 1988, updated 2002.

Hutchings, David F.: *Queen Elizabeth*: From Victory to Valhalla. Kingfisher Publications, 1990.

Hutchings, David F.: RMS *Queen Mary*: Fifty Years of Splendour. Kingfisher Railway Productions, 1986.

Hutchings, David F.: *Titanic*: 75 Years of Legend. Kingfisher Railway Productions, 1987. Reprinted as *Titanic*: A Modern Legend. 8th edition, 1995.

Kludas, Arnold: Great Passenger Ships of the World (5 volumes). Patrick Stephens, Ltd., Cambridge, 1976 – 1977.

Lloyd's Registers (Various years): Lloyd's Register, London.

Miller, William H.: Picture History of the *United States*. Dover Publications, Inc., Mineola, New York, 2003.

Miller, William H. and Hutchings, David F.: Transatlantic Liners at War: The Story of the *Queens*. David & Charles, Newton Abbott, 1985.

Miller, William H. and Correia, Luís Miguel: SS *Canberra* of 1961. Liner Books, Lisbon, 1997.

Miller, William H. and Correia, Luís Miguel: SS *France* / SS *Norway*. Liner Books, Lisbon, 2002.

Mitchell, Alan: Splendid Sisters. George G. Harrap & Co., Ltd., London, 1966.

Moody, Bert and, later, Hornsby, David: Ocean Ships (various editions). Ian Allan, Ltd., Shepperton.

Moody, Bert: A Pictorial History of Southampton Docks. Waterfront Publications, later Kingfisher Publications, various editions and dates.

Newall, Peter: Union-Castle Line: A Fleet History. Carmania Press, London, 1999.

Rabson, Stephen and O'Donoghue, Kevin: P&O: A Fleet History. World Ship Society, Kendal, 1988.

Villiers, Alan: The *Cutty Sark*: Last of a Glorious Era. Hodder & Stoughton, Ltd., London, 1953.

Williams, David L. Glory Days: British Ferries. Ian Allan, Ltd., Shepperton, 2003.

# Periodicals and Newspapers

Dorset Evening Echo.

Lloyd's List.

Marine News.

Sea Breezes.

Ships Monthly.

Shipbuilding & Shipping Record.

Southampton Evening Echo.

# Selected 'wwwebography'

baycrossings.com

college.hmco.com

crosswinds.net

cuttysark.org.uk

faktaomfartig.com

hms-victory.com

iwm.org.uk

mvdoulos.org

maritimematters.com

navysite.net

redduster.f9.co.uk

ss-shieldhall.co.uk

theshiplist.com

tallship-fan.de

thayer.dartmouth.edu

tugtalk.com

worldshipny.com

Printed by
**TISAK ZAMBELLI, RIJEKA**
October 2006

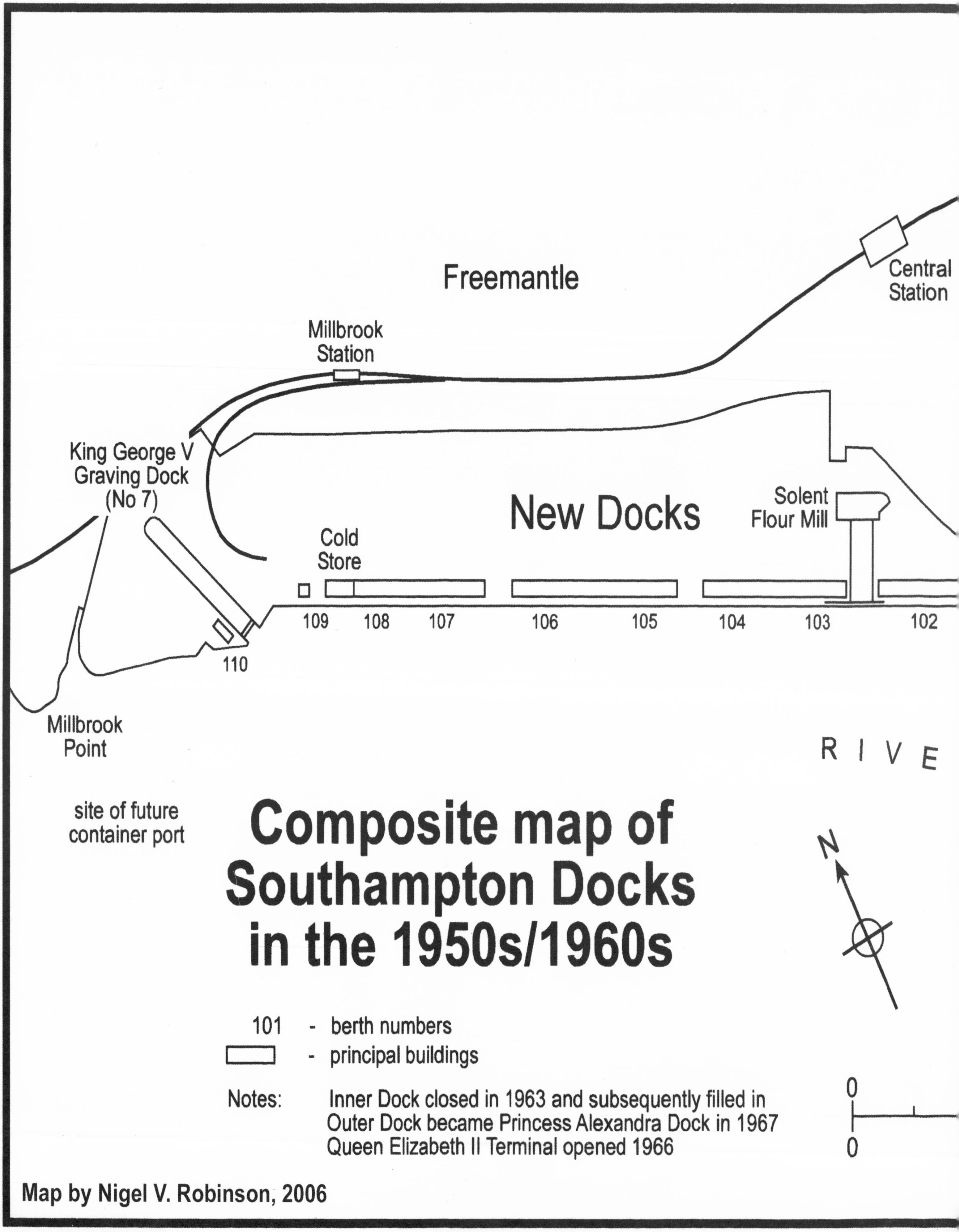

Freemantle

Millbrook
Station

Central
Station

King George V
Graving Dock
(No 7)

New Docks

Solent
Flour Mill

Cold
Store

| 109 | 108 | 107 | 106 | 105 | 104 | 103 | 102 |

110

Millbrook
Point

R I V E

site of future
container port

# Composite map of Southampton Docks in the 1950s/1960s

N

101   -   berth numbers

☐   -   principal buildings

Notes:     Inner Dock closed in 1963 and subsequently filled in
Outer Dock became Princess Alexandra Dock in 1967
Queen Elizabeth II Terminal opened 1966

0

0

**Map by Nigel V. Robinson, 2006**